SIKKIM
A Guide and Handbook

RAJESH VERMA

SIKKIM

A GUIDE AND HANDBOOK

(with road, town and trekking maps)

Also includes a General Knowledge Quiz on Sikkim with many new questions

In memory of my mother Raj Rani Verma

RAJESH VERMA

First Edition:	Apr '90
Second Edition:	Sept '91
Third Edition:	Oct '92
Fourth Edition:	Apr '93
Fifth Edition:	Jan '95
Sixth Edition:	Oct '95
Seventh Edition:	Mar '96
Eighth Edition:	Oct '97
Ninth Edition:	Apr '99
Tenth Edition:	Jan '00
Eleventh Edition:	Apr '02
Twelvth Edition:	Mar '04
Thirteenth EditionJan '05	
Fourteenth Edition	May '06
Fifteenth Edition	Mar '07
Sixteenth Edition(Bengali)	Mar '08
Seventeenth Edition	Feb '09
Reprint	Dec '10
Eighteenth Editiion	Apr '12

Text, Wordprocessing, Cartography, : Rajesh Verma
Maps & Photographs

Published By: : Rajesh Verma

Although all care has been taken to ensure accuracy of information provided in the book, the author assumes no responsibility for loss to the reader due to any errors or omissions in this publication. The hotels and travel agents mentioned in the book are only representative and does not suggest any special preference.

Front Cover: Changu Lake;A Thanka being unscrolled at the Pemayanste monastery; A Nepali milkwoman; Local jewellery

Back Cover: A panoramic view of the Kanchendzonga range from Ganesh Tok, A paddy field; Rafting on the River Tista; An orchid; Snow Leopard

Price : US$ 4.50

CONTENTS

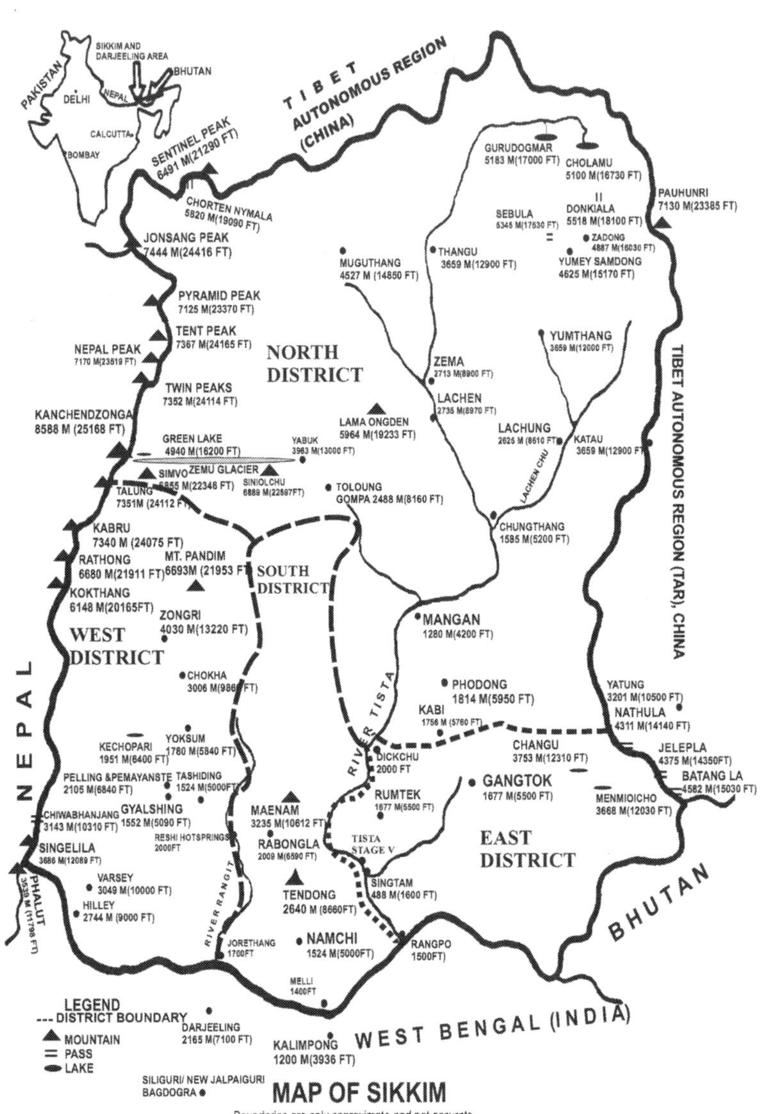

MAP OF SIKKIM

Boundaries are only approximate and not accurate
Map preparation & Copyright: Rajesh Verma

PREFACE

Long sequestered in the laps of the Himalayas, Sikkim has evolved into a favourite destination with new tourist attractions being added every year. This book has been written keeping in mind the increasesd requirement for information on Sikkim.

My earlier job of installing radio-communication equipment for the Police Department took me to the remotest corners - some involving days of walking through lush green valleys and over high passes, bivoacing in caves - and enabled me to experience Sikkim's rustic splendour and village life and study the local way of living closely which has been described at many places in this book. I am grateful to many people - yakherders, porters, monks, villagers, police personnel and foresters posted in remote areas - who regaled me with stories of local beliefs and folklore during my travels and have indirectly contributed to this book by providing a wealth of information.

As a member of a local environment group "Green Circle", I was intensively involved in ecology related work in Sikkim - organising environment and afforestation camps, workshops, quiz programmes, cleaning up fragile areas like the Tsomgo lake of garbage and implementing the AUSAID funded Litter and Spit Free Zone on M.G. Marg. As a part of our advocacy programme we took initiatives like getting the authorities to agree to make it compulsory for all vehicles plying to Alpine areas to carry small garbage bags so that passengers do not throw out wrappers and vitiate the landscape. Thanks to my "Green Circle" friends with whom I enjoyed working.

My association with the Syari Government Employees Welfare Assocaition gave me an opportunity to use innovative methods to resolve parking problems in the locality. Door to door collection of garbage was initiated by me. These initiatives resulted in creation of jobs: parking attendants and garbage collectors. By viewing parking and garbage not as problems but opportunity and resource we opened up whale of avenues. As Vice President of National Association for the Blind, Sikkim Branch and also member of various other organisations dealing in disablities, I was involved in use of Information Technology tools to make the disabled acquire skills that would make them employable and not reliant on compassion and charity. The outcome of my experiences with these associations gave me an insight on various issues dogging Sikkim and have been reflected in the book. It also prompted me to add a chapter on NGOs and Community Initiatives this edition. Thanks to all those with whom I was associated.

And finally, I am grateful to my wife Sunila and daughter Vernica for their immense patience and bearing with my rather irregular routine while I was preparing the manuscript. Thanks also to Ashish Pradhan who has helped me with the maps.

They say even the height of Mount Kanchendzonga is increasing a couple of centimeters every year. Therefore in order to keep abreast with the changes, I endeavour to take out an edition every year so that all the facts and figures are updated. Twice or thrice every year when I realise that the only exercise that I am getting is pushing files from the IN tray to the OUT tray in the office, I put on my trekking shoes and go out exploring and this enables me to add new trekking routes to the book. This edition particularly has many new maps and sketches.

I am sure this information packed book will be found useful by the readers.

Rajesh Verma
r_verma32@hotmail.com

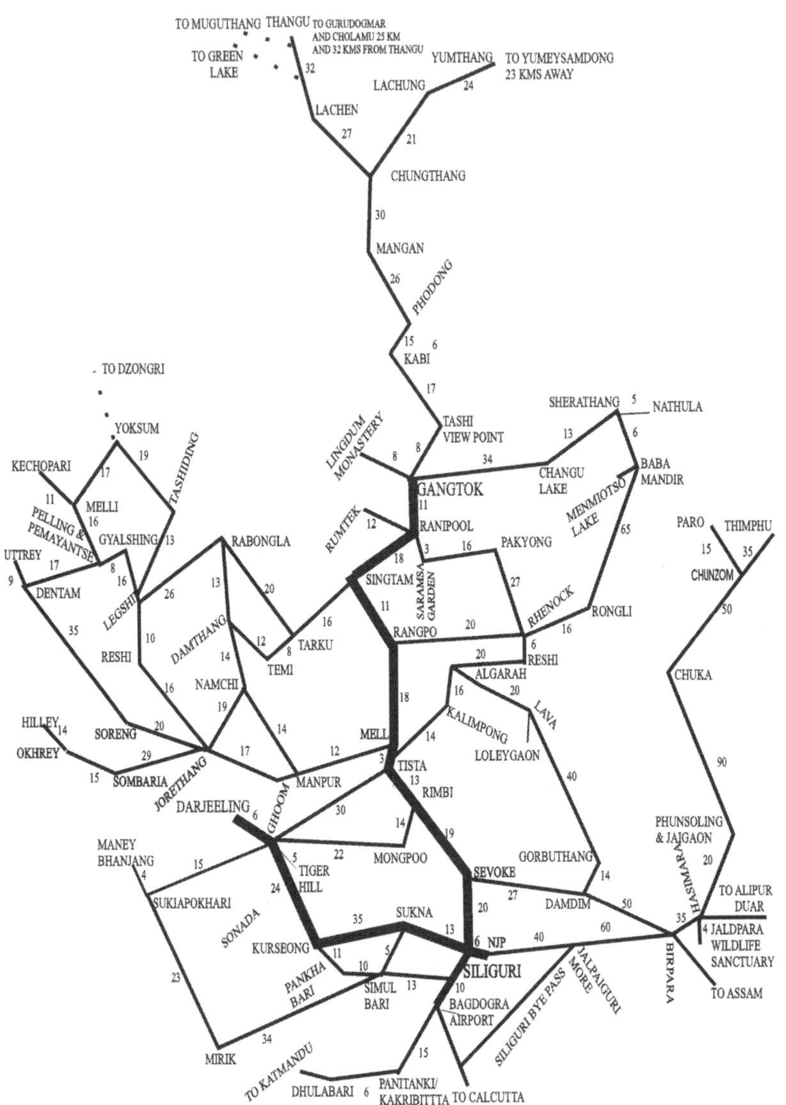

IMPORTANT ROADS OF SIKKIM, DARJEELING AREA & A PART OF BHUTAN

Not to Scale Distances in kilometers Trekking Routes have been depicted elsewhere in the book Map Preparation & Copyright: Rajesh Verma

The source of the Tista river: the Tista Khanste glacier on the plateau

The Roro chu river below Gangtok

A bridge over the river Tista

A jeep wades through the Meyong chu waterfall

The author at Donkiala pass, 18400 ft overlooking the Cholamu lake and the Tibetan plateau

Marmot

Rhubarb plant

Kiangs - the rare Tibetan wild ass

A Bhutia House

A Herd of Yaks

A Tika ceremony

A Nepali Rai girl

A Lepcha girl

A Nepali Subba lady

A local made carpet

A local face

A Lepcha priest

SIKKIM - INTRODUCTION AND PHYSICAL FEATURES

Sandwiched between the kingdoms of Nepal in the west and Bhutan in the east lies a small stretch of rugged land just 115 kilometres by 65 kilometres - the Indian state of Sikkim. On its northern border towers the plateau of Tibet whereas it shares its southern border with West Bengal which is another state of India. On the world map it is just a speck with an approximate latitude of 27 degrees North and longitude of 88 degrees East but its small size of 7096 sq km belies its richness of culture, customs, heritage, flora and fauna all telescoped into one. By travelling a few hours within Sikkim one can traverse from sultry tropical to temperate and then to alpine climates-and from almost sea level to 18000ft. Although Mount Kachendzonga at about 28000 ft is the highest point in Sikkim, there are places like Melli at 1100 ft which have a lower altitude than say Hyderabad (1700 ft) and Jaipur (1400 ft). A couple of hours of travel can take you from the almost the rainest region on earth to a cold desert where clouds do not dare to venture and where it hardly rains. No wonder Sikkim is a bio-diversity hotspot - Sikkim has only 0.2percent of the area of India but has 26 percent of its biodiversity- species of flora and fauna -wild animals like marmots and the red panda, a wide range of flora from primulas to orchids. The pristine and unspoilt natural beauty includes alpine landscapes and thick luxuriant tropical forests, rivers in torrents and peaceful lakes - a true Shangrila and a veritable kaledioscope.

By travelling a few kilometers, one can leave a city like Gangtok with all modern amenities and reach a quaint village that seems anachronistically from a different age and having names like Bringbong and Passingdon.

Sikkim is a nice place to be in. It is not dogged with the social problems and economic problems like discrimination against women being faced by other states. Crime is negligible and the state is not troubled by insurgency. There are hardly strikes and bandhs in the state. Even when there is an All India Strike, life in Sikkim goes on as normal. Sikkim also has been the first state to ban the use of plastic carry bags and use of fertilizers and pesticides as a step towards becoming an organic state.With a literacy of 82%, the Government has also launched a Total Computer literacy programme.

Sikkim was earlier a protectorate of India with a monarchy government but in 1975 it metamorphosed as the Twenty Second state of the Indian Union. The population of the whole state is only 5,40,000 as per the last census-less than a populated colony of Delhi. It is well connected to the rest of the country by rail and air through Siliguri about a 100 kms away from Gangtok.

Surrounded by three countries, Sikkim has a 220 kilometres long border with Tibet, 100 kilometres with Nepal, 30 kilometres with Bhutan and 80 kilometres with West Bengal. Because of absence of habitations on both sides of the international border there is hardly any infiltration.

Within the state there is a good road network and more roads are being constructed at a frenzied pace. It is possible to reach Gangtok from places as

	GANGTOK	RUMTEK	TSANGO LAKE	BABA MANDIR	NATHULA	PHODONG	MAGAN	CHUNGTHANG	YUMGTHANG	LACHEN	LACHUNG	NAMCHI	YOKSUM	RABONGLA	TASHIDING	GYLAHING	KECHOPARI	RANGPO	MELLI	KALIMPONG	DARJEELING	SILIGURI	PHUNSOLING
RUMTEK	22																						
TSANGO LAKE	34	75																					
BABA MANDIR	47	59	13																				
NATHULA	52	60	17	5																			
PHODONG	40	62	74	87	92																		
MAGAN	66	88	100	113	118	26																	
CHUNGTHANG	96	118	129	143	148	56	30																
YUMGTHANG	141	163	198	221	193	101	75	45															
LACHEN	123	145	157	170	175	83	57	27	72														
LACHUNG	117	151	152	168	169	77	51	21	24	48													
NAMCHI	84	85	118	131	136	124	153	180	226	207	201												
YOKSUM	123	124	198	221	216	163	189	219	264	246	240	104											
RABONGLA	66	66	99	112	117	105	131	161	206	188	116	24	58										
TASHIDING	88	89	122	153	140	128	154	184	229	211	155	57	19	39									
GYLAHING	83	84	117	30	135	123	149	179	224	206	142	51	33	56	29								
KECHOPARI	120	121	154	167	172	160	186	216	261	243	200	67	28	59	40	27							
RANGPO	40	41	74	87	92	80	106	136	181	163	157	61	130	47	80	83	110						
MELLI	58	59	92	105	110	98	124	154	199	181	175	62	112	88	86	89	116	3					
KALIMPONG	75	98	109	122	127	115	141	171	216	198	191	65	128	99	91	94	212	28	17				
DARJEELING	97	86	131	144	149	137	163	193	238	220	180	39	151	83	107	128	139	57	39	50			
SILIGURI	110	114	144	157	162	150	176	206	251	233	217	123	167	152	167	162	189	66	55	66	68		
PHUNSOLING	222	200	297	310	315	314	288	318	363	345	339	201	286	228	241	270	305	185	167	181	200	152	
THIMPHU	397	375	472	506	490	489	467	493	538	520	514	376	461	403	416	445	480	360	342	356	375	327	175

DISTANCES BETWEEN IMPORTANT PLACES IN KILOMETERS

far flung as Lachen and Okhrey within four hours making hardly any place in Sikkim remote. There is a good and reliable shared Taxi- Jeep facility from all places in Sikkim to and from Gangtok. Language communication for outsiders also poses no problems. Although Nepali is the most widely spoken language in Sikkim, everyone seems to know Hindi and English. In spite of rapid development, Sikkim continues to be a small place and everything about it is simple including the names of its four Districts: North, South, East and West. Everyone seems to know everyone.

Sikkim is located in the eastern part of India and therefore the time seems to be slightly skewed as Indian Standard Time(IST) is infact the local time of Allahabad. . It dawns early (as early as 3.30 am in June) and also becomes dark early (as early as 4.30 pm in winter)

PHYSICAL FEATURES

Sikkim may have a small size, but this is amply compensated by formidable physical features. It are the physical features like the rivers and mountains that define the boundaries of the state with its neighbours. The edge of the Tibetan plateau more or less demarcates the northern border of Sikkim with Tibet. The eastern boundary with Tibet is represented by the Chola range whereas the border with Bhutan is constituted by the Pangolia range. In the west the Singelila range forms the watershed as well as the border between Nepal and Sikkim. Parts of the rivers Rangit, Tista, Ramam and Rangpo-chu combine to define the border of Sikkim with West Bengal. The terrain of Sikkim is so rugged that from the air it looks as though a giant plough had been carelessly run through it. Because of the relatively low latitude of Sikkim (27 degrees north) and its proximity to the Tropic of Cancer, the snow line above which permanent snow is found is about 20,000ft. Habitations are found till altitudes of 17,000 ft. This is in sharp contrast to Eurpoe where the Alps at a latitude of approximately 45 degrees north comparitively are tiny tots and the highest Mt. Blanc at an altitude of 15,000 ft remains perenially under snow.

The humidity in Sikkim is relatively higher because of its proximity to the Bay of Bengal and also due to the rich rain forest coverage. Therefore a temperature of 25 degrees celcius at Gangtok is considered terribly hot whereas the same temperature at Delhi is considered mild and pleasant.

With the change in seasons, the mountains and rivers change colours like a chamelon: the mountains are dark green in summer and brown in winter and the rivers muddy brown in summer and green torquise blue in winter.

Mountains, Glaciers and Passes

Sikkim has a very rugged and formidable topography and flat lands are difficult to come by- from the air Sikkim looks as though someone has run a giant plough thorugh the land. The towering mountains that define this paradise of nature also create a barrier to efficient agriculture. It are these mountains that fall directly in the path of the monsoon clouds making the state one of the wettest in the country. In some areas the peaks are as jagged as primitive spearpoints and in others they look like the top of icecones. There are even mountains that have the shapes of huge canyons.

Most of the peaks above 6100 metres (20000 ft) lie towards the western border of Sikkim. On the western border lies the third highest mountain of the world- the Kanchendzonga, 8588 metres (28168 ft) high- the very name suggests majesty and challenge. It is a huge mass that straddles Nepal and Sikkim but its summit lies in Sikkim.Other peaks that stand at altitudes of above 6100 metres (20000 ft) are Kabru, which is also the second highest mountain in the state, Siniolchu, Pandim, Rathong, Kokthang, Talung, Kanglakhang, Simvo and Jonsang. On the eastern border the most imposing peak is Paunhri, at an altitude of about 6700 metres (22000 ft). The other imposing mountains that are slightly less than 6100 metres (20000 ft) are Masthonangye, Yabukjakchen, Narsing and Lamaongden.

Viewed from different locations, the mountains adopt various shapes. For instance Mount Siniolchu from Gangtok has a shapeless ugly profile. But from the Green Lake area this very mountain is an epitome of perfection and is compeltely symmetrical. Similarly Mount Kanchendzonga from Gangtok looks like a volcano, but from Pelling it looks very different.

Through the centre of Sikkim runs another mountain ridge in the north to south direction. This mountain ridge separates the Tista and Rangit Valley and ends at the confluence of the two rivers. The peaks of this ridge are Tendong at 2640 metres (8660 ft) and Maenam at 3235 metres(10612 ft). Most of the peaks of Sikkim have remained unscaled because the Sikkimese consider them sacred and feel that they will lose their sanctity if climbed. From the Sikkim side, Kanchendzonga has been scaled a few times but the climbers have returned back a few feet from the summit in deference to the religious feelings of the Sikkimese. Kanchendzonga itself means Houses of the Five Treasures and it is believed that holy treasures have been kept by the Gods on the summit. The gnarled topography tends, however to smoothen out in the upper reaches of the Tista river in the Lachen Valley where the Tibetan Plateau juts into Sikkim.The Tibetan plateau gets hot during the summers and as a result an area of pressure exists over it that draws monsoon clouds over the plains of India resulting in their fertility but sometimes being the cause of floods.

A glacier, simply put, is a slow moving river of ice. It flows from high mountain peaks through rocky valleys, carrying off unmelted snow that has compacted over many years into a solid, creeping ice stream. Glaciers also carry with them rocks and these are deposited in the form of small mountains called moraines. There are many glaciers in Sikkim but the most important ones are the Zemu Glacier, Rathong Glacier and the Lonak Glacier. Of late the shrinking glaciers because of climate change has been making news. The status of glaciers has become a sort of barometer for measuring climate change.

The mountain ranges are interspersed with passes which can be used to cross from one side to another. On the eastern Chola range the most important passes are the Nathula at 4242 metres (14140 ft) and Jelepla at 4305 metres (14350 ft) and Bhutan la at an altitude of about 4509 metres (15030 ft) - the first two lead to the Chumbi valley in Tibet and the third to Bhutan. Another important pass on this range that also leads to the Chumbi valley is the Chola pass. On the west between the border of Sikkim and Nepal, the most important pass is Chiwabhanjang which has an altitude of 3090 metres (10300 ft). The other pass on the west is Kang la. In the north the important passes are Chorten Nyimala, which at 5730 metres (19100 ft) is also the highest usable pass in Sikkim, and Kongra-la. Lungnala connects the Lachen valley to the Lonak valley in North Sikkim. Donkiala pass is another pass in North Sikkim that links up the Lachen valley to the Lachung valley.

Lakes

On the face of it, one would not expect to find lakes on such a rugged terrain. But surprisingly, Sikkim does have lakes though not very large in size. These lakes are both spring fed as well as river fed. They also form the source of many rivers. On the highway between Gangtok and Nathu-la, 34 kilometres from Gangtok lies the serene Changu (Tsomgo) Lake at an altitude of about 3693 metres (12310 ft). Two other lakes nearby are the Bidang cho and the Menmecho. Kechopari lake is another well-known lake that lies on a bifurcation of the route between Gyalshing and Yoksum. The highest concentration of lakes is on the Western border north of Chiwabhanjang towards the Base Camp. Laxmipokhari, Lampokhari, Majurpokhari, twin lakes of Ram-Laxman are a few of the lakes in this area. Dud Pokhari and Samiti Lake are two other lakes situated in this area. Gurudogmar, which is the largest in Sikkim and Cholamu are some other beautiful lakes and are in North Sikkim.

Rivers

The river that flows right across the length of Sikkim is the Tista snaking through the deep gorges taking tributaries as it goes. Its major tributary is the Rangit which originates from the Rathong Glacier and meets it at the border between Sikkim and West Bengal. The river Ramam a tributary of Rangit, a part of the river Rangit itself and Rangpo chu a tributary of Tista define the Southern border between Sikkim and West Bengal. Tista originates from the Lake Cholamu where it is hardly a stream. No one can imagine that this innocuous looking stream would transform into a thundering mighty river less than a hundred kilometres downstream. From an altitude of almost 5400 metres (18000 ft), the Tista plummets down in less than 80 kilometres to 1620 metres (5500 ft) at Chungthang - a veritable waterfall. From Chungthang onwards till the border with West Bengal the Tista descends just another 900 metres (3000 ft) over a course of about a 100 kilometres. The other smaller tributaries of the Tista river are Zemu chu, Lonak chu, Lachung chu,Talung chu, Bakcha chu. While the river Tista flows in the North-South direction its tributaries tend to flow in the South West or South East directions.

Fed by runoff from glaciers and copious snow and rain, Sikkim's rivers flow fast and furious - a tempting source of hydropower. Because of their natural steep gradient, these perennial rivers have a potential of generating thousands of megawatts of electricity. Many hydroprojects have come up in the state which are selling power to the neighbouring states bringing much needed revenue to Sikkim.

Hot springs

Sikkim has many hot-springs known for their medicinal and therapeutic value. The most important are the ones located at Phurchachu (Reshi), Yumthang, Borang, Ralang, Taram-chu and Yumey Samdong. All these hotsprings have high sulphur content and are located near the river banks. The average temperature of the water in these hot springs is 50 °C

CLIMATE

Temperatures

The temperatures that a particular place experiences varies considerably with altitude. At places of low altitude, like Singtam, Rangpo and Jorethang, the temperatures vary between 4 °C to 35 °C. Places like Gangtok with moderate altitudes of about 1800 metres (6000ft) experience temperatures between 1 °C and 25 °C whereas at altitudes above 4000 metres (13100 ft), the temperature never rises above 15 °C and remains much below the freezing point during the winters and great part of the spring and autumn. At higher altitudes, temperatures can change for instance from + 25 °C to -25 °C within minutes

Rainfall

Sikkim is one of the rainiest regions in India. Because of the proximity of Sikkim to the Bay of Bengal and the fact that the mountains of the state come directly in the path of the monsoon clouds, most parts of Sikkim experience torrential rains during summers. So much so that even a small depression over the Bay of Bengal triggers off a downpour in Sikkim. Even during spring and autumn moisture laden clouds formed due to local evaporation, continue to batter a greater part of Sikkim. It is only during October to March that there is hardly any rain and the weather remains more or less clear.

Rainfall however varies considerably from place to place because of the hill features. The northern border of Sikkim experiences comparatively low rainfall because the monsoon clouds dry out by the time they hit the northern barrier. For the sake of comparison, Gangtok registers an average of 325 cm rainfall per annum whereas Muguthang in the extreme north experiences an average rainfall of only 60 cm per annum. Most of Sikkim does not experience high intensity winds. However, at many hill tops and passes, winds and blizzards having high speeds blow. Given below is the average maximum-minimum temperature and average rainfall over the last ten years at Gangtok and the probability of seeing clear skies.

Month	Jan	Feb	Mar	Apr	May	Jun	Jul	Aug	Sep	Oct	Nov	Dec
Max	13.5	11.9	16.6	20.7	22.3	21.5	22.5	22.5	21.8	19.9	16.1	13.0
Min	2.0	3.6	10.0	12.1	15.0	17.4	17.7	17.7	16.9	13.0	9.4	6.7
Rainfall cm	2.7	6.5	10.3	30.4	54.0	57.0	66.0	57.0	49.8	13.7	4.7	2.7
Chance of clear skies	90%	90%	75%	40%	30%	10%	1%	2%	5%	50%	98%	98%

Although the figures above pertain to Gangtok which is at an altitude of about 2000 metres it could be considered representative of the whole area after you make corrections based on the altitude. The rainfall would decrease at higher altitudes and so would the maximum-minimum temperature.

THE PEOPLE

Communities, cultures, religions and customs of different hues intermingle freely here in Sikkim to constitute a homogeneous blend and present a kaleidoscopic picture. Hindu temples coexist with Buddhist monasteries and there are even a few Christain churches, Muslim mosques and Sikh Gurdwaras. Although the Buddhists with monasteries all over the state are the most conspicuous religious group, they are infact a minority constituting only 28% of the population. The majority, 68% profess Hinduism. The predominant communities are the Lepchas, Bhutias and the Nepalis. In urban areas many plainsmen- Marwaris, Biharis, Bengalis, South Indians, Punjabis- have also settled and they are mostly engaged in business and government service. Because of development and construction activities in the state, a small part of the population consists of migrant labourers from the plains and from Nepal: plumbers, masons and carpenters from Orissa, Bihar and West Bengal and Sherpas who are hired by the army to maintain the roads at high altitudes. There are also a few thousand Tibetan Refugees settled in Sikkim. Many locals have names that are indistinguishable from those of Hindi speaking states in India: Singhs, Sharmas, Bhandaris, Pradhan etc. The communities celebrate an eclectic range of festivals which mean a lot to rural folks who normally do not have any other means of recreation.

Of the violent invasions that Sikkim had to face over the centuries from Nepal and Bhutan, there is hardly any trace today; but a quieter invasion is taking place; that of cultures from outside at the cross roads of Gangtok and other towns of Sikkim. Cultural and economic forces are reshaping the way of life of the Sikkimese. This can be seen by taking a walk down the M.G. Marg of Gangtok: boys and girls sporting the latest fashions probably picked up from a new Hindi movie or BBC s Clothes Show gaily tromp up and down. An open Jeep carrying jubilant footballers who have won a match passes by - they are singing Daler Mehndi's popular Punjabi song "Ho Jaygi Balle Balle " at the top of their voices.

The cable TV is definitely attempting to remould the cultural landscape of Sikkim. You should not be surprised if you come across a village girl somewhere in the wilderness dressed in a Punjabi Kurta Pajama singing a Hindi number "Didi tera dewar diwana ...." while tending to her herd of cattle. Inspite of such powerful external influences, Sikkimese have proved to be resilient accepting the benefits of progress while retaining their ethnic identity.

In Sikkim, women are not confined to home and the hearth. You purchase your vegetables from a lady puffing away at her bidi (local made cigaratte). And in the small local restaurant you go to, you are greeted by a burly woman behind the sale counter lined with bottles of beer who asks you in Nepali " Ke Khanu Honcha?" (What would you like to eat?). At a busy traffice intersection a smartly turned out woman police constable is busy regulating the traffic while another is issuing a ticket to an errant woman driver. On construction sites, women work side by side with men, carrying material in wicker baskets and

Foods and Drinks

The discovery of a new dish does more for the hapiness of mankind than the discovery of a star - Althem

Sikkimese are essentially rice-eaters. Alcoholic drinks are popular both amongst men and women. Beef eating is common amongst the Bhutias. It is not uncommon to see Marwari plainsmen gulping down Momos and Thukpa and Bhutias partaking to Indian dishes like Puris and Dosas - a true sign of national integration. A typical diet of a working Sikkimese consists of dal bhat (lentils and rice) with meat for breakfast; a light lunch of momos; and an early dinner consisting of noodles. Some of the local cuisines are:

Momo

Momo is a very popular Tibetan delicacy in Sikkim. It is prepared by stuffing minced meat, vegetables or cheese in flour dough and then moulding them in the form of dumplings. These are then steamed for about half an hour in a three tiered utensil that has bone or tomato soup in the lowest compartment. Steam from the boiling soup rises through the perforations in the containers above and cooks the dumplings. Momos are taken alongwith soup and home made chilly sauce. It is available in most of the local restaurants.

Thukpa

It is noodle soup with vegetables. Thukpa is readily available in most of the local restaurants.

Phagshapa

Phagshapa is strips of pork fat stewed with radishes and dried chillies.

Sael Roti

This Nepali cuisine is prepared by grinding a mixture of rice and water into a paste. The paste is then poured into hot oil and deep fried. It is normally eaten with potato curry. Normally not available in restaurants but is widely prepared during parties.

Niguru with Churpi

Niguru is a local fiddlehead fern and its tendrils when light fried with churpi (cheese) forms an irresistible dish. Normally not available in restaurants but is prepared as a household dish.

Gundruk

Gundruk are leaves of the mustard oil plant that have been allowed to decay for some days and then dried in the sun. These dried leaves are then cooked alongwith onions and tomatos and forms a tasty dish.

Chang (Thomba)

Chang is a local beer which is made by fermenting millet using yeast. It is sipped from a bamboo receptacle using a bamboo pipe. The receptacle which has millet in it is topped with warm water a couple of times until the millet loses its potency. Chang can sometimes be strong and very intoxicating indeed.

Kinama

It is fermented soya beans. Quite popular in villages.

pulversing stones. Women, even those belonging to the conservative Marwari community run many of the shops in town. In the Government Sector, more than fifteen percent of the employees are women.

Hindi movies are a craze with the locals here and Hindi music is invariably played at all functions here. Even the cultural shows held during the Buddhist festival week of Lossong (Sikkimese New Year) get eclipsed by the blare of Hindi songs.

The Lepchas

Lepchas are said to be one of the original inhabitants of Sikkim. It has not yet been established from where the Lepchas originally came to Sikkim. There are some theories which indicate that the Lepchas came from the border of Assam and Burma. Other theories speak of the Lepchas having migrated to Sikkim from Southern Tibet. No matter from where they have original roots, the fact that is clearly established is that they are of Mongoloid descent. The Lepchas are now predominantly Buddhists but many of them are also Christians having been converted to this faith by the missionaries.

Before adopting Buddhism or Christianity as their religion, the earliest Lepcha settlers were believers in the Bon faith or Mune faith. This faith was basically based on spirits, good and bad. Witchcraftry and exorcism were very common. They worshipped spirits of mountains, rivers and forests which was but natural for a tribe that co-existed so harmoniously with the rich natural surroundings. The well-known deities of the Lepchas are Itbumoo, Rom, Itbu Debu Rom, Kongchen Konglo and Tamsang Thing, who is also said to have invented the Lepcha script. One major festival of the Lepchas is the Namsoong which marks the beginning of the New Year. A highlight of this festival is the week long mela or fair held at Namprikdam at the confluence of Tista and Tolung-chu near Mangan in North Sikkim. The Lepcha priests are known as Bomthing and they perform intricate ceremonies to invoke the blessings of the spirits.

The Lepcha (Dzongu) folklore is rich with stories. One of the very popular story has a parallel with the legend of the Tower of Babel. It describes that the Rongs or Lepchas once attempted to ascend to Rum or Heaven by building a tower of earthern pots. When Rum was about to be reached, God thought he must put an end to this venture. He made them speak in different tongues with the intention of creating confusion. The man at the top of the tower shouted "Kok vim yang tale" (Pass the pole with the hook) but the men at the bottom heard the words "Chek tala" (cut it down). The tower was hacked down and its remains are still found in Daramdin near Sombaria in Western Sikkim.

The Lepcha population is concentrated in the central part of Sikkim. This is the area that encompasses the confluence of Lachen and Lachung rivers and Dickchu. The

Games and Amusement

Archery

This is a much loved outdoor game and is played during the festival months of December and January. The bows and arrows are made of bamboo and the targets each measuring about 30 by 100 cms are kept at the end of the range which is usually 100 metres in length. 11 archers constitute each team with each participant shooting 2 arrows. The method of calculating scores is quite complex as arrows that land close to the target also win points. The team that first scores 33 points wins the match. Spectators and team members stand along the range and dodge misfired arrows with dexterity. During the break, the spectators partake to the local beer, chang and snacks in the lawns. The whole atmosphere is that of festivity. Archery competitions are held in which teams from as far as Bhutan participate.

Majong

Essentially a dice game of Chinese origin, it is very popular in Sikkim.

Chawri or dice

This is a very popular dice game and is played using two dices which are shaken in a wooden bowl which is then upturned on a leather strap with a loud thump and a shout. The score is kept using small sea shells which are known as chawris.

terrain here is rugged and Lepcha dwellings are perched precariously on the steep hillsides. No wonder the word Lepcha means the Ravine folk. They mostly live on agriculture of paddy, cardamom and oranges.

Life in a Lepcha dwelling is very simple. In a Lepcha hut which is usually made of bamboo and is raised about five feet above the ground on stilts, there are usually just a couple of rooms.

Lepchas is very rich in vocabulary related to the flora and fauna of Sikkim.

Lepchas are very good at archery. Archery competition are held very frequently by the Lepchas. Hunting of wild animals using bows and arrows and fishing are favourite pastimes of the Lepchas.The male Lepcha wears a dress called a Pagi made of cotton which is striped. The dress comes down to the knees. It is fastened on the shoulder by a pin and a belt is worn round the waist. Lepcha men keep the hair in the form of a plaited pigtail. The Lepcha women wear two piece dress. The upper garment or the blouse is called the Tago whereas the lower part which resembles a petticoat is called Domdyan.

The polyandry marriages are permitted amongst the Lepchas although this is now becoming very rare. The nuptial customs are quite intriguing. After both the parties have evinced interest in establishing marital relations, the boy's maternal uncle approaches the parents of the girl with some bottles of liquor, scarf and some money. The marriage can easily be ended but the husband has to pay some money to the girl's parents.

Folk dances of Sikkim

Folk dances and songs are an ingrained part of Sikkimese culture. Most of the dances relate to the beauty of the natural surroundings, some depict the harvest season and others are performed for good luck and prosperity. Many of the musical instruments that accompany the dances are unique to Sikkim. Some of the popular dances are described below:

Nepali Folk Dance Maruni

Although this dance is associated with the festival of Tihar meaning "Festival of Light", because of its popularity it is performed even on occasions like marriages. Tihar is celebrated to mark the return of the Hindu god Rama from exile. During this festival Maruni dancers richly dressed in colourful costumes and resplendent with ornaments and noserings called "dungris" go on a house to house visit. The dancers are usually also accompanied by a clown called "Dhatu waray". Sometimes Maruni dances are performed to the accompainment of the nine instrument orchestra known as "Naumati Baja".

Nepali Folk Dance Tamang Selo

Tamangs are a Nepali community and the "Tamang Selo" dance is performed to the rhythmic sound of the "Dhamphu" musical instrument which the dancers carry in thieir hands. This dance is therefore also called the "Dhamphu Dance".

Lepcha Folk Dance Zo-Mal-Lok

This dance portrays the sowing and the subsequent harvesting of paddy. The dance is performed by the Lepcha farmers to reduce the drudgery and monotony of working in the fields.

Bhutia Folk Dance Tashi Sabdo

This dance describes the custom of offering "Khadas" or scarves.

Tibetan Yak Dance

This dance is performed to honour the yak, an animal on which man is completely dependent upon for survival at high altitudes.

The other popular dances are Subba Chabrung Dance, Bhutia Talachi, Tibetan Singhi Chaam, the Sherpa Sebru Naach, Gurung Sorathi, Bhutia Lu-Khang-Thamo, Lepcha Kar Gnpk Lok, Bhutia Gha-to-Kito, Lepcha Dhamra Jo, Bhutia Be-yul-mista, Lepcha Mon-Dryak-lok, Nepali Dhaan Nach and Bhutia Chi-Rimu

ॐ Hindu festivals

Nepali Hindus constitute the majority community in the state. Some of the colourful festivals that they celebrate are described below.

Dasain

This fortnight long festival usually falls in the month of October. Also known as Durga Puja, this festival symbolises the victory of the Hindu Goddess Durga over the forces of evil. On the first day barley seeds are sown in the soil and their growth a few inches foretells a good harvest. The next important day, a week later is Fulpati meaning the "day of flowers". Maha Astami and Kala Ratri follow Fulpati. The next day is Navami. The 10th day of of the festival is known as Vijay Dashmi and also marks the victory of Lord Rama over Ravana. During this day people smear their foreheads with coloured rice and the barley sprouts which were sown on the first day of Dasain are picked and placed over the ears.

Tihar

Tihar is the "Festival of Lights" and symbolises the return of Lord Ram to his hometown from exile after victory over Ravana and covers a period of five days. The festival honours certain animals on successive days. The first day known as "Kak Tihar" is dedicated to crows and they are offered rice and some if caught are even garlanded. On the second day, which is known as "Kukkur Tihar", dogs are garlanded. On the third day the cows are honoured with garlands and their horns are painted in bright colours. It is the turn of the bullocks on the fourth day.

Deepawali, which falls on the third day is considered to be the most important day when goddess Lakshmi comes visiting every home which is lit bright with candles and electric lights.

The fifth day is also known as Bhai Tika in which brothers visit the homes of their sisters and they apply tikas vermilion to each others foreheads. It is also an occasion for exchanging gifts. During Tihar, traditional carols called Bailo or Deusi are sung.

The genesis of Deosi and Bhailey is related to a Kirat King Balihang. It is believed that he fell seriously ill. The God of Death Yama came to take him but Balihang's sister, who was guarding him sent back the messengers with directions that Yama could take her brother after he fulfilled certain conditions. Yama was told to wait till Panchami i.e. Bhai Tika. He could take Balihang away only after the colour of the Tika had faded away, or the water she had sprinkled around him, dried or the flower which she had prepared his garland had wilted. Yama granted her wish. Balihang's sister was, however, much more ingenious than Yama had given her credit to be. She carefully chose the ingredients of the Tika to make sure that it did not fade. Rice grains, she knew would not lose their colour quickly giving her brother enough time to recover from his illness. She then mixed oil in the water and sprinkled around him to keep it from drying and on the third day she stringed a garland made of Makhamali, a flower which does not wilt for years. The Tika did not fade, the water did not dry and the flowers did not wilt for days together and Balihang recovered. Balihang's sister sent messengers across the country to announce her brothers recovery. Dewsi and Bhailey are supposed to be these messages.

Dasain and Tihar means a lot to the local Hindus. Even in-patients in the hospitals leave to be at home with their families.

Continued...

Hindu festivals (continued)

Saraswati Puja

This festival falls in the month of January and honours the Hindu Goddess of Knowledge "Saraswati". School children place their study books in front of the statue and seek blessings for doing well in their studies.

Magh Sakranti

This festival takes place in mid January and marks beginning of the lengthening of days. Fairs are held on the banks of the confluence of rivers. It is an occasion for villagers to gather, meet each other and make purchases.

Maha Shivratri

Observed in the month of February, this festival commemorates the marriage of the Hindu God Shiva to Parvati. In temples dedicated to Shiva, day and night long prayers are held. Devotees of the god keep a fast on this day. The Shiva Lingam is worshipped by washing it with milk, curd and honey. Offerings of bael leaves are slo made to the Lingam.

Holi

Although a festival that is observed mainly in the Hindi speaking areas of India, this festival is gaining popularity in Sikkim too. People visit homes of friends and relatives and smear each other with colour. Holi falls in the month of March and marks the advent of the spring season. This festival essentially celebrates the killing of the demoness Holika by Lord Krishna.

Chaite Dasain or Ramnami

Observed to commemorate the birth of the Hindu God Rama, this festival is celebrated by holding Melas or fares at various places. One place where a small Mela is held during this occasion is Tendong when villagers from surrounding areas undertake the ardous trek up to the peak. Of late this festival is being celebrated in a big way at Aritar lake near Rhenock

For business-men, Ramnami marks the end of the financial year during which the books of accounts are closed.

Raksha Bandhan

Another festival that has its origins in the Hindi heartland of India, it is becoming quite popular with the people of Sikkim. Sisters tie threads to the wrists of their brot hers and wish for their long and prosperous life.

Janamastami

This festival commemorates the birthday of Lord Krishna. Temples are decorated with colourful lights and prayers are held in various temples across the state. The birth of Lord Krishna took place in the mid-night of Janamastami.

Vishwa Karma Puja

This festival takes place on 17th September every year and honours Vishwa Karma - the God of Machines. Statues of this deity are put up in temporary sheds called pandals and worshipped especially by those who are involved in handling machines like drivers and mechanics.

Rangey Mela

A little known festival, it is unique to Namchi. Held in the month of July, an effigy of Rangey Bhoot (ghost) is burnt at Namchi Bazar, a day before the Mela.

The Bhutias

These are people of Tibetan origin. They migrated to Sikkim perhaps somewhere after the fifteenth century through Bhutan. They are evenly distributed throughout the state of Sikkim. In Northern Sikkim, where they are the major inhabitants, they are known as the Lachenpas and Lachungpas. The Lachenpas and the Lachungpas who mainly inhabit the areas around Lachen and Lachung respectively have their own traditional legal system known as Zamsa to settle disputes. Zamsa means public meeting place and the village headman, who is also known as the Pipon metes out justice and is chosen once in a year by the villagers voting by the show of hands. The Pipon takes all decisions regarding the village life like when the crops should be harvested. The Bhutia aristrocrats are known as the Kazis. The language spoken by the Bhutias is Sikkimese which is in fact a dialect of Tibetan language. The script is the same. Bhutias constitute about ten percent of the total population of Sikkim. Bhutia villages are large as those compared to those of Lepchas.

Marriage in a Bhutia family is arranged through negotiations by the paternal or maternal uncle of the boy who goes to the bride's place with gifts to ask for the hand in marriage for his nephew.

The traditional dress of the male member is known as the Bakhu which is a loose cloak type garment with full sleeves and is fastened at the neck on one side and near the waist with a cotton belt. They wear loose trousers. The ladies dress consists of a silken Honju which is a full sleeve blouse and a loose gown type garment fastened near the waist tightly with a belt. In the front portion they tie a loose sheet of multi coloured woollen cloth made of special design. This is called Pangdin and is a symbol of a married woman. Ladies are fond of very heavy jewellery made of pure gold.

The Nepalis

The Nepalis now constitute more than 80 percent of the total population of Sikkim.

The Nepalis introduced the terraced system of cultivation and this brought large tracts of hilly terrain to yield crops productively.

A major sub-cultural stock of the Nepalis are the Kiratis who include Limbus, and Rais. Originally most of them were hunters and shepherds and semi-nomadic. The Limbus who are also called Yakthambas (yak-herders or traders) are divided into three sects: Kashigotra, Bhuiphuta and the Lhasagotra (Tsongs). Each Kirati sect has a dialect of its own. Some of the tribes of the Kiratis are animists (attributing the soul to non-living things like mountains), whereas the others are either Hindus or Buddhists. The deities of the Limbu community are Sri Janga,Tagyera Ningwa Poma and Yuma Shamma. The Rai community also constitute a sizeable population of the state. Some other communities of the Nepalis are the Newars, Sharmas, Basnets, Thakuris, Chettris Mangars, Kamis, Damais and Karkis.

The language spoken by Nepalis is understood all over by the state. This language is similar to Hindi and uses the Devanagri script. The great Hindu epic Ramayana has been translated to Nepali by a Nepali poet named Bhanu

Bhakta who lived in the ninteenth century. The birthday of Bhanu Bhakta holds a special significance for the Nepalis specially to those belonging to the intellectual class. During this day special functions, debates and essay competitions are held in memory of the great poet and writer.

Bhanu Bhakta, the Nepali poet

SAKEWA - AN IMPORTANT RAI FESTIVAL

The Rai community in Sikkim celebrate Sakewa to invoke the blessing of godess Chandi for an abundant crop and favourable weather. Sakewa falls on baisakh purnay (fifteenth day of the fifth month of the Nepali calender) coinciding with the sowing season. Sakewa can therefore also be interpreted as Bhoomi Puj. The Mangpa (priest) performs the prayer. One person beats the hongken (drum) loudly. The mangpa then dances to the single drum beat. The silis, as the dance is called consists of hundred and eight characters of various animals and birds. After the performance of the puja the worshippers partake to wachipa which is a dish made of chicken feathers.

The Rais also observe Sakewa in their homes. Three lungs (stones) are installed in the prayer room to make a furnace called Samkha. The lungs have unique names: Suptulung, Taralung and Shakhalung. While invoking the blessings of the goddess, a fire is lighted in the furnace and the names of the forefathers are called out aloud while offering food, millet, ginger and water. The pot used for the water is called Wabuk or Salawa.

HISTORY OF SIKKIM

The story of Sikkim echoes the land itself - an ardous landscape of peaks and valleys that rise and fall like its tumultous history. The history pertaining to Sikkim before the seventeenth century is not well documented but it is said that somewhere in the thirteenth century a prince named Guru Tashi in Tibet had a divine vision that he should go south to seek his fortune in Denzong " the valley of rice". As directed by the divine vision he along with his family which included five sons headed in the southern direction. The family during their wanderings came across the Sakya kingdom in which a monastery was being built at that time. The workers had not been successful in erecting pillars for the monastery. The elder son of Guru Tashi raised the pillar single handedly and thereby came to be known as Khye Bumsa meaning the superior of ten thousand heroes.

The Sakya king offered his daughter in marriage to Khye Bumsa. Guru Tashi subsequently died and Khye Bumsa settled in Chumbi Valley and it was here that he established contacts with the Lepcha chieftain Tetong Tek in Gangtok. Khye Bumsa was issueless and it was with the blessings of Tetong Tek who was also a religious leader, that Khye Bumsa was finally blessed with three sons. Out of gratitude Khye Bumsa visited Tetong Tek a number of times thereafter which ultimately culminated in a treaty of brotherhood between the two chieftains at a place called Kabi Longtsok. This treaty brought about new ties of brotherhood between the Lepchas and Bhutias.

Khye Bumsa was succeeded by his third son Mipon-Rab. The fourth son of Mipon-Rab was Guru Tashi and it was he who shifted his family and tribe to Gangtok. The Lepchas had meanwhile broken down into small clans and thereafter came under the protection of the descendants of Guru Tashi.

When colonial powers of Britain, Portugal and France were making inroads into the shores of the Indian continent, history of another kind was also being made in Sikkim. Events were taking place that would lead to the establishing a monarchy in Sikkim. As compared to the dynasties in India which left behind rich architectural marvels, the early monarchs in Sikkim built no permanent structures . But the very fact that a monarchy was founded here in an area that was at that time covered densely with forests, mostly uninhabited, remote and inaccessible was itself a watershed event.

The great grandson of Guru Tashi was Phunstok and events led to his becoming consecrated as the first king of Sikkim. Phunstok was born in 1604. It would now not be out of place to digress to events that were taking place in another sphere. The rifts between the Yellow Hat Sect and the Red Hat Sect of the Buddhists in Tibet had led to the followers of the latter to flee southwards to Sikkim and Bhutan to escape prosecution.

Out of the Red Sect Saints who came to Sikkim in the seventeenth century was Lama Latsun Chembo. He felt that he had a mission to establish a Buddhist monarchy in the hidden country of Denjong. After a long journey he reached a place called Norbugang where he was met by two other holymen.

They were Sempa Chembo and Rinzing Chembo. The place where they met was later named as Yoksum meaning the meeting place of the three superior ones. These three great holymen had the mission to establish a Buddhist monarchy in this country which was made up of small clans. But whom should they choose as the monarch? They sent a search party in the easterly direction. The search party went in search for a man called Phunstok who was found at Gangtok. He is the same Phunstok of whom a mention had been made earlier and was the great grandson of Guru Tashi.

Phunstok left for Yoksum with his family and followers and was consecrated as the King of Sikkim in the year 1642 with the title of Chogyal which means the king who rules with righteousness. Phunstok was also conferred the surname Namgyal.

Phunstok Namgyal and the three saints immediately got to the task of successfully bringing the Lepcha tribes under the Buddhist fold. Politically, Sikkim expanded its borders which included Chumbi valley, the present Darjeeling district and a part of present day Nepal and Bhutan. The capital of Sikkim was established in Yoksum itself. It was also then that Sikkim derived its name from "Su" "Khin" which in the Limbu language means "New House" signifying the new palace that the first king constructed.

Phunstok Namgyal was succeeded by his son Tensung Namgyal in 1670. Tensung Namgyal shifted the capital from Yoksum to Rabdanste near present-day Gyalshing. Tensung Namgyal married thrice. One of his wives was the daughter of the Limboo chieftan Yo Yo Hang. His son Chakdor Namgyal from the second wife succeeded him in the year 1700. However his half sister Pendeongmu, whose mother was from Bhutan, claimed that she was entitled to the throne. Because of this fact, serious difference arose between her and Chakdor Namgyal. In order to snatch the throne she went to the extent of taking the help of the Bhutanese to invade Sikkim, and evict her brother. Chakdor Namgyal had to flee Sikkim and the Bhutanese forces occupied the capital Rabdanste. In the process, Kalimpong which was a part of Sikkim was lost to Bhutan. Kalimpong later became a part of British India following a war between Bhutan and the British.

Chakdor Namgyal remained in Lhasa for about seven years and was reinstalled as king with the help of the Tibetans. Chakdor also choreographed many Lama dances especially the ones pertaining to the Phang Labsol festival. He also introduced the system of sending one son from each family to the monastery. When the Chogyal Chakdor Namgyal was ill at the Ralong hot springs in 1716, his half sister Pendeongmu had him murdered. She was later caught and strangled to death. Gyurmed, Chakdor Namgyal's son succeeded him in 1717. Gyurmed Namgyal's reign was uneventful.

Gyurmed Namgyal was succeeded by his illegitimate son Phunstok Namgyal in 1733. Phunstok Namgyal was born posthumously. His reign was marked by an increase in the Lepcha influence in the Sikkimese court. Bhutan tried to occupy Sikkim, but the forces of that country were driven back. The Nepalis on the western border of Sikkim started becoming brazen in their imperialistic designs and made frequent attacks into Sikkim's territory.

Phunstok Namgyal was succeeded by his son Tenzing Namgyal in 1780. During the reign of Tenzing Namgyal, Nepali forces occupied large chunks of Sikkimese territory. They attacked Rabdanste and the Chogyal had to flee to Tibet. The Nepalis excursions emboldened them to penetrate even into Tibet. This led to the Chinese intervention and Nepal was defeated. In the Sino-Nepal treaty, Sikkim lost some its land to Nepal, but monarchy was allowed to be restored in the country. Tenzing Namgyal died in Lhasa and his son Tsudphud Namgyal was sent to Sikkim in 1793 to succeed him as the monarch. Rabdanste was now considered too insecure because of its proximity to the Nepali border and Tsudphud Namgyal shifted the capital to a place called Tumlong.

The defeat of Nepal by the Chinese did little to weaken the expansionist designs of the Nepalis. They continued to make attacks into the neighbouring British territories and Sikkim. British India successfully befriended Sikkim. The British felt that by doing so the expanding powers of the Gorkhas would be curtailed. Britain also looked forward to establishing trade links with Tibet and it was felt that the route through Sikkim was the most feasible.

War between Nepal and British India broke out in 1814 and came to an end in 1816 with the defeat of the Nepalis and the subsequent signing of the treaty of Sigauli. As a direct spin-off, British India signed another treaty with Sikkim in 1817 known as the treaty of Titalia in which former territories which the Nepalis captured were restored to Sikkim. H.H. Risley writes in The Gazetteer of Sikkim,1894, that by the Treaty of Titalia British India has assumed the position of lords paramount of Sikkim and a title to exercise a predominant influence in that State.

The British became interested in Darjeeling both as a hill resort and an outpost from where Tibet and Sikkim would be easily accessible. Following a lot of pressure from the British, Sikkim finally gifted Darjeeling to British India on the understanding that a certain amount would be paid as annual subsidy to Sikkim. The gift deed was signed by the Chogyal Tsudphud Namgyal in 1835. The British appointed a superintendent in the ceded territory. The British however did not pay the compensation as had been stipulated and this led to a quick deterioration of relation between the two countries. The Chief Minister in the king's court, Tokhang Namgyal, also popularly known as Pagla Dewan had strong anti-British convictions and this aggravated the situation further. The relations deteriorated to such an extent that when Dr Campbell, the Superintendent of Darjeeling and Dr. Hooker visited Sikkim in connection with the latter's botanical research, they were captured and imprisoned in 1849. The British issued an ultimatum and the two captives were released after a month's detention. In February 1850, an expedition was sent to Sikkim which resulted in the stoppage of the annual grant of Rs 6,000 to Maharaja of Sikkim and also annexation of Darjeeling and a great portion of Sikkim to British India.

In November 1860 that the British sent an expeditionary force to Sikkim. This force was driven back from Rinchenpong in Sikkim. A stronger force was sent in 1861 under the command of Colonel J.C. Gawler that resulted in a showdown and the signing of a treaty between the British and Sikkimese the same year. This treaty signed by Ashley Eden and Sidekong Namggyal on 28th March 1861 cancelled all the previous treaties signed between Britain and Sikkim and Sikkimese territories in occupation by British India were restored to Sikkim. After the signing of this treaty, the Raja of Sikkim came to be known as Maharajah.

Tsudphud Namgyal was succeeded by his son Sidekong Namgyal in 1863. The British Government started the payment of annual subsidy of Rs 6,000/- in 1850 for Darjeeling. In an attempt to keep good relations with Sikkim, the British enhanced the subsidy to 12,000/- per annum.

Chogyal Sidekong Namgyal died in 1874 issueless and was succeeded by his half brother Thutob Namgyal.

In 1886 a secret treaty was signed in Galing in Tibet btween Sikkim and Tibet agreeing that Sikkim was a part of Tibet. This came as a shock to the British India.The Britishers started building of roads in Sikkim. This was viewed with suspicion by Tibet and in 1886, some Tibetan militia occupied Lingtu in Sikkim near Jelepla pass. In May 1888, the Tibetans attacked Gnathang below Jelepla but were driven away. In September of the same year the British under the command of Brigadier General Graham called for reinforcements and the Tibetans were pushed back from Lingtu. A memorial was built at Gnathang for the British soldiers who died in the engagements.

Alarmed by the defeat of the Tibetans and apprehending that they would lose influence over Tibet, the Chinese began negotiations with the British that finally resulted in the signing of the Anglo-Chinese convention on 17th March 1890. This treaty clearly defined the boundary between Sikkim and Tibet and recognised British India's direct control over the internal and external affairs of Sikkim and prohibited Sikkim to have direct links with any other country without the permission of the British.

The Britishers appointed Claude White as the first Political Officer in Sikkim in 1889 and Chogyal Thutob Namgyal was virtually under his supervision. Claude White played a pioneering role in bringing about radical changes in the administrative setup as well as improving the economy of the state by introducing revenue earning agricultural methods. In the process however there was a large influx of people from outside the state to till the land. To protect the interest of the Bhutia and Lepchas, White marked lands belonging to them that could not be sold to other communities. This practice still continues till date with land belonging to Bhutias and Lepchas not being permitted to be sold to other communities.

Thutob Namgyal shifted the capital from Tumlong to Gangtok in 1894. The Sir Thutob Namgyal Memorial Hospital (STNM) hospital built in 1917 is named in the memory of Thutob Namgyal who died in 1914.

Towards the last quarter of the nineteenth century, plainsmen especially, the Marwaris started to come to Sikkim for trade. Jetmull & Bhojraj established a bank at Gangtok in 1899 and soon became the offical bank of the Government and remained so till the seventies.

The Garden Party at the Gangtok Residency in 1890

An Excerpt from "Sikkim and Bhutan" by J. Claude White, the first Political Officer of Sikkim

My first garden party would have seemed very quaint to European eyes. I had invited the Maharaja and Maharani, with the members of Council, and all Kazis and headmen with their wives and families. A goodly crowd assembled about four hours before the appointed time and lined the road just outside the Residency grounds, sitting about on the grassy edges until they were told they might come in, determined not to be late. Most of them had never seen, much less tasted European sweets or cakes, and when tea-time came they simply cleaned the tables of everything, and what they could not eat they carried away in the front of their voluminous coats. They emptied the sugar basins, and even took the spoons and liqueur glasses, and it all took place so quietly while my wife and I were with the Maharaja and Maharani and more important guests in another tent, I hardly realised what was going on.

The spoons and glasses, which I think they wanted as mementos of the good time they had had, were returned, on the Phodong Lama and Shoe Dewan remonstrating, and they departed very happily, declaring they had highly enjoyed their entertainment, and that all their heads were going round, a polite way of saying I had not stinted the drinks. They were always a very cheerful crowd and very pleasant to deal with, though indolent and improvident.

After my house was finished, nothing pleased them more than to be allowed to wander round the rooms, especially the bedrooms. They never touched anything, but liked to see how we lived and what European furniture was like.

Almost every market day little bands of women dressed in their best clothes would arrive with a few eggs or a pat of butter to make their salaams to my wife and a request that they might be allowed to go over the house, and their progress was marked with exclamations and gurgles of laughter at the strange ways of Sahib-log.

While the house was building, the Maharani came several times to see how it was getting on, and told me I had built the walls much too thin and it would never stand. In their own houses and monasteries the walls are very thick, from 3 feet to 4 feet 6 inches, and have always a small camber. However, later on I had the best of the argument when, in the earthquake of 1897, the Palace, notwithstanding its thick walls, collapsed entirely and had to be rebuilt, while the Residency, though badly cracked, remained standing.

Jetmull & Bhojraj,
BANKERS AND MERCHANTS, SUDDER BAZAR, CART ROAD, GANGTAK BRANCH, (SIKKIM.)
BANKING DEPARTMENT,
Gangtak the 18th July 1906.
No. 179

An interesting Letterhead

The letterhead of Jetmull & Bhojraj who established a bank at the Ridge Road at Gangtok in 1899. Jetmul and Bhojraj were Marwari businessmen. A market called Sudder Bazar existed till the early nineteen twenties on the Ridge, then called the Cart Raod, before it shifted to present day M.G. Marg.

Alarmed by the growing Russian influence in Tibet and also to assert itself, the British sent an expedition led by Col Francis Younghusband to Lhasa via Jelepla in 1904. Many villagers were forced to work as labourers in the expedition and were punished with flogging in the event of their not participating. Lambodar Pradhan a son of Luchmidas Pradhan was given the task of hiring the villagers as labourers. The expedition met with resistance from the Tibetan army which was defeated and a treaty was dictated by Younghusband on Tibet on 7th September 1904. The treaty was known as the Lhasa Convention. The treaty secured monopoly trading privileges in Tibet for the British. Tibet agreed to adhere by the Anglo-Chinese Convention of 1890 and to recognise the border between Sikkim and Tibet.

Thutob Namgyal was succeeded by his son Sidekong Tulku in 1914. Unfortunately he did not live long and died in the same year. He was succeeded by his half brother Tashi Namgyal who promulgated many reforms in the state. Evil Practices like Jharlangi, Bhethi, Kuruwa and Khalo Bhari were in existence.

Jharlangi was the system of unpaid labour recruited by the Government for the purpose of construction of road and bridges. The British expeditions resorted to Jharlangi extensively. Bhethi was the system of each household providing unpaid labour to Mandals and Kazis for a fixed number of days in a year. Kuruwa was again a type of labour conscripted to carry the luggage of Government officials passing through the villages. Khalo Bhari, as its name implies, were goods that were packed in black tarpaulin to be illegally exported to Tibet These evil practices were abolished by Tashi Namgyal. In a bid to tone up the administration by providing incentives, many were awarded the medal 'Dorjee Pema' the highest medal.

Claude White was succeeded as Political Officer by Charles Bell. The Political Officers who followed Charles Bell and served for about a couple of years each during the pre-independent period were O'Connor, Bailey, Campbell, Weir, Gould Macdonald, Williamson, Hopkinson, Richardson, Ludlow, Sherrif, Dhondup, Rivett-Carnac, Fletcher, Russell, Hailey, Battye, Sakerr, Kennedy, Vance, Worth, Sinclair, Gloyne, Davis, Mainprice, Flinch, Dark, Thornburgh and Robins.

Harishwar Dayal was appointed as the first Indian Political Officer to Sikkim after Independence. He was succeeded by Balraj Kapur, Appa B. Pant, Inderjit Bahadur Singh, V.H. Coelho, N.B. Menon, K.S. Bajpai, B.Singh and Gurbachan Singh in that order till the merger of Sikkim with India.

In 1949, John Lall joined as the first Dewan or Principal Administrative Officer (PAO) of Sikkim. The Dewan was the highest bureaucrat and the head of administration. He was on deputation to the State administration from the Government of India. During the Chogyal's absence, he used to function on his behalf. John Lal was succeeded by Nari Rustomji and then Baleshwar Prasad followed by R.N. Haldipur and I.S. Chopra. In 1969, the title of PAO was changed to Sidlon which in Tibetan language means Prime Minister.

Many Sikkimese fought for the British during the Second World War. Notable among them was Ganju Lama who was decorated with the Victoria Cross (VC)

SOME INTERESTING DOCUMENTS

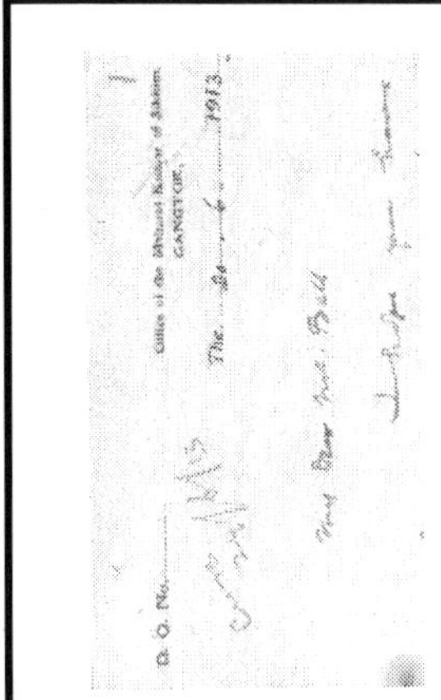

Prince Sidekong Tulku got a part of his education at Oxford. He wanted to implement many reforms. This is part of a copy of the letter that he wrote to Political Officer Camb Bell voicing his concern about the drunkards in the town and suggesting that ...'people found drunk in the Bazar or on the thoroughfare be prosecuted and fined..........' Sidekong Tulku succeeded the throne in 1914 but unfortunately died the same year

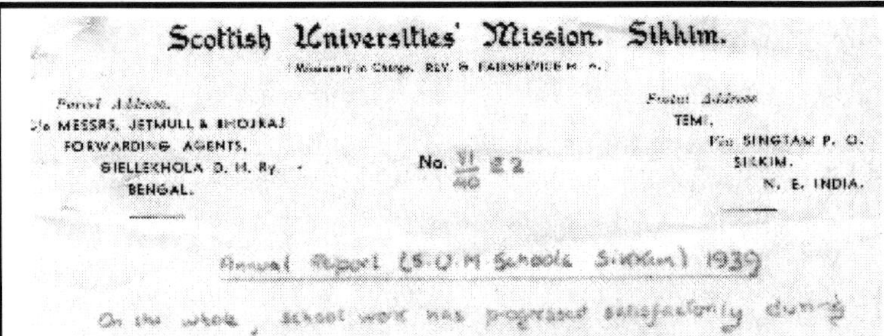

Scottish Universities' Mission. Sikkim.

Parcel Address.
c/o MESSRS. JETMULL & BHOJRAJ
FORWARDING AGENTS.
GIELLEKHOLA D. H. Ry.
BENGAL.

Postal Address
TEMI,
Via SINGTAM P. O.
SIKKIM.
N. E. INDIA.

No. VI/40 22

Annual Report (S.U.M. Schools Sikkim) 1939

On the whole, school work has progressed satisfactorily during

All Departments and units were required to submit a report of their activities annually to the Secretary to the Maharaja which was then compiled and forwarded to the Political Officer.

A part of the report submitted in 1939 by the missionary school, Scottish Universities' Mission, at Temi is reproduced here. The parcel address has been given as Gielle Khola in the letterhead. A narrow gauge railway line existed till Gielle Khola near Tista till 1951 when it was washed away by floods.

for demonstrating exemplary bravery on the Burma front.

During the late fifties, a goods ropeway from Gangtok to Thegu, short of Nathula was constructed to make the trade between Sikkim and Tibet more efficient as it was felt that getting the goods down from Nathula on mules resulted in a wastage of time and money and traders would prefer this mode of transport for their goods. However, the ropeway could hardly be used for the purpose it was built for as the Indo-China war of 1962, resulted in the closure of borders between the two countries. During the early sixties, the Sikkim Distilleries at Rangpo and the Fruit Preservation Factory at Singtam were established. In 1953 the institutions of the Executive Council and State Council came into being to assist the Chogyal. These councils consisted of elected and nominated Executive Councillors

Tashi Namgyal died in 1963 and was succeeded by his son Palden Thondup Namgyal. By the beginning of 1970 there were rumblings in the political ranks and file of the state which demanded the removal of monarchy and the establishment of a democratic setup. This finally culminated in wide spread agitation against Sikkim Durbar in 1973. There was a complete collapse in the administration. The Indian Government tried to bring about a semblance of order in the state by appointing a Chief Administrator Mr. B.S. Das. Further events and elections led to Sikkim becoming transformed from a Protectorate to an Associate State. On 4th September 1974, the leader of Sikkim Congress, Kazi Lendup Dorji was elected as the Chief Minister of the State. The Chogyal however still remained as the constitutional figure head monarch in the new setup. Events leading to the confrontation between the Chogyal and the popular Government caused Sikkim to become a full fledged state of India on 16th May 1975. Mr. B. B. Lal was the first Governor of Sikkim.

After B.B.Lal the office of Governor were held by H.J.H Taleyarkhan, K. Prabakar Rao, B.N. Singh, T.V. Rajeshwar, S.K.Bhatnagar, Admiral R.H. Tahiliani, P.Shiv Shankar, K.V. Raghunatha Reddy, Chaudhary Randhir Singh, K.N. Sahini , V Rama Rao (R.S. Gavai was also Governor for one month during V Rama Rao tenure) and B.P Singh.

ELECTIONS IN SIKKIM BEFORE THE MERGER

In 1947 when India became independent, Tashi Namgyal was successful in getting a special status of Protectorate for Sikkim. This was in face of stiff resistance from local parties like Sikkim State Congress who wanted a democratic setup and accessation of Sikkim to the Union of India. In fact this party got the Maharaj to agree to install a five member interim government including two nominees of his own. The first popular government was therefore installed in May 1949. But things did not work out properly and a month later the ministry was dissolved and the monarchy system allowed to continue. On 5th Dec 1950 a treaty was signed between India and Sikkim that ratified the status of Sikkim as a Protectorate with Chogyal as the monarch. Under this treaty, the Defence and Foreign Affairs of Sikkim was to be looked after by India. The Postal system and Currency would also be Indian.The internal administration would be looked after by the Chogyal. A new party which

P. T. NAMGYAL - THE LAST KING OF SIKKIM

(An Excerpt from Sikkim Coronation Souvenir)

Miwang Chogyal Chempo Palden Thondup Namgyal, Twelfth Consecrated Chogyal of Sikkim, was born at Gangtok on 22nd May 1923. The Chogyal Chempo was the second son of the late illustrious Chogyal Sir Tashi Namgyal. The Chogyal started his schooling at Saint Joseph's Convent, Kalimpong, at the age of six. In 1935 he continued his studies at Saint Joseph's College, Darjeeling, and completed his studies at Bishop Cotton School, Shimla, in 1941. He could not study further because of the untimely demise of Prince Paljor, the heir apparent, who was then serving as an officer in the Royal India Air Force.

As the heir-apparent, Crown Prince Palden Thondup Namgyal underwent the Indian Civil Service training course at Dehra Dun in 1942 and thereafter returned to his country. The young Crown Prince started taking an active interest in the administration of his country.

In August 1950 he married Sangey Deki, daugther of Yapshi Phodrant of Tibet. Sangey Deki died in June, 1957. In March, 1963 he married Miss Hope Cooke of the United States of America. The Chogyal had three issues from the first wife - Tenzing, Wangchuk and Yangchen. From the American wife- Palden and Hope.

After the death of his father, Palden was crowned as the Twelfth Chogyal of Sikkim on 4th April 1965. The Evening Standard dated 5th April 1965 had this to say about the Coronation

A King was crowned in the bright sunshine this morning in the Himalayan land of Sikkim where there are giant butterflies and pandas and four hundred different species of wild orchid - a day chosen by the astrologers as "entirely favourable." The Mahayana Buddhist ceremony at the splendid pagoda-type Royal Chapel was remarkable. The chapel, every inch decorated with pointed carving and tassels and cylindrical banners hanging from the ceiling, was packed with a strange cross section of the world and cameramen were flashing and whirling and jostling. Monks and Lamas in their tall red hoods grouped round the Chogyal, were deep in their religious rites and quite unaware of the commotion. The King mounted his golden throne, covered with 13 cushions signifying 13 stages of perfection at the auspicious hour. He sat cross-legged and serene in his golden brocade robes, lined with red satin and embrodiered with lotus flowers, while he was presented with innumerable objects (symbolising moral virtue, compassion, altruism, stability and power) and listened to the rhythmic chanting of the lamas and monks. Speeches in English and Sikkimese followed the ceremonial taking of tea. The King read a speech from the throne in English thanking the people for their loyalty, remembering his father with reverence and thanking India for her kindness.

All the ceremonies were presided over by Sikkim's spirits, who live on the summit of the Kanchendzonga, whose snowy peak smiled through the window facing the throne.

Sikkim became an integral part of India in May 1975 following which Palden Thondup Namgyal no longer remained the Maharaja: the three hundred year old monarchy thus came to an end. A few years later he became estranged with his wife Hope. In 1977 his eldest son Tenzing died in a car accident. Palden Thondup Namgyal died of cancer in 1982 - a dejected man. His son Prince Wanchuk presently stays in the "Palace".

was pro Maharaja was launched by the name of National Party was formed.

The first general election was held in 1953 on the basis of this parity formula. Of the twelve seats, six seats were reserved for the Bhutia, Lepchas, six for the Nepalis. Besides these five seats were to be filled by nomination by the Maharaja. A Bhutia Lepcha candidate was to be first elected in a primary election by the Bhutia Lepcha voters only. In order to finally qualify these persons elected by the Bhutia-Lepcha voters would be confirmed in the general election. For the purpose of the elections, Sikkim was divided into four territorial constituencies: Gangtok, North Central, Namchi & Pemayantse. The twelve seats were distributed amongst these four constituencies. For instance Pemayantse had 3 seats (2 Nepalis and 1 Bhutia) and a voter in this constituency had to cast three votes one each for the seats. So in effect one man had three votes in the Pemayantse constituency.

The election process was further complicated as a candidate in order to get elected would not only have to secure the highest number of votes from his community but also a minimum percentage of votes from the other community. The system of calculating votes was as follows:

> ***The candidate securing the highest number of votes of the community which he represents will ordinarily be required to have secured at least 15 percent of the total votes of the other community for which seats have been reserved to entitle him to be returned. If, however, he fails to secure 15 percent of the votes of the other community, the candidate securing the next highest votes of his community and who has also succeeded in securing 15 percent of the votes of the other community will be eligible to be returned, provided the difference between the number of votes of his community secured by him and the highest candidate does not exceed 15 percent of the votes secured by the latter. If the difference is in excess of 15 percent the latter will be regarded as returned, not withstanding that he shall not have secured 15 percent of of the votes of the other community.***

Such a pattern of calculating votes was therfore biased and all the political parties of Sikkim, except the National Party, agitated against this and demanded "One man one vote".

Along with the state council, an executive council was also constituted. It consisted of the Dewan and four elected members from the State Council. The second general elections were held in 1958.The seats in the council were raised from 17 to 20;2 new elective seats one general and the other reserved for the Sangha Monastery were included.The number of nominated seats were raised from 5 to 6. In 1960 a new political party The Sikkim National Congress emerged by the merger of the Sawtantra Dal, Praja Samalen and the dissidents of the Sikkkim State Congress and the National party. Kazi Lendup Dorjee was unanimously elected as the president of the party.

The third general elections were held in 1967. Four more seats were added and the break up was: 7 Bhutia-Lepchas, 7 Nepalis, 1 Sanga, 1 Tsong, 1 SC/ ST, 1 General and 6 nominated. During the end of 1969 a new party named Sikkim Janata Party was formed by Lal Bahadur Basnet.

The fourth general general election were held in 1970. In October 1972, the Sikkim State Congress and the Sikkim Janata Party merged together to form the Sikkim Janata Congress. The fifth general election was held in 1973 but triggered off wide protests in the State on charges of rigging and the demand of one man one vote voting pattern. In order to bring normalcy to the state a process of conciliation between the Chogyal and the political parties through the Government of India began and resulted in the tripartitie agreement of the 8th May 1973 with an aim to setting up a more democratic constitution and ensuring greater legislative and executive powers for the representatives of the people. The signatories were the Chogyal, the Foreign Secretary, Government of India and the representatives of the three political parties.

ELECTIONS AFTER THE MERGER

Following the Tripartite Agreement, the State was divided into 32 constituencies: 15 seats were reserved for the Bhutia-Lepchas, 15 for the Nepalis, 1 for the Schedule Caste/Schedule Tribe and one for the Sangha.The Chogyal would continue to be the constitutional head and the Assembly would have no powers to question him or his family. The head of the administration would be a Chief Executive from India. The first election for the Assembly was held in April 1974 and the party of Kazi Lendup Dorjee, Sikkim Congress swept the polls by winning 31 seats. The Government of Sikkim pressed hard to have closer ties with India and on 5th September, 1974, the Constitution (Thirty-fifth amendment) was passed in Parliament to up-grade the status of Sikkim from a protectorate to an associate state of the India. However differences between the Chogyal and the Assembly got aggravated to such an extent, that the Sikkim Assembly unanimously adopted a resolution, on 10 April, 1975, abolishing the institution of the Chogyal and declaring Sikkim as a constituent unit of India. The Assembly also resolved to submit its resolution to the people of Sikkim by way of a general referendum. About 60,000 votes were cast in favour of the resolution whereas 1,500 against. Consequently the Lok Sabha and the Rajya Sabha passed the Thirty-Eight Constitution Amendment Bill, which received the assent of the President on 16th May 1975 and made Sikkim the 22nd state of the Indian Union.

The next election was held in October 1979. Prior to the elections, however, an Ordinance, called the Representation of the People (Amendment) Ordinance, 1979 was issued in which the seat reservation for the Nepalis was withdrawn. Out of the 32 seats, 12 seats were reserved for Bhutia-Lepchas, 2 seats for the Scheduled Caste and one seat for the Sangha. The other seats were general. Many parties dubbed this Ordinance as the Black Bill because it completely did away the seat reservations for the Nepalis.The Sikkim Janata Parishad led by N.B.Bhandari secured 17 seats and formed the government. In 1981 the Sikkim Janata Parishad joined the Congress(I) and became the Sikkim Pradesh Congress(I). In 1984 the government of N.B.Bhandari was dismissed by the governor on the ground that he had lost the support of the M.L.A's. B.B. Gurung was installed as the new chief minister but his ministry lasted only 13 days and President's rule was imposed. N.B. Bhandari formed a new party called the Sikkim Sangram Parishad which won 31 of the 32 seats in the General Elections in 1984. In the 1989 elections N.B. Bhandari was returned to power the third time by sweeping all the 32 seats. On 17th May 1994, dissidents toppled the Bhandari Government on the controversial issue of income tax concessions to the tribals. Mr. Sanchaman Limboo was installed as the Chief Minister as head of the party called the Sikkim Sangram Parishad (Sanchaman). In the Assembly election held on 17th Nov. 1994, a regional party, the Sikkim Democratic Front was returned to power and its leader Mr. Pawan Chamling was installed as the Chief Minister of Sikkim. The Sikkim

Some old Sikkimese Laws and Customs

(Excerpted from the book "A Gazetteer of Sikhim" by H.H. Risley, 1894. These laws and customs are of course no longer prevalent)

Marriage Customs of the Sikhimese

If the eldest brother takes a wife, she is common to all his brothers. If the second brother takes a wife, she is common to all the brothers younger than himself. The eldest brother is not allowed to cohabit with the wives of the younger brothers. Should there be children in the first case, the children are named after the eldest brother, whom they call father. In case 2, after the second brother, &c.Three brothers can marry three sisters, and all the wives are common, but this case is not very often seen. In such a case the children of the eldest girl belong to the eldest brother, & c., if they each bear children. Should one or more not bear children, then the children are apportioned by arrangement. Two men not related can have one wife in common, but this arrangement is unusual. A man occasionally lends his wife to a friend, but the custom is not general and uncommon.

If a girl becomes pregnant before marriage and afterwards marries the father of the child, the child is considered legitimate, but the man is fined a bull or its equivalent, which go to her relatives. Should the man by whom the girl was made pregnant not marry her, and should she afterwards marry another, the child remains with the woman's brothers or relatives. A woman is not considered dishonoured by having a child before marriage.

Taking another's wife or adultery

The old law runs that if any one takes a Raja's or Lama's wife, he may be banished, have his hands cut off, or his penis cut off. He may also have to pay a weight in gold equal to his penis and testicles. For violating woman of different position 3 oz. of gold have to be paid to the woman's relations and 4 gold srang to the Government, besides many things in kind.

For violation of a woman of the same position, 2 or 3 gold srang and several kinds of articles have to be paid. If the woman goes of her own accord to the man, he has only to pay 1 gold srang and three kinds of articles.

Democratic Front was returned to power in 1999, 2004 and then in 2009.

On the national front, the members who were elected from Sikkim for the Lok Sabha are S.K. Rai, C.B. Katwal, Pahal Man Subba, N.B. Bhandari, D.K. Bhandari, Nandu Thapa, D.K. Bhandari, Bhim Dahal and Nakul Rai in that order. L.S. Saring was the first Rajya Sabha member from Sikkim followed by Kesang Namgyal Paljor, Karma Topden , Kalzang Gyatso Bhutia P.T. Gyamsto O.T. Lepcha and Hissey Lachungpa.

IMPORTANT BUDDHIST FESTIVALS

After Buddha attained Nirvana, differences of opinion arose in the religion causing the formation of new sects. Finally in about 100 AD a split took place and caused the formation of two schools, which later became known as the Hinayana (Southern) and the Mahayana (Northern). The Hinayana adhered to more primitive Buddhism, which was primarily a philosophy with rules and ethics and emphasized on realisation of Nirvana (freedom from the cycle of birth and rebirth) only for oneself by directly worshipping the Buddha. The Mahayana schools believes in attaining Nirvana by worshipping the dieties called Bodhisattvas who do not want to attain Nirvana until they have freed all the humanity from suffering. The Mahayana has a wider base as it believes in attaining Nirvana for oneself as well as all suffering humanity.

The native religion of Tibet was called Bon which is said to be founded by Shenrab Mibo. This religion was fused and refined by Buddhism by Guru Padmasambva and this gave birth to the Red Hat Sect of Buddhism. The Red Hat sect was further reformed by Atisha and the Kadampa sect was established. Tsong-kha-pa modified the Kadampa and led to the formation of the Yellow Sect.

Tibetan Buddhism is therefore divided into the Red and Yellow Sects. The Red Sect comprises of the Nyingma, Kargyu and Sakya lineages and the Yellow Sect consists of the Gelugpa lineage. Whereas the Nyingma Sect is associated with Guru Padmasambva, the founders of Kargyu and Sakya are said to be Marpa and Khon Konechog Gyalpo respectively. The sects and the lineages are differentiated from each other by the rituals performed, monastic discipline and the founder. However the differences tend to blur with rituals of one lineage overlapping the other.

The Tibetan sacred books are called the Kanjur and the Tanjur. The Kanjur correspond to the original teachings of the Buddha and has three sections or Tripitakas whereas the Tanjurr are related to the teachings of the commentaries of the teachings. Each year or *lo* of the Buddhist calender is named after an animal these animals being: rat, bull, tiger, rabbit, garuda, snake, horse, sheep, monkey, hen dog and pig. Similarly each month of a year is named after an animal. These being: Tag (Tiger), the 11th month, Yeo (Hare) the 12th month, Druk (Dragon), the 1st month, Drul (snake), the 2nd month, Tah (Horse), the 3rd month, Lug (sheep), the 4th month, Trel (Monkey), the 5th month, Jya (Bird) the 6th month, Khye (Dog), the 7th month, Phag (Pig), the 8th month, Jewa (Mouse) the 9th month and Lang(Ox), the 10th month.

The count of the first month of the year according to astrological calculation begins from Tiger, the 11th month. The twelve months are grouped into four seasons of three months each. They are Chiyid-ka, the spring; Yar-ka, the summer, Ton-ka, the autumn and Gyun-ka, the winter.

FESTIVALS

Saga Dawa

This is the "Triple Blessed Festival" and is considered as the holiest of the holy Buddhist festivals. On this day in different years of his life, Lord Buddha took birth, achieved Enlightenment and passed away attaining Nirvana; three important events celebrated in the festival of Saga Dawa.

Lord Buddha was born in Lumbini in Nepal to King Sudhodhna and Queen Maha Maya of the Sakya Clan around 560 BC. He was named Siddhartha and his parents took all the pains to make his life comfortable and keep him ensconed from the miseries of the world. At the age of twenty-nine, realisation dawned upon Prince Siddhartha that all the worldly pleasures were transient and unreal and that the ultimate truth lay elsewhere. He renounced the world and after wandering for many years in search of the truth reached Sarnath in Uttar Pradesh (India), where he meditated under the Bodhi tree and attained Enlightenment at the age of thirty five. Buddha, the Enlightened One, left for his heavenly abode at the age of eighty-one at Kusinara on attaining Nirvana or deliverance into bliss.

At Gangtok, a highlight of Saga Dawa is the procession carrying the Holy books of the teachings of Buddha from the Tsuklakhang Monastery in the Palace around the town.

This festival is held on the full moon of the 4th month of the Buddhist calender around the end of May and early June.

Drukpa Teshi

This festival celebrates Buddha's first preaching of the four Noble Truths to his first five disciples in a deer park at Sarnath. The first is the Noble Truth of suffering. The Second Noble Truth is the truth of the origin of suffering Karma and Delusion and their causes. The third Noble Truth is the cessation of the suffering or the attainment of Nirvana. The fourth Noble Truth is the truth of the Eight Fold Path leading to Nirvana. The eight fold paths are 1. Right Understanding 2. Right Thought 3. Right Speech 4. Right Actions 5.Right livelihood 6.Right Effort 7. Right Mindfulness 8. Right Concentration.

The day falls on the fourth day (Teshi) of the sixth Tibetan month (Drukpa) around August.At Gangtok, Drukpa Teshi is marked by prayers at the Deer Park and at a secluded place called Muguthang in extreme North Sikkim the festival is celebrated by holding a Yak race.

Guru Rinpoche's Trungkar Tsechu

The birth anniversary of Guru Padmasambva, also known as Guru |Rinpoche, is celebrated in Sikkim with great pomp. A procession, which originates from the Chorten, carrying the statue of the Guru is taken out around the town of Gangtok. In the evening dramas and concerts depicting the life of the Guru are held.

Phang Lhabsol

This festival is quite unique to Sikkim. It was popularised by the third Chogyal of Sikkim, Chakdor Namgyal. In this festival the snowy range of

Kachendzonga is worshipped for its unifying powers. This festival marks the signing of the treaty of brotherhood between the Lepchas and Bhutias by Khye Bumsa and Tetong Tek when the local deities were invoked to witness the occasion. In fact Phang means witness. On this day, the guardian deity is portrayed by masked Lama dancers as a fiery red-faced deity with a crown of five skulls, riding a snow lion. To lighten the mood of the spectators, jesters called 'Atchars' play antics during the Chaams.This festival is held on the 15th day of the 7th month around August and September. Of late the festival is celebrated in a big way at Rabongla.

Lhabab Dhuechen

This festivals symbolises the Descent of Buddha from the heaven of the thirty three gods after visiting his mother. Dhuechen means" festival", Lha means "heaven" and Bab means "descent".

Legend says that Queen Maha Maya, the mother of Lord Buddha, did not live long after his birth and took rebirth in Trayastrimsa or the heaven of the thirty Gods. After attaining Enlightenment, Lord Buddha through spiritual powers came to know about the whereabouts of his mother and at the age of forty-one ascended to the heavens alongwith thousands of his followers. Lord Buddha stayed in heaven for three months during which he delivered sermons to his mother and other celestial beings. Lord Buddha had left behind on earth one of his disciples, Maudgalyayana, as his representative. This disciple and other devotees of the Lord could not bear the long separation and longed to hear his preachings. Maugalyayana, who possessed miraculous powers, was exhorted to go up to the heaven to request the Lord to return back to the earth. The gods were not willing to let Lord Buddha return back to earth but Maugalyanana suggested that as the earthly beings did not have the powers to visit heaven, the celestial beings could come to the earth to attend his preachings. Lord Buddha finally relented and descended to the earth at a place called Sankasya along a triple ladder that was prepared especially for the occasion by Viswakarma, the God of Machines.

Losoong and the Chaams (Lama Dances)

Losoong marks the end of the harvest season and also the end of the tenth month of the Tibetan Year. As it falls in the eleventh month of the Tibetan calender it is not the real New Year in the sense of the word. Also known as Sonam Lossar, it is in fact an agriculture New Year when rice and grains are plentiful and the weather is moderate in sharp contrast to the actual new year Lossar which falls in a lean season and when it is extremely cold. Before Losoong a ceremony called Gutor is performed by monks in the monasteries. Kagyed (Eight teachings of the Guru) dance forms an important part of the Gutor ceremony and is held on the 28th day of the 11th month at the monasteries at Enchey, Palace (Tsulakhang), Phodong and old Rumtek. The other religious dances or Chaams that are performed prior to Losoong are Rolchaam (cymbal dance),

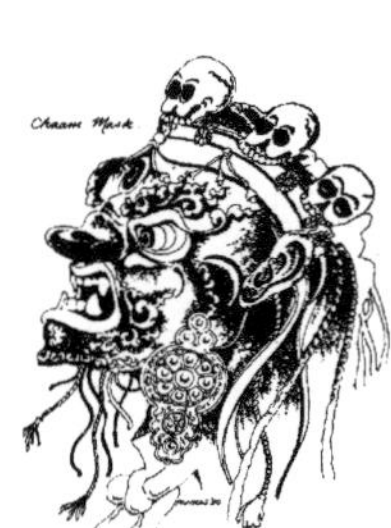

Tshamche (animal headed mask dance), Shyak (dance of horned animals), Namding (dance of winged animals), Thakshobalap (dance of the beasts of prey), Hdur (skeleton dance), shanag (black hat dance), Thoma Tshoglen (dance of wrathful deities) and Shawa chaam (stag dance). The dances symbolise the exorcizing of the evil spirits of the year and the welcoming of the good spirits of the new year. They also essentially represent the victory of the good over evil. The Head Lama or Dorjee Lopen of the Monastery and the Music conductor or Rolpon supervise the performance of the dances. Men become gods during the dances and don attires with mystical symbols.

The orchestra consists of Gyaling and Kyaling, which are trumpets, dungkar (conch), nga chen (drums) and rolmo and silnyen which are types of cymbals.

The Rolchaam is unique to Sikkim and was introduced by Chogyal Chakdor Namgyal. The Rolchaam is performed by 12 dancers.

The twelve animals depicted in the Tshamche chaam are : Singhi (snow lion), male and female Shawas (deer), Lang (Bull), Shyak (yak), Tel (monkey), Chachug (garuda), cha (bird), Hookpa (hawk), druk (dragon), chusing (crocodile), ta (tiger) and dul (snake). The Tshamche chaam is performed admist the reading of prayers from the Guda, which is a prayer book.

In the Shyak and Namding chaam there is no reading of scriptures from the Guda. Shyak has four dancers representing the yak, bull , garuda and stag. In the Namding chaam birds like the the eagle, garuda, parrot and owl are represented.

The Shanag (black hat dance) is particularly impressive. This dance celebrates the killing of the trecherous King Langdarma of the Yarlung dynasty in the ninth century by a monk, Pelkyi Dorjee, using a dagger hidden in the voluminous sleeves of his garment. King Langdarma was virulently anti-Buddhist and had been prosecuting monks and destroying monasteries. Black hat dancers, who normally number 12, carry phurpa (daggers) in the left hand and a bandha (skull cap) in the right hand. The masks used during the dances are usually made of wood but some dancers use copper masks. In order to protect their faces from the mask's sharp edges, the dancers wear padded caps covering the forehead, the neck and the sides of the faces. The caps are held in position by scarves. The mask is much larger than a human face and the dancers see through the mouth or the nostrils of the masks.

The chaamgo (dancing dress) is made of high quality brocade. A pair of Lham (boots) made of colourful cloth is another important item of the costume of a chaam dancer. The dancers move circular and clockwise around a phya dar (flagpole) Atchars or clowns provide comic relief to the audiences during the breaks between the dances and keep it laughing. At the Chaams at Lachung monastery, the audience come with heaps of eatables and drinks - chang, tea, pork, rice etc. and sit cross-legged in front of Choksee tables partaking to the food as they watch the dances.

The first day of the eleventh month marking the actual beginning of Losoong is known as Tshe Tchi. Prayers are held and the elders bless the younger members of the family by applying Chimma (flour) to the head or the shoulders.

On the second and third days people visit each others homes and exchange greetings. On the fourth and fifth day community feastings take place. The anti-climax of the Losoong festival is Nyempa Guzom, on the sixth and seventh day when it is said that nine evil spirits meet and therefore it is considered inauspicious to venture out. People generally stay at home and rest accompanied by a few bouts of drinking and gambling.

Lossar

It is the Tibetan New Year also known as the Gyalpo Lossar, and is marked with lot of gaiety and festivity. It falls normally in the month of February. At Pemayanste, Chaams are held two days before the Losar. These Chaams are similar to the one held during Losoong.

Bumchu

This festival is held at the monastery at Tashiding in the month of February or March. During the festival, the pot containing the Holy water is opened by the lamas of the monastery. The level of water in the pot foretells the future for the forthcoming year. If the water is to the brim, it prophesies bloodshed and disturbances. If the pot is almost dry it signifies famine and if it is half full, it foretells a year in which peace and prosperity will prevail. Bum in fact means "pot or vase" and chu means "water".

A part of the holy water is distributed amongst the gathering of devotees and the pot is replenished with river water, which has been collected one day before from the Rathong Chu river, and sealed at the end of the festival to be opened only in the next Bumchu.

The Kalchakra Puja

Drawing:Dinesh Pradhan, Green Circle

A mention of the two bodies of Buddhism, Hinayana and Mahayana has been made at the beginning of this chapter. To attain Nirvana or Enlightenment and Freedom from suffering one of the paths offered is Tantrayana which emphasises the Tantric or mystic aspect of Buddhism involving complex and esoteric rituals. Anutara Yoga Tantra or the Supreme Tantra is one of the class of Tantrayana which combines male tantras and female tantras out of which Kalchakra is one of the deities. The rituals and meditations performed to Kalchakra with the ultimate aim of attaining Nirvana or Buddhahood is known as the Kalchakra Puja. The Dalai Lama is presently the ultimate authority in teachings of Kalchakra Puja which His Holiness performs to initiate the disciples. His Holiness holds the Kalchakra Mass Initiation Puja usually once in three years

Kalchakra deity is usually represented in union with his female consort Viswamata. The body of Kalchakra is blue in colour and has multiple necks, shoulders and faces. The many hands of Kalchakra hold various implements. Viswamata, the consort of Kalchakra, has a yellow coloured body, four faces and eight hands. Like in other Buddhist rituals, the Kalchakra Puja also centres around the Mandala which consists of rites, offerings and the deities that concern the Puja.

IMAGES AND SYMBOLS

Monasteries and many buildings in Sikkim are richly decorated with symbols and icons. These symbols are painted or embossed on the walls or on Tankas. These paintings may depict the life of Buddha or some Tibetan saint, the Wheel of Life or a deity surrounded by lesser deities.

Wheel of Life

The wheel of life is one of the purest Buddhist emblems. This emblem can be seen in the entrance of almost all monasteries. This emblem is also widely depicted on Thankas or religious scrolls.

The circular form of this wheel symbolises the ceaseless worldly existence. This wheel is held in the clutches of a monster with its claws and teeth and signifies the passionate clinging of the people to exist in this world. The hub of the wheel contains a cock, a snake and a pig. The cock signifies lust or desire, the snake signifies anger and the pig symbolises ignorance and stupidity. These are shown in the centre of the wheel as it is said that they are the root cause of the trouble on earth.

In the intermediate circle of the wheel of life, the five worlds are drawn as advised by Lord Buddha. The rim between the intermediate world and the innermost circle of ignorance, lust and envy is drawn in half white and half black. White area symbolises good deeds and black symbolises bad or evil deeds. People going upwards in white portion represent people who have performed good deeds in their life time and are now going to take rebirth in the world of gods. People going in the black portion indicate hell or the world of animals.

In the intermediate circle there are five parts that of which the two upper parts symbolise heavenly and human worlds. The remaining three worlds in the lower part symbolise sinful deeds leading to a world of animals, ghosts and hell. Outer most circle shows 12 phases of life.

Eight Lucky signs and their significance

The eight signs are called as Tashi Tagyein Tibetan. These auspicious signs are intimate with life and teachings of Buddha. These eight lucky signs manifest themselves in paintings and in the form of carvings on furniture and can also be seen on the walls of buildings. The eight lucky signs have been explained briefly below

1.**The Dug (Parasol):**The Parasol of authority symbolises the authority of Buddha. The parasol protects the head from the scorching heat of sun just as the law protects the mind from the scorching passion.

2.**The Bhumpa (Vase):**The vase represents a repository of limitless material wealth, good health and long life.

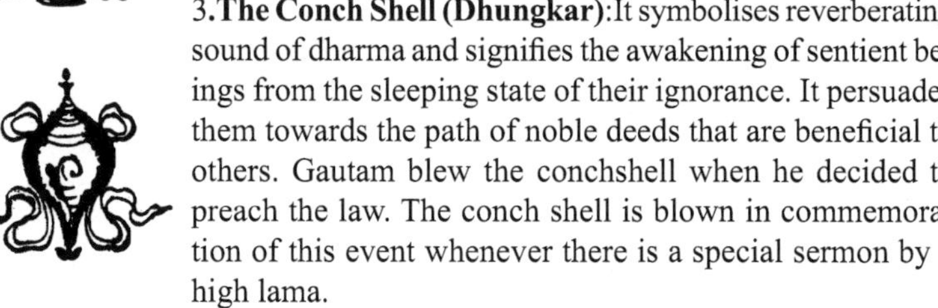

3.**The Conch Shell (Dhungkar)**:It symbolises reverberating sound of dharma and signifies the awakening of sentient beings from the sleeping state of their ignorance. It persuades them towards the path of noble deeds that are beneficial to others. Gautam blew the conchshell when he decided to preach the law. The conch shell is blown in commemoration of this event whenever there is a special sermon by a high lama.

4.**The Banner of Victory (Gyaltsen):**This symbol signifies the fortune of having victory of good over the evil forces which hinders the success of noble goals and also proclaims the victory of piety over evil. It is used in processions.

5.**A Pair of Golden Fishes (Sernya):**Symbolises resurrection of eternal life, rebirth etc. The pair signifies the ability to swim with ease without obstruction in the ocean of this world. They may also be taken to symbolise the eye of perception as fish can see through muddy water. The fish couple suggests mutual aid and indispensability between male and female in material life.

6.**The Lotus Flower (Pema)**:It symbolises the ultimate goal namely enlightenment. As the lotus comes out of dirt but does not carry any dirt similarly law is free of all earthly matters.

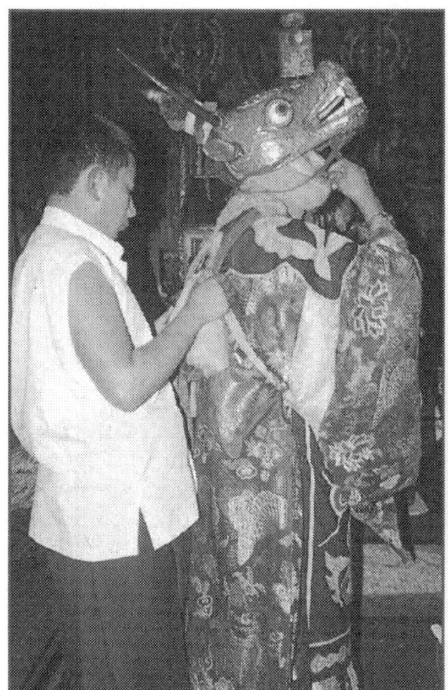

Dancers get ready for the Lama Dance

Drummers at the Saga Dawa Festival

A Thanka being painted

A Wall Painting at a Monastery

A Mantra being engraved

Monks carry the Eight Lucky Signs

Glimpses of the Saga Dawa Procession

A Lama Dancer

Carrying Statue of Buddha

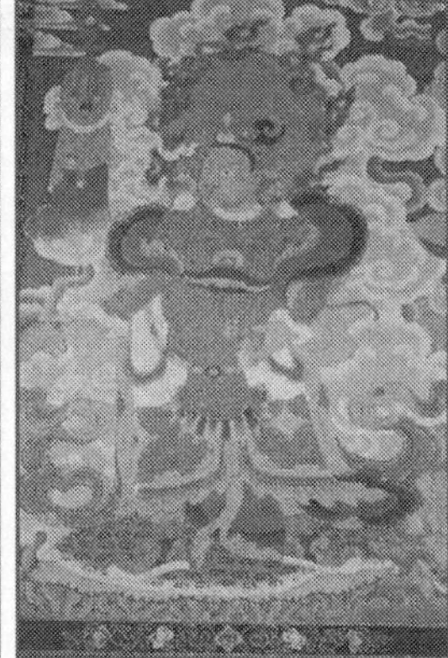

God of Direction of East

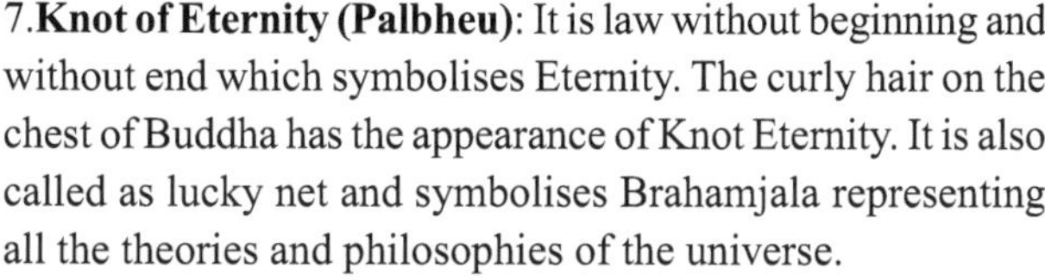

7.**Knot of Eternity (Palbheu)**: It is law without beginning and without end which symbolises Eternity. The curly hair on the chest of Buddha has the appearance of Knot Eternity. It is also called as lucky net and symbolises Brahamjala representing all the theories and philosophies of the universe.

8.**The Wheel Of Dharma (Choekyi Khorlo)**:It symbolises the propagation of Buddha's teaching. The first sermon setting in motion of the cycle of law is symbolist in a wheel with eight spokes, which stand for the eight fold path.

Mandalas

A mandala is a mystic pictorial representation of the universe. In the centre of the mandala is a divinity with whom the meditating practitioner aims to merge. Many types of mandalas are painted on thankas.

HOLY IMPLEMENTS & STRUCTURES

The Prayer Flag

The Prayer Flags can be seen almost anywhere in Sikkim - on hill-tops, on building-tops - an integral part of the landscape of Sikkim. These flags have prayers inscribed on them. There are four types of Prayer flags. Lungta or wind Horse are strips of clothes attached with bamboo poles. These flags have the figure of a horse with the mystical jewel on its back. Chopen or luck flag are long, narrow and oblong in shape. These type of flags are tied on twigs of trees, bridges and top of hills. Gyalsten or Victorious Banner have a large amount of holy text on them including the eight lucky signs. Glan-po stob ryyas or Vast lucky flag include symbols such as crossed dorjee in the centre with a peacock.

Chortens

Chortens or stupas dot every nook and corner Sikkim. Chortens are normally found concentrated around monasteries. In old times, the chortens were built as relic holders but now they are erected in memory of Lord Buddha or some Buddhist saints. Though chortens vary in size with some as high as a four storeyed building, their shapes are more or less the same. The shape of the chorten symbolises the five elements of nature namely earth, water, fire, air and ether to which a body is transformed after death. The rectangular base represents the earth whereas the globe atop this depicts water. Resting on the globe is a triangular structure which signifies fire. On the tip of the triangular is a crescent that represents air. Nested in the crescent is a small oval structure which symbolises ether.

Bell & Thunderbolt

The Bell and the Thunderbolt signify the two truths. The Bell or Thrilbu symbolises that everything in the end is void and the Thunderbolt or Dorjee signifies the immortality of Truth. The Bell is held in the right hand and the Thunderbolt in the left during rituals.

Prayer wheel & Rosary

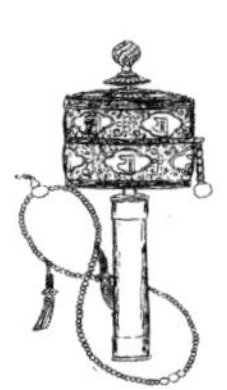

The Prayer Wheel is a religious implement on which some holy mantra is inscribed and which is held in the hand and rotated with the motion of the wrist. There are also the bigger type of Prayer Wheels which surround monasteries or chortens. For instance, Phurba-Chorten near Tibetology in Gangtok is surrounded by 113 prayer wheels which are rotated by devotees when they go around the chorten. One can also see Prayer wheels in streams the flowing water of which rotate them. The Rosary consists of 108 beads made of small pellets of wood, ivory or precious stones. While telling the beads, holy mantras are chanted to invoke the blessings of the gods.

Khada or Scarf

Khadas are long length of silk cloth in the form of a scarf that besides being used as an offering to the gods are also presented at social occasions be it a marriage, birthday or funeral.

The method of presenting khadas varies according to the status of the person it is being offered to. To one who is superior to you, you should raise it in both hands to the height of the forehead while to the one who is of equal status, you have have to raise it in both hands at a level with your shoulders and present it in his hands. You can also accept one in return from him whom you presented. To one who is below in status or age you should put the scarf around his neck with the free ends kept hanging in front. To the bereaved, the khada is folded and offered.

BODHISATTVA (BUDDHAS IN THE MAKING)

Most of the monasteries in Sikkim contain the idols of the Bodhisattvas Avalokitesvara, Padmasambva and Manjusri.These and some other Bodhisattvas are briefly described below. Some monasteries also have an image of some form of Buddha. There are a few monasteries which emphasise the Tantric form of worship and have the Bodhisattva depicted in the Yab-Yum (Father-Mother) pose with a female shakti.

Avalokitesvara or Chenrezi

He is the leading celestial being in Buddhism and the Lord of Compassion. He is said to be the saviour of beings alive. He is manifested in 108 different forms. The most popular form is with 11 heads. The Dalai Lama is said to be the reincarnation of Avalokitesvara.

Amitaba or Opame

This deity holds a pot of ambrosia in his hand. His earthly manifestation in Tibet is the Panchen Lama.

Padmasambva

He was a Guru who travelled to Lhasa in the eight century and was instrumental in spreading Buddhism in Tibet. He is depicted normally holding a Thunderbolt in his right hand and a bowl made of human skull in the left hand. There are three heads on the spear beside the Guru: a skull, a head with blood and flesh and a head with signs of life. The heads represent the doctrine of Three Bodies.

Mirlrepa

This great mystic of Tibet renounced all earthly possessions and he has only a bowl of human skull for storing food. He always has his right ear pointing towards the sky as if in constant communication with the Almighty.

Manjusri

He is also known as the Deity of Knowledge and carries a Sword of Wisdom in the right hand.

ཨོཾ་མ་ཎི་པདྨེ་ཧཱུྃ།

The mystic mantra "OM MANE PADME HUM" meaning "Hail Jewel in the Lotus"and is found engraved on prayer wheels and also inscribed on Medangs which are roadside holy walls

Why festival dates change every year

Buddhist and Hindu festivals follow the Lunar Calendar (each month has 28 days). They add an entire month(Adhik Mas) every three years. This means that the festivals will fall back on the English (Gregoriann) calendar and then jump ahead to its earlier position, which is why Diwali jumps between November and October. The same is the case with Loosong which jumps between first week of December to the last week of December. Sometimes Losoong spills over by one or two days to January next year and this sometimes leads to a situation when you have two Losoongs in the same year in the English calendar The year 2009 had two Losoongs.

Invoking the gods to stop the rains

In drought stricken areas around the world, priests are normally requested to invoke the gods to shower rain. But in Sikkim the scenario is different. Rains are almost perennial in nature and fearing the festivities during festivals will get washed away, a monk who specialises in appeasing the rain gods is approached. Puja is performed and lo and behold there is no rain during the festival.

This is borne by the fact that on Saga Dawa which falls in the middle of the monsoon season invariably always goes dry at least during the time the procession is going around the town. It just could not be a coincidence.

Death and funeral rites

The funeral and death ceremonies are very intricate; death itself does not mean an end but is a step for a reincarnation to another life. Rituals and prayers must performed in a manner that this transformation happens in the most favourable way. The ceremonies, which go on for many days, can entail huge expenditures involving hiriing of monks, purchase of ritual offerings, feeding the mourners who come to pay their condolences and visit of monasteries by the bereaved.

After death, the body is placed in cross-legged curled pose in the coffin which is kept in the premises of the house. Monks perform prayers and rituals using trumpets and cymbals sitting in front of the body. Meals are served to the deceased throughtout the period following death and until the rituals are over.

Visitors pay their condolences by handing over a folded khada and some money to the eldest of the bereaved family. Food and refreshments are served to the visitors.

The cremation takes place on the day decided by the astrologer and it could be even a week after the death has taken place. The funeral procession is led by a monk carrying a thanka and the coffin is flanked by monks blowing trumpets and conches and sounding the cymbals. When the funeral pyre is lit, the family members and well-wishers throw mud in the fire and wish that the deceased has a good reincarnation. The ashes of deceased are usually dispersed in the river or mixed with clay.

The Kutse Shegu ceremony is held on the 49th day following the death and is aimed to purify the atmosphere. Invitations are sent to well-wishers to visit the house of the deceased. Food and drinks are offered to the visitors. Also those who could not pay their condolences earlier do so now by offering a folded khada and some money to the bereaved.

The origin of Thankas

Thankas are religious scrolls on which are painted pictures of gods.In the mid seventeen century when Buddhism made inroads into Tibet and beyond most of the people of Central Asia were basically nomadic herders as so many are even today. Unlike townsfolk, the nomads had no fixed abode so they could not worship their gods in private chapel. Thankas were devised so that could be rolled up and carried to wherever they were going and which at the appointed worship time they could individually unroll and place at a high ground to make into their temple.

FLORA AND FAUNA OF SIKKIM

Because of the altitudes that vary right from sea level to summits that touch the skies, the flora and fauna naturally covers a wide and myriad spectrum. Nowhere in the world in such a small area can one find flora and fauna of all varieties - tropical to the alpine. Sikkim has one of the richest assemblages of habitat in the world. Even in the seemingly lifeless northern plateau of Sikkim a dream like vision of ducks and wildasses often greet the visitor. Sikkim's botanical and zoological richness and diversity is awe-inspiring, boasting of more than 4000 species of plants and 30% of all the birds found in the Indian Sub-continent. No wonder Sikkim has been a dream of naturalists. Dr. J. Hooker during the middle of the last century surveyed in the detail the botanical wealth of Sikkim and his findings were embodied in the publication Himalayan Journal that is still considered as an authoritative document. Dr. Salim Ali an ornithologist has given a detailed account on birds in his book "The Birds of Sikkim". Besides these there are many other books available on the flora and fauna of Sikkim.

DISTRIBUTION OF FLORA AND FAUNA

Sikkim can basically be divided into three zones. The tropical, from almost sea-level to about 1500 m, the temperate from 1500 m to 3500 m and the alpine above 3500m. Till about 3000 m, there are terraced farmlands in which rice, maize, barley and millet are grown. Sometimes even at high altitudes, vegetation grows defying the hostile surroundings. Cardamom, oranges, apples potatoes and ginger are grown in abundance in the state.

The lower altitudes towards the south harbour Jungle cats, Mongoose, House sparrows etc. The jungles of the south are teeming with plantains, bamboos, tree ferns, walnut, sal and oak. Orchids also abound in areas with moderate altitudes. In fact orchids are the pride of Sikkim and there are almost 600 species of them in Sikkim. They come in a wide variety of colours and sizes. The most popular orchids of Sikkim are Cymbidiums, Vanda, Cattaleya, Hookeriana, Farmeri, Dendrobium Amoenum. The variety Nobile Orchid (Dendrobium nobile) has been declared as the State Flower of Sikkim.

In the temperate zone the fauna comprises of Common Langur, Leopard cats, Red Panda, Musk deer, Himalayan Black Bear and the Flying Squirrel. The flora consists of the oak, cherry, alurel, chestnut, maple and the birch.

In the arid cold alpine regions of Sikkim, roam the snow-leopard and wild ass amongst rhododendrons. There are about 30 species of Rhododendrons in Sikkim and are found above the height of 3000 m. The Rhododendron Grande is over 10 m tall whereas the Rhododendron Nivale grows barely a few inches above the ground. When Rhododendrons flower between the month of April and July, it is a sight to behold with hillsides becoming shrouded in colour. The variety Rhododendron niveum has been declared as the State Tree of Sikkim.

At the treeless altitudes above 4000 m curious types of flowers in colours of blue, red, violet blossom during summer just a few inches above the ground. The stones and rocks also get coloured by lichens and mosses in amorphous patterns as though someone was doing abstract art on them. Jatamasi, a medicinal plant, also thrives at altitudes above 4500 m and is found especially in North Sikkim. Rhubarb, a herbaceous plant with a yellowish thick stem grows in the barren cliffs of North Sikkim. Primulas are found in abundance in altitudes above 3500 m.

VEGETATION

Crops & Cereals

Rice, maize and millet are grown here. However the production of rice is not sufficient to meet the local demand and it has to be imported from the plains alongwith other cereals like wheat etc.

Vegetables

All vegetables of daily consumption like peas, potatoes, cauliflower, cabbages, radishes, turnips, carrot etc grow here. Cabbages grow in abundance in Lachung and is exported out of the state. Potatoes are also grown in huge quantities in Hilley and Ribdi above Sombaria. Besides these two vegetables, the others have to be brought in from other states because of limited production locally.

Intense Ultra-violet rays and relatively good sunshine at higher altitudes result in radishes and turnips assuming huge proportions each sometimes weighing upto a kilogram. The Tibi Beans which are endemic to the Lachung area also are huge in size,

Cash crops

Sikkim tea is well-known for its exotic flavour and is grown at Temi in government-owned tea-gardens. Cardamom grows in abundance mostly in the Dzongu area of North District. Farmers have now also extensively taken to the agriculture of ginger.

Fruits

Oranges are grown in abundance in the southern parts of Sikkim and apples grow in North Sikkim. Other fruits that grow in limited quantities are plums, peaches, papayas, and bananas.

FAUNA

Yaks

Yaks belong to the cattle family and can survive only at altitudes above 3000 m. They live on alpine shrubs and can go without food for days together. Because of the long and thick hair that grows on its flanks, legs and tail and its thick hide, yaks can comfortably sleep and rest in the snow. Yaks forage on their own and do not require grooming, stabling and care as required by other domesticated animals.

Yaks have been domesticated in Sikkim and are used as beasts of burdens as well as for their meat and milk which though produced in small quantities is very thick. Yak milk is extensively used for preparing Churpi which is hardened

cheese. The hide and hair is used for making crude canvas and tents. Crossbreeds of yaks with cows are known as Dzo and these can survive at lower altitudes.

Shapi

A rare animal that inhabits the alpine region is the Shapi. It was discovered only in 1938 by a German doctor Ernest Schalfer in the Lachen valley area and is peculiar to Sikkim although it definitely looks similar to the Himalayan Tahr. There are only a very few such animals and it is high on the endangered list. The Shapi has the size of a mountain goat and has a long white mane and curved horns.

Blue Sheep

Also known as the Baharal, Blue Sheeps occupy one of the highest ecological niches in the world - the Green lake basin and also the area around the Donkia pass.

Tibetan Wildass

Locally it is called the Kiang and is found usually in big herds on the plateau in the Cholamu lake area.

Red Panda

It has been declared as the State Animal of Sikkim, is about 1 m in length when full grown and belongs to the raccoon family. It is an aboreal animal and inhabits treetops and is found in altitudes between 2000 m and 3000 m. It feeds mostly on bamboo leaves.

Birds, Butterflies, & Fish

Just like the plants and animals, the avifauna (birds and butterflies) of Sikkim are also very diversified. The 500 species of birds range from the majestic Bearded-Vulture with a wing span of over 3 m to the Olive Ground Warbler just a few inches in length. Other colourful birds are the emerald dove, fairy blue bird, king-fisher, ashy woodpecker, sultan tit and the emerald cuckoo. Many migratory birds like the Ruddy Shelduck also visit Sikkim.

There are also a wide variety of pheasants in various colours. The Blood Pheasant is declared as the State Bird of Sikkim. Over 600 species of butterflies have been identified in Sikkim. These are found at almost all altitudes.

Various types of fishes are also found in the lakes and rivers of Sikkim. There are 45 species of fish in Sikkim which include the trout and salmon which are migratory in nature. Another important migratory species of fish is the Mahseer.

As far as the reptiles are concerned, Sikkim is said to have 40 species of these. These include various types of lizards and snakes like the grass-snake, the krait and the cobra. In the amphibians, toads are found in good number especially during the monsoons.

PARKS & SANCTUARIES

In order to protect the rich flora and fauna of Sikkim from the poacher, the Government has established parks and sanctuary. Extensive afforestration programmes are being undertaken and this has played a role in preventing encroachment.There is a basic difference between National park and Sanctuary,

SOME MEDICINAL PLANTS OF THE SIKKIM HIMALAYAS

Nardostachys grandiflora, commonly known as Spikenard and Jatamasi in Nepali. It is a perennial shrub about 40 cm in height and thrives above 4000 m. It finds a wide spectrum of uses as a tonic, antispasmodic, diuretic, laxative. Its roots are used to prevent eplileptic fits. The roots are also used as incense specially for religious offerings

Aconites, commonly known as Monkshood and Bikh locally is found at altitudes between 2500 m and 4000 m. Growing to an height of about 1 m, they are very poisionous. Their roots are however effective against rheumatism and fever but care has to be taken to administer the correct dosage.

Artemisia vulgaris, commonly known as Indian Wormwood and Titopati locally grows upto altitudes of 2000 m. Attaining a height of about 4 ft, their leaves are used as an antiseptic.

Piper longum, commonly known as Long Pepper and locally as Pipla grows on the foothills of the Himalayas upto an altitude of 1000 m. It is a creeping herb. Its fruits are used as a tonic and a medicinne for diseases like asthma. The roots are used as an antidote to snake bites.

Picrorhiza kurrooa, known as Kutki locally grows at altitudes ranging twetween 3000 m and 5000 m. It grows to a height of about half feet and its roots are used as a purgative and have also been found effective against malaria.

A national park is an area which is sstrictly dedicated to conserve the wild flora fauna and natural habitat whereas a sanctuary is an area for the conservation for only one type of species.

Kanchendzonga National Park(KNP)

KNP encompasses an area covering 1784 sq km. It is bounded in the north by the Tent Peak and the ridge of the Zemu glacier. The eastern boundary of this park comprises of the ridge of the Mountain Lamaongden. The southern boundary includes Mount Narsing and Mount Pandim. The western boundary comprises of the mighty Kanchendzonga which presides over its namesake park and the Nepal Peak. Being bounded by such formidable features, it is no wonder that the park has remained ecologically untouched and therefore has provided a natural protection to the flora and fauna it shelters. The fauna includes the Snow leopard, Himalayan Black Bear, Red Panda, Barking deer and many other species. The KNP is surrounded by biosphere which combines nature conservation with sceintific research, environmental training, environmental education monistoring and demonstration. Many places in this park have perhaps never been trod by man and it is very likely that new species may be discovered here.

Fambong Lho Wildlife Sanctuary

This is located about 20 kilometres from Gangtok and covers an area of about 5200 hectares above the road between Singtam and Dikchu with the highest point at a place called Tinjure where a wooden observation tower of the Forest Department exists. The Sanctuary is the home of Himalayan Black Bear, Red Panda, Civet cat and many varieties of birds and butterflies.

KANCHENDZONGA NATIONAL PARK & WILDLIFE SANCTUARIES

Maenam Wildlife Sanctuary

It is located in South Sikkim above the town of Rabongla and covers an area of about 3500 hectares with its highest point being at Maenam at 10,600 ft. It shelters the Red Panda, Leopard cat, civet cat, blood pheasant, black eagles and other animals of the temperate forest.

Singba Rhododendron Sanctuary

It is located near Yumthang in north Sikkim and contains a vast variety of rhododendrons. When in blossom the rhododendrons provide a riot of colour to this small 33 hectare park.

Kyongnosla Alpine Sanctuary

It is situated around the area adjoining the Changu lake and covers an area of about 400 hectares.

Varsey Rhododendron Sanctuary

This Rhododendron Sanctuary lies in the West corner of Sikkim.

Mountains scarred by landslides suggest that development activities are taking a toll on the environment and the flora and fauna are definitely being affected. The loss of topsoil, soil instability, degeneration of agriculture land and shrinking of catchment areas of the rivers are issues that are cause for concern. The alpine areas of Sikkim in particular which look so powerfully big and formidable are ironically most vulnerable and sensitive to environment degradation. High altitude soil is not readily regenerative and therefore overgrazing of yaks and sheep in alpine meadows has led to many stretches of land becoming barren.Man has realised that forests form an indispensible part of our life support system and placed their conservation high on the agenda. Perhaps in the thousands of species of flora in Sikkim, some of them unique to this state and not found elsewhere, are some which await to be discovered to provide life saving drugs to fight diseases like cancer and AIDS that are stalking mankind. It is truly said that in the wildness is the preservation of the world.

The best protection for the species is the people who know and care about them. The need for development and the preservation of the ecology have to be balanced and one should not be allowed to overwhelm the other. We do not require an asteroid to destroy us. Like the anecdotal bull in the china shop we are destroying the world ourselves -slowly and irrevocaly without realising it. Emission of green house gases is causing global warming and this cuts across borders and nations. But we have saviours in the form of trees. Quietly they stand absorbing the noxious gases.Perhaps the trees in Sikkim at some given moment would be absorbing carbon-dioxide emitted by a coal fired power station in China and releasing pure oxygen in return. Sikkim has the capability of earning good Carbon credits and doing carbon trading given the good forest coverage.The forest coverage in the state is steadily increasing due to the green initiatives of the state. Grazing in forest areas has been banned and the use of chemical fertilizers banned as a step to make the state completely organic. Felling of trees is banned: Government also feels that trees can be more productive if left standing. Sikkim is perhaps the only state in the country to set up a Glacier Commision to study the effect of climate change on its glaciers.

ENVIRONMENT RELATED SLOGANS

Environment is high on the agenda of the State Government Extensive afforestration programs, setting up of Smriti Vans and ban on grazing have improved Sikkim's forest coverage consiederably. With the Government exhorting all house owners to paint their buildings green , Sikkim is on its march ahead on becoming a truly green state. The Green Mission was launched on 27th Feb 2006 and this is manifested in various slogans that have been put up on road sides.

Life is green when trees are seen
Plant a sapling earn a blessing
Wealth of the plains depends on the health of the hills
You have not inherited the land from the past, but borrowed it from the future
Nature has everything to meet Man's need but not his greed
The trees are gods great alphabet with them he writes in shining green
Across the world his thoughts serene
Nature breaths through the trees
Save trees to save life
Trees can reduce the carbon footprint to a tiptoe
Plastic is Drastic
Mother planet is showing us the red warnlng light be careful she is saying to take care of the planet is to take care of our own house
He who plants a tree plants a hope
We are not passengers on spaceship earth, we are all crew
If you see a dust bin, throw the wrapper in

I noticed this following poignant poem written in honour of trees at an exhibition

Trees are the kindest things I know
They do no harm they simply grow
The more they are the much it is better
So let us take a pledge and come together
Stop deforestration and work without buts
Plant two more for every tree that is cut
Against the difference all should care
So greenery can spread everywhere

Anakisha Jain, Army Public School Gangtok

Argali-handmade paper contributing to the local economy

Argali(edgeworthia gardneri) is a native quick growing plant of Sikkim. Found in abundance and growing in wild throughout the mountainous state, Argali has been traditionally used to make hand made paper.. The bark of the plant is peeled and beaten into pulp, dried and pressed into paper. The paper is lightweight, longlasting and insect resistant.

The Borong-Polok Handmade Paper Unit in South Sikkim is a successful venture which involves 50 households who supply Argali and are involved in the manufacture of the paper. The simple papermakeing process provides a sustainable means of economic livelihood for the local community without pollution or the cutting of trees.

THE STATE ADMINISTRATION AND ECONOMY

THE GOVERNMENT DEPARTMENTS

The official website **sikkim.gov.in** of the Government of Sikkim that is being maintained by Department of Information Technology can be browsed for details on the various organs of the government.

This is the official government emblem which adorns most official correspondences and documents. It is also embossed or painted at the entrances of many Government buildings. It is an exquisite and intricate icon of two winged horses protecting a shield and a conch. Written below in Tibetan are the words "KHAM SOOM WANGDI" which means "CONQUEROR OF THE THREE REGIONS".

Like any other state of the Indian Union, Sikkim has a Chief Minister, Council of Ministers and MLAs chosen through the electoral process. The Chief Minister and the Council of Ministers are in charge of various Departments. Some of the Departments and a few of the Government Undertakings have the ruling party MLAs appointed as their Chairpersons. The bureaucracy in the State is headed by the Chief Secretary. Each Department or a group of them is put in charge of a Secretary or Commissioner who is usually an Indian Administrative Service Officer.

The various Departments in the Government of Sikkim are

1. Animal Husbandry,Livestock,Fisheries & Veterinary Services Department (earlier Animal Husbandry & Veterinary Services Department) 2. CM Secretariat (earlier Chief Ministers Office) 3.Commerce & Industries Department (earlier Industries Department) 4.Co-operation Department 5.Cultural Affairs & Heritage Department (earlierCultural Affairs Department 6.Department of Personnel AR Training P G,Career options & Emp,Skill Dev & CM's Self employment Scheme (earlier Department of Personnel Administrative Reforms & Training) 7.Development Planning Economic Reforms and N.E Council Affairs Department (earlier Planning & Development Department) 8.Ecclesiastical Affairs Department 9.Election Department10. Energy and Power Department 11.Excise Department 12.Finance,Revenue and Expenditure Department (earlierFinance Department) 13.Food Security & Agriculture Development Department (earlierAgriculture Department) 14.Food C.S. and Consumers Affairs Department 15.Forest ,Wild Life & Environment Management Department (earlier Forest & Environment Department) 16.Health Care,Human Services & F W Department(earlier Health & Family Welfare Department) 17. Home Department 18. Horticulture & Cash Crops Development Department (earlier Horticulture Department) 19. Human Resources Development Department (earlier Education Department) 20. Information & Public Relation Department 21. Information Technology Department 22. Irrigation & Flood Control Department 23. Labour Department

LEGEND

- ● BAC
- ★ POLICE STATION
- ✚ HOSPITAL/ PHC
- ◣ FIRE & EMERGENCY SERVICES

DISTRICT MAGISTRATES

1. Gangtok - 03592 - 202922
2. Namchi - 03595 - 263734
3. Gyalshing - 03595 - 250742
4. Mangan - 03592 - 234234

○ SDMs

1. Pakyong - 03592 - 257827
2. Rongli - 03592 - 255887
3. Ravangla - 03595 - 260841
4. Chungthang - 03592 - 276910
5. Soreng - 03595 - 253282

SUPERINTENDENT OF POLICE

1. Gangtok - 03592 - 284416
2. Namchi - 03595 - 263726
3. Gyalshing - 03595 - 250763
4. Mangan - 03592 - 234242

★ POLICE STATIONS

1. Sadar - 03592 - 202033
2. Rangpo - 03592 - 240835
3. Pakyong - 03592 - 257834
4. Rhenock - 03592 - 253840
5. Ranipool - 03592 - 251712
6. Singtam - 03592 - 233762
7. Rongli - 03592 - 255623
8. Sherathang -
9. Kupup -
10. Mangan - 03592 - 234284
11. Phodong - 03592 - 262992
12. Lachen -
13. Lachung -
14. Chungthang - 03592 - 214988
15. Geyzing - 03592 - 210266
16. Soreng - 03595 - 255658
17. Kaluk -
18. Sombaria - 03595 - 245270
19. Uttrey -
20. Legship -
21. Namchi - 03595 - 250819
22. Jorethang -
23. Ravangla - 03595 - 257358
24. Melli -
25. Temi - 03595 - 270203
26. Hingdam -

◣ FIRE & EMERGENCY SERVICES

1. Gangtok - 03592 - 202011/101
2. Singtam - 03592 - 233722/101
3. Rangpo - 03592 - 241055
4. Pakyong - 03592 - 257695/101
5. Singtam - 03592 - 233722
6. Namchi - 03595 - 26388/101
7. Jorethang- 03595 - 257327/101
8. Ravangla- 03595 - 260782/101
9. Gyalshing 03595 - 250810/101
10. Mangan - 03592 - 234266/10

✚ HOSPITALS AND PHCS

1. STNM, Gtk - 03592-202059
2. Singtam - 03592-235379
3. Rongli - 03592-253896
4. Pakyong - 03592-257885
5. Rangpo - 03592-240362
6. Samdong - 9674256914
7. Sang - 03592-236860
8. Machong - 9557591735
9. Gyalshing - 03595-251089
10. Senek - 03595-243267
11. Yoksum - 03595-241205
12. Dentam - 03595-255311
13. Rinchenpong - 03595-245244
14. Mangalbaria - 03595-252204
15. Soreng - 03595-253273
16. Sombaria - 03595-254248
17. Mangan - 03592-234344
18. Phodong - 03592-263965
19. Passingdong - 9434153059
20. Chungthang - 03592-276947
21. Dikchu - 9614540024
22. Hee-Gyathang - 9474512636
23. Namchi - 03595-263830
24. Jorethang - 03595-263233
25. Melli - 03595-270245
26. Namthang - 03595-241260
27. Yangang - 03594-243222
28. Temi - 03595-261663
29. Ravangla - 03595-260612
30. Bermiok Tokal- 9434445859

BACs

1. Gangtok - 03592 - 284093
2. Ranka - 03592 - 214100
3. Pakyong - 03592 - 257274
4. Rhenock - 03592 - 253584
5. Duga - 03592 - 240246
6. Rhegu - 03592 - 255909
7. Khamdong - 03592 - 242376
8. Rakdong Tintek - 03592 - 245284
9. Parakha -
10. Martam
11. Namchi - 03595 - 264262
12. Ravangla - 03595 - 260222
13. Yangang - 03592 - 243426
14. Melli - -
15. Temi - Tarku - 03592 - 261556
16. Namthang -
17. Jorethang -
18. Yuksom -
19. Dentam - 03595 - 241206
20. Daramdin - 03595 - 254485
21. Gyalshing - 03595 - 251050
22. Soreng - 03595 - 253126
23. Kaluk - 03595 - 253126
24. Wok - 03595 - 252415
25. Magan - 03592 - 234610
26. Chungthang - 03592 - 276847
27. Passidong - 03592 - 234241
28. Kabitingda - 03592 - 237426
29. Hee- Martam -

□ FOOD GODOWNS

1. Chungthang - 9434131427
2. Dikchu - 9733307565
3. Mangan - 9648747700
4. Gangtok - 9434127200
5. Pakyong - 9476364740
6. Rangpo - 8972685033
7. Ranipool - 9434446043
8. Rhenock - 9454409913
9. Rongli - 9547121305
10. Singtam - 9832013224
11. Makha - 9679009858
12. Ravangla - 9832392094
13. Temi - 9733235564
14. Yangang - 9734943917
15. Namthang - 9434409060
16. Jorethang - 9832015067
17. Melli - 9434235363
18. Namchi - 9434184235
19. Dentam - 9733064503
20. Gyalshing - 9733271660
21. Kaluk - 9733327413
22. Legship - 9735917708
23. Sombaria - 9679907080
24. Soreng - 9593384092
25. Thingling - 9733065965
26. Bermoik - 9475384136
27. Chongrong - 9434221427
28. FCI Jorethang - 9434103251
29. FCI Rangpo - 9733275211
30. Lanchung Sub-godown - 9593883672
31. Lachen Sub-godown - 9434179069

24.Land Revenue & Disaster Management Department (earlier Land Revenue Department) 25. Law Department 26. Mines, Minerals & Geology Department (earlier Mines & Geology Department) 27. Parliamentary Affairs Department 28. Printing & Stationery Department 29. PWD Building & Housing Department 30. PWD Roads & Bridges Department 31. Rural Management and Development Department (earlier Rural Development Department) 32. Science & Technology Department 33. Sikkim Police (headed by Director General of Police) 34. Social Justice, Empowerment and Welfare Department 35. Sports & Youth Affairs Department 36. Tourism Department 37. Transport Department 38. Urban Development & Housing Department 39. Water Security and Public Health Engineering Department. (earlier Public Health Engineering Department)40. Raj Bhawan (not a Department in the real sense of the word but has a Secretary) The Ecclesiastical Affairs Department, which deals in the management of the affairs of the monasteries of the state, is unique to Sikkim and is not found elsewhere in the country.

There are many Central Government offices also in the state. These are Department of Telecommunications, Department of Postals, Accountant General, All India Radio, Doordarshan, Botanical Survey of India, Census, Central Excise, Customs, Central Public Works Department, Central School, Central Water Commission, Central Reserve Police Force, Field Publicity, General Reserve Engineering Force (GREF), Geologicial Survey of India, Indian Council of Agricultural Research (ICAR), Inter State Police Wireless, Meteorological Department, National Sample Survey Organisation, Government of India Press, Press Information Bureau, Ayurvedic Research Centre, Special Bureau, Spices Board, Subsidiary Intelligence Bureau (SIB) and Small Industries Service Institute.

The State is divided into four districts: North, South, East and West each with a District Collector. There are also nine subdivisions which are Gangtok, Pakyong, Rongli, Namchi, Soreng, Gyalshing, Rabongla, Mangan and Chungthang.

PANCHAYATS AND VILLAGE ADMINISTRATION

For effective administration of the villages, the State is divided into 159 Gram Panchayat Units. The Gram Panchayat is responsible for construction of village roads, sanitation, management of lands, registering births and deaths and other matters pertaining to day to day village life. The Government provides funds for the purpose of the development activities. Each Gram Panchayat unit has a few revenue blocks under it: covering the 453 revenue blocks (villages). Each Gram Panchayat consists of five persons: a Sabhapati (equivalent to a Sarpanch or village headman), a Up-Sabhapati, a Sachiva and 2 members who are elected for a period of five years through an election. The Gram Panchayats of each district get together and elect a Zilla (District) Adhakshya. There are therefore four Zilla Adhakshyas. At Lachen and Lachung in North District, the traditional Pipon system has been allowed to continue is very nominal and is paid more as a token of ownership of land.

ECONOMY- PRESENT STATUS, PROBLEMS AND PROSPECTS

The major problems confronting the state are rising unemployment and dropping percapita income because of internal resources that have not been exploited. The economy of the state essentially depends on the huge amout of Central grant that it gets. So far the State Government has been the major employer in the state and is now buckling under huge establishment costs. For a population of 5.5 lacs the State Government directly employs 30,000 persons - the highest government employee to population ratio in the country - and the government can no longer continue to provide direct employment. The roads and building construction activity in the state, which got a considerable boost immediately after Sikkim became a part of India, till now was a good source of employment for the labourers and provided income for the local contractors. With roads and bridges constructed in almost every corner of the state, there is now a steady decline in employment from this source.

There is therefore an urgent need to exploit other sources of income as well as find way and means to generate internal resources to rejuvenate the Sikkimese economy. The Government of Sikkim has taken up an ambitious capacity building and skill development programme and local youth are now getting jobs in the private sector out of the state. The key sectors of the economy and the related watershed events are discussed below

Agriculture and Horticulture

The Nepali immigrants during the last century introduced terrace farming in the state. This gave a considerable boost to the agricultural yield. Paddy and maize are grown in the tropical and temperate regions of the state. Barley, millet and buck-wheat are grown in certain areas.

Cabbages grow in abundance in the Lachung area and its yield is sufficient to meet the requirements of the state. Potatoes grow in abundance in the Ribdi area in Western Sikkim and are even exported out of the state. Cardamom (big variety) copiously grows in the humid areas of the state and Sikkim is a major supplier of this commodity to the Indian market. Apples grow in limited quantities in the Lachung valley whereas oranges are found in the southern areas of the state. The climate and soil also lends itself to the growth of ginger especially in South Sikkim. The Temi Tea Estate annually produces about 150 tons of high quality tea which carries a high premium in the international market. Vegetables are also grown in limited quantities but are not sufficient to meet the local demand and therefore have to be brought in from outside. In the upper reaches of North Sikkim Jatamasai plant grows in abundance and is exported out of the state for manufacturing incense.

Horticulture holds a very good promise for Sikkim. The climate of Sikkim is conducive to the growth of both apples and oranges. However, because of overgrowth, the yield of these fruits is almost non-existent. It can be revived for commercial exploitation through cross-breeding and use of appropriate manure. Peaches, plums and many other fruits can also be commercially viable if their cultivation is taken up scientifically. If Himachal Pradesh, which has a terrain and climate similar to Sikkim, has a sizable income from horticulture there is no reason why this state also cannot. Orchids and cutflowers have a good market in the plains and this certainly requires to be exploited. Although there is a Fruit Preservation Factory at Singtam to can various fruits and produce squashes, but there is a further scope of this coming up in the private sector. High yielding crops also need to be propagated amongst the marginal farmers in the state so that the state becomes self sufficient atleast in paddy.

High tansportation costs and the lack of a proper marketing structure where farmers can easily sell their products has been a banein the development of horticulture in the state.

Animal Husbandary

Most of the cattle in the state have been cross-bred with the Jersey and Holstein Fresians species and this has led to the milk yield increasing considerably. Sikkim is self-sufficient in milk more than 25 percent of which is pasteurized in the chilling plants and sold in polypacks. At the higher altitudes, yaks, goats and sheep are used to provide milk products, meat and skin. Yak cheese is exported out of the state to Darjeeling and Kalimpong. The few poultry farms are not able to meet the local demand and therefore eggs have to brought in from the plains.

Poultry can also be a good source of income. There is a great demand for Sikkimese Apso dogs and their breeding can be taken up on a large scale to provide good income. The rearing of Angora rabbits for their wool has been taken up on an experimental basis: it should be taken up in a big way and and can come up as a big cottage industry. Yaks form the mainstay of the economy in the high altitudes; their rearing should be taken up commercially for milk products, meat and skin.

Power

The first power plant in Sikkim was established below the Sichey Busty area in Gangtok in 1927. It worked on water power and had a capacity of only 120 KW and met the needs of the capital. In 1965 a 2 MW Hydroelectric was commissioned on the Rongnichu and was named the Jali Power House. In 1969, a hydel project with a capacity of 50 KW was established at Manaul near Mangan to cater to the power needs of North District. A year later a micro-hydel station was setup at Rothak near Jorethang in West Sikkim. In the early seventies a 200 KW hydroelectric station was commissioned at Rimbi near Yoksum. The first major hydroelectric project was established in the mid-seventies at Lower Lagyap near Ranipool by harnessing the three streams Roro chu, Yalichu and Takchemchu.

The other hydroelectric projects in the state are the Lachen (100 KW), Upper Rongnichhu (8MW), Mayongchu (4 MW), Kalez Khola (2 MW), Lachung (200 KW) and Rathongchu (30 MW).

The National Hydroelectric Power Corporation (NHPC) in the year 2001

HYDEL PROJECTS IN SIKKIM

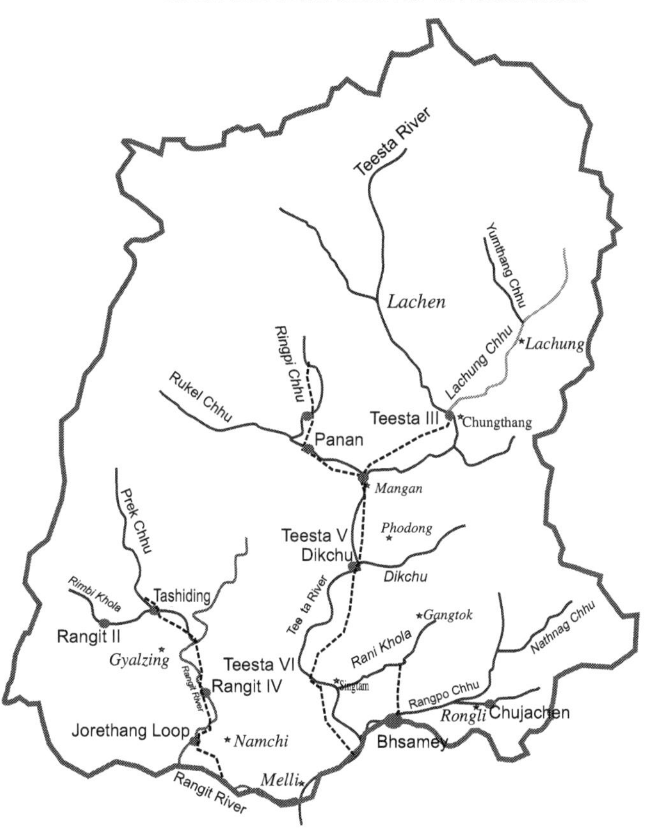

INDEX

- Boundary Line
- Hydro Power Projects
- Rivers
- Tunnels

North District

Project Name		Capacity in (MW)
Teesta III	- Teesta Urja	1200
Teesta V	- NHPC	510
Panan	- Himagiri Hydro Energy Pvt. Ltd.	300

East District

Project Name		Capacity in (MW)
Ronghichu	- Madhya Bharat Power Co. Ltd.	96
Chujachen	- GATI Infrastructure Ltd.	99

South District

Project Name		Capacity in (MW)
Teesta VI	- Lanco Enegry Pvt. Ltd.	

West District

Project Name		Capacity in (MW)
Rangit II	- Sikkim Hydro Ventures Ltd.	60
Rangit IV	- Jal Hydro Enegry Pvt. Ltd.	120

commissioned its 60 MW hydroelectric project at Legship on the River Rangit. and Stage V on River Tista which is generating 510mMW.

95 percent of the villages in the state are electrified.

Rivers and streams criss-cross the topography of the state and the waters in these can be harnessed to provide almost limitless hydro-electric power. It is said that the state has a potential for generating more than 10,000 Megawatts of electricity. Even after a decade it is felt that Sikkim will not have a requirement of more than 50 MW. If properly tapped, hydroelectricy therefore can provide an attractive source of generating revenue by means of selling the surplus power to the neighbouring states.There is also a good scope for privatising generation of power especially in the micro-hydel segement.

Tourism

The last few years have seen a considerable surge in the number of tourists visiting the state - perhaps because of unrest in other tourist spots in the country like Kashmir. However, tourism as a major source of income still remains unexploited. Sikkim has the most unparalleled beauty on earth - exotic lakes, verdant landscapes and breathtaking views. Unfortunately, most of these places are in the restricted areas and to visit them entails getting permission from various sources and this can take months together. Even most locals do not have easy access to the restricted areas making them feel like outsiders in their own state. A beginning has been made by opening Changu, Nathula and Yumthang to foreign visitors but this is not enough - definitely more requires to be done - if Sikkim has to earn a respectable revenue from tourism and make it the mainstay of its economy. The concerned Central Government agencies must open up new areas to tourists considering the thaw in relations with China. Boating, rafting, angling, bird-watching and yak-rides are some other activities that can also be fruitfully developed to provide much required revenue. Cultural carnivals and Light and Sound Programme at the White Hall can be thought of as presently tourists do not how to spend their evening.

Conference tourism in which big companies organise their workshops and seminars is also making inroads in Sikkim. Buddhism circuit tourism has also good prospects.

A boom in tourism in the state will result in concomitant rise in the demand for local handicrafts. Manufacture and sale of this commodity can be source of income for the locals.

Information Technology

Information Technololgy is in its nascent stage in the state and requires to be put on a firm footing. There is an engineering college that offers graduate level courses in computers.Many private institutes like APTECH, NIIT, ZEd are running Diploma and other short term courses at various places in Sikkim. Information Technology is well poised to become a service oriented industry on the lines of Tourism. Information Technology can help to introduce better governane through the use of information tools. It can aid in income and employment generation especially through Information Technology Enabled Services. It can empower the rural communities to reduce the digital divide.

Computerisation in the State Government began as early as 1988 with the Sikkim Police pioneering it. However computerisation has been limited to offifce automation in areas like paybilling. Computers are yet to be used for Management Information System and E-governance.

The high literacy rate, familarity with English, pleasant climate and absence of labour problems are conducive to the development of IT enableeechnology is organising a annual national Exhibition and Conference since 2009. Such a step would help in getting big companies to invest in Sikkim and contribute towards conference tourism.

As its commitment towards development of this sector, the Government created a new Department of Information Technology. It is presently involved in computerising various government departments and training government employees in the use of computers. It has set up a website for the government wherein the Sikkim Herald (the official mouthpiece of the Government), government Gazettes, rules and regulations etc have been hosted. Prices of agricultural commodities are also being hosted so that farmers can access these and are not fleeced by the middlemen. 45 Common Service Centres have been established in places as remote as Lachen and Okhrey. Each centre is equipped with 6 computers and a direct satellite link and would be accessible to the members of the public. The Department is playing more of a role of a facilitator and capacity builder to stimulate IT in the private sector.

Telecommunication

Till the nineteen eighties, most of the telecommunication within the state was being catered to by the Sikkim Police through its wireless network. The scenario has changed considerably since then. The remotest areas of Sikkim have been connected on the telephone by the Bharat Sanchar Nigam Limited (BSNL).Optical Fibres have also been laid interconnecting all important towns and villages in the state- a boon for those who require wide bandwidth to work on the internet.

Roads and Bridges

The first roads in Sikkim were cart roads. These roads were later strengthened and broadened to take vehicular traffic. A cart road was built from Siliguri to Tista in 1860 and in 1861 another road was built from Darjeeling to Tista. A few years later the road was extended to Kalimpong. The border dispute between Tibet and British India prompted the construction of a cart road from Kalimpong via Pedong, Rongli to Jelepla in late seventies of the last century. In the early eighties a cart road was constructed between Gangtok and Tumlong, the then capital of Sikkim. The late eighteen eighties saw the construction of a cart road between Tista and Gangtok. Suspension bridges were also constructed at Tista, Rangpo and Singtam. In the early 1920s, motor vehicles arrived at Darjeeling and the road between Darjeeling and Tista was broadened to accommodate them. The road between Tista and Gangtok was also broadened in the mid 1920s. In the late thirties concrete bridges were constructed over river Tista at Sevoke and Tista, the latter of which was washed away in the floods of 1968. The road scenario in the state has undergone dramatic changes since then. Roads, the total length of which run to almost 1,600 kms, have been constructed to almost each and every corner of Sikkim bringing modern amenities to the doorsteps of the people of the state.

In the absence of any other means of communication, roads form the backbone for transporting men and material in the state. The economy of the state is very much dependent on roads. At many places the roads require to be improved by widenening them and replacing bridges with a low tonnage capacity. Roads in many areas are prone to landslides and alternate routes need to be developed.

Transportation

The first motorised vehicles arrived at Gangtok in 1925 and were "Beetles" - very small in size just suited for the small roads of this area. In the early thirties a private taxi service using a Dodge car was started between Gangtok and Siliguri by a Bihari businessman. In 1944, the Government established the Sikkim State Transport with a couple of Dodge and Mercedes Benz trucks and a few Willy Jeeps. In 1955, the organisation was nationalised and called the Sikkim Nationalised Transport. Since then this Department has grown in size manifold and with its fleet of 150 buses and 200 trucks provides passenger and freight service to the remotest parts of Sikkim. It also runs bus services to Siliguri, Kalimpong and Darjeeling. Although Sikkim Nationalised Transport continues to monopolise most of the routes in Sikkim, private buses are permitted to operate between Gangtok and the important towns in North Bengal. Sikkim now has more than 10,000 vehicles including about 1,000 two wheelers.

A broad gauge railway line is being constructed till Rangpo.

Rural Development

Rural Development brings the economic benefits to the grassroot levels. Through the medium of the Panchayats, the government implements various schemes to provide employment and for the upliftment of the rural poor.

The Mahatma Gandhi National Rural Employment Gurantee Act provides for 100 days employment to all unemployed in Rural areas by engaging them in construction works related to various schemes. The Integrated Rural Development Programme (IRDP) and the Development of Women and Children in Rural Areas (DWCRA) are schemes that provide income generating assets through financial assistance to the rural poor. The Training of Rural Youth for self-employment (TRYSEM) is another scheme that offers courses in different trades like carpet weaving and other cottage industries.

Rural water supply schemes that provide potable water have been extensively implemented in the villages of Sikkim. Rural sanitation is another aspect that has received concerted attention. In order to permit easy inter-village communication, foot-bridges have been widely constructed over rivers and streams as a part of the programme to develop the rural scenario.

Education and literacy

The first modern primary schools were opened in Sikkim by the missionaries. Finnish missionaries of the Scandinavian Mission Alliance established schools in 1880s at Khamdong, Sang, Dentam, Lachen, Chakung and Mangan. Later the Scottish missionaries also established many schools. The Government established a boarding school called the Bhutia school at Burtuk at Gangtok in 1895. This was followed by the opening of another school almost ten years later called the Nepali School in the Lal Bazar area of present day Gangtok. In 1925 these two schools were combined to form the present day Tashi Namgyal Academy. A Scottish missionary established the present day Paljor Namgyal Girls' School in 1924. With the passage of time, more and more schools were opened and presently there are about 1,400 schools in the state including about 1,200 primary and pre-primary schools. There are approximately 7,000 teachers for a student population of 1.3 lacs the highest teacher-student ratio in the country. The percentage of literacy in the state stands at about 80 percent. There are also many Buddhist monastic schoools and Sanskrit Pathshalayas. A Government run Sheda (Monastic College) called teh Nyggmipa School of Higher Studies -from Class 9 to MA - exists at Gangtok for those interested in pursuing higher studies in Tibetan and Buddhism. It is affliated to a University at Banaras. Two private Shedas also exist - one at Rumtek and the other near Tashi View Point in Gangtok.

Education can come up as a major service oriented industry in Sikkim in lines of places like Dehra Dun, Mussorie and Shimla. The Government should encourange the opening of schools and colleges of excellence. A welcome beginning has been made following the establishment of an Engineering College and a Medical College by the Manipal Group.

Forests

Early in this century when Sikkim was a rolling wilderness of forests and most of it hardly inhabited, the need was even then felt to preserve the forest and properly manage our natural resources. The Forest Department was established in 1905.

With a forest cover of almost 40% consisting of a wide spectrum of species of flora, the Forest Department faces the daunting task of preserving this natural heritage. It has adopted many schemes to prevent deforestation. Afforestation schemes, nurseries, environmental programmes have all contributed in preventing the loss of forest cover. The forest department is also involved in propagating sericulture by supplying mulberry saplings to interested silkworm rearers.

Sikkim is endowed with thick forests that cover almost 40 percent of the area. Forests can be exploited commercially for wood for construction, handicrafts and fuel. A saw-mill and a plywood factory somewhere down-stream on the Tista is a viable proposition. But cutting of trees can lead to an ecological imbalance and therefore has to be matched with a concerted reforestation programme.

Health and Family Welfare

The first modern hospital was establised in 1917 at Gangtok. The state now has 5 hospitals, 25 Primary Health centres and 150 Primary Health Sub Centres.

A private medical college and a hospital has being established at Gangtok. This hospital has the most modern and sophisticated health care facilities and compares with the best in the country. The State Government has also launched a scheme to provide free medical check up and treatment to all in the state.

Metals and Minerals

Exploration of minerals and oil has not yet been carried out in Sikkim in the real earnest. Extensive mining of copper was done during the last century by the Nepalis in South Sikkim and the Pachey Khani area. The mines were open pit ones and the lack of the necessary technology at that time prevented deep mining. There is a strong case to re-explore these areas to determine whether they contain commercially exploitable deposits of copper. If commercially viable deposits of minerals are found in Sikkim they can be a good source of revenue for the state.

Human Resources

Capacity Building aspect of the younger generation is the corner stone to the policy of the Government. Unless the people are empowered through long-term training, any opportunity created in the State in government and non-governmental sectors will not translate into income generation of local people and augmenting local economy. Therefore, the Government have established a separate Directorate of Capacity Building in the State to spearhead various skill development training programmes in the State and also help in providing placement. Under the Directorate, a number of livelihood schools have been set up in the state that provide vocational training in trades like welding, plumbing, electrical fittings, driving, tailoring - all having immense demand in the job market. The Information Technology Department has been an integral part of this capacity building campaign to organize computer training and skill development programme for people over the last 10 years. Approximately over 20,000 people all across the state have been trained in various aspects of the usage of computers. The aim is to make Sikkim a completely computer literate State.

The country has a growing requirement of police and para-military forces to tackle the internal security problems and communal unrest. The Sikkimese are by and large physically strong and sturdy people and the Government should take steps to raise battalions that can be requisitioned by the Centre for deployment in other parts of the country for internal security purposes. Such battalions will constitute a good source of employment for the locals without any burden on the state exchequer as most of the expenditure would be met by the Central Government or the borrowing organisation. Sikkimese sportsmen are also doing well: Baichung Bhutia, footballer and Jaslall Pradhan, boxer are Arjuna award winners.

Industry and Trade

Althogh presently restricted to a few items, there is a every likelihood that full fledged trade between India and China will reopen through Sikkim in the near future and the state should seize this opportunity to bolster its economy.

It should avoid being relegated to being just a corridor between the two countries. Traders in Sikkim should be permitted to directly carry out business with their Chinese counterparts as was done before 1962 and this would certainly bring in a considerable amount of foreign revenue.

What has inhibited the development of industries in the state are high transportation costs. Therefore products and services that have a good local demand or that can be transported out without incurring too much expenditure should be produced in the state. Electronics industries, software parks, educational institutions and hospitals of excellence should be encouraged to be established and can play an important role in the economic development of the state. With the ban on the use of plastic bags in the state, the need of an alternative immediately been felt. The manufacture of paper carry bags by recycling paper can come up as a major cottage industry in the state.

Non Resident Indians (NRIs) and foreign companies should be encouraged to invest in the state; they would definitely be forthcoming because of the political stability in the state, the absence of labour problems and cheap labour. When neighbouring West-Bengal which is by and large anti-capitalist can woo the NRIs to invest their money, there is no reason why Sikkim cannot follow suit. The Government has been holding meetings with prospective investors and also the Confederationof India Industries (CII).

Environment

Environmental issues are high on the agenda of the State Government. There is an urgent need to protect the rich bio-diversity of Sikkim from the threats of development. Landslides and other natural calamaties has prompted the Government to adopt various measures to protect the environment. Sikkim became one of the first states to ban plastic carry bags and the Sikkim Bio-degradable Act was enacted in 1999 that prohibits the dumping of garbage in undesignated places. The Government has banned grazing in Forest Land to preserve the forest coverage. As its commitment towards environment, it scrapped the Rathong-chu Hydel Project on which the work had already begun. In 1999, the Chief Minister of Sikkim, Mr. Pawan Chamling was declared the most Green CM based on a survey conducted by Centre for Science and Environment - a tribute to the state for its commitment to keep the environment clean. In January 2002, the State Government in association with a local NGO Ecotourism and Conservation Society of Sikkim (ECOSS) sponsored a South Asian Regional Conference on Ecotourism which was attended by representative from the SAARC countries. The Smriti Van programme has been a success in Gangtokin which Government has alloted pieces of barren land to various NGOs for afforestation.

However much more needs to be done in the field of environment. Huge quantities of garbage-organisc waste, paper, plastics, glass, batteries- are being generated in the towns: this requires to be segregated and recycled. Recycling units to convert paper and cotton waste into paper bags should be encouraged. Vermicomposting using earthworms to convert organic waste to manure should be introduced. LPG (Liquefied petroleum gas) and kerosene should be made widely available in the remotest corners of the state so that cutting of wood for fuel is reduced. Good telecommunication facilities, videoconferencing and telemedicine should be introduced so that people travel less and pollution is reduced. Neighbourhood watchdog schemes involving the community to ensure a clean environment may also be considered.

The best tool towards ensuring a clean environment is education. Awareness campaigns, cleanup drives, workshops, advertisement in the press, quiz programmes, and tree planting programmes can all contribute towards changing the mindset of the people and making them more environment conscious. But 'catching them young' is perhaps the best way of imbibing an environment culture: environment education as a part of the school syllabus and curicullum can have very long term benefits.

Other issues

The Government of Sikkim is already playing the role of a facilitator and watchdog. Development in various sectors like tourism, horticulture, information technology education should be through public-private partnership. NGOs should be involved in the area of healthcare and environment.

To provide a sense of direction, the Government prepared two landmark documents 'Sikkim-the people's vision' and 'Sikkim Human Development Report' which were released by the Prime Minister in New Delhi in September 2001. Packed with statistics on Sikkim, the reports also have identified the various thrust areas that can be developed to improve the economy and the human resources of the state. The reports have set the goal of putting the state on an accelerated path of eco-friendly sustainable development.

Developmental activities should however be balanced with the need for preserving the environment and the ecology. The pressures of development are already having their impact on Gangtok: a jungle of concrete buildings, clogged sewer lines, the cacophony blare of motorcars, an occasional traffic jam and overcrowding in the streets.

When hills come tumbling down, buildings collapse and the green landscape is scarred here and there by landslides- people start rethinking " Is it a place worth staying or visiting for a holiday" This is what happened at Gangtok in June 97, when more than 50 people died in landslides. The disaster was attributed to rampant and unplanned construction and clogged drains from which water flowed out and triggered the landslips. Although natural calamaties are the making of the God, they can be minimized if proper precautions are taken. Urban planning must be done in a manner that makes the cities and towns blend with the natural landscape.

A report Natural Calamities - Some Observations and Suggestions prepared by the local environment group Green Circle states "In the scriptures it is mentioned that ' if one cuts the land, destroys the cliffs, cuts down the trees,this will disturb the gods and the owner spirits of the land. It will anger all the Nagas and the owner spirits and thus create epidemics of disease and famine. The land will be destroyed by in-fighting and quarreling' We must therefore pause to consider the fundamental law of nature that 'we can only take as much as we can give.' It should be the need and not greed that should dictate our activities."

Inspite of rapid development and also rising unemployment, Sikkim still exudes charm and magic - the people are friendly and the high level officials are easily accessible making the Government very responsive to the problems of the people. Even the Chief Minister meets the public five times a week at his official residence and the Ministers and Secretaries can be met almost without any appointment at all.

Disasters in Sikkim

The mountains, lakes and rivers that we so eucolise can become monsters and unleash disasters like landslides and floods. Sikkim has had its fair share of disasters in living history the most promenient ones are as under:

1897 Earth Quake caused extensive damage to the Palace

1934 Earth Quake

1951 Flooding and landsldies that destroyed the railway line till Geil Khola

Oct 1968 A cloudburst and minor Tremor triggered a landslide on a tributary of Tista. The resulting pondage exerted pressure on the naturnal dam which gave way after two or three days sendig a wall of water gushing down the valley wreaking havoc and death. The Andersen Bridge at Tista was washed away. Gangtok was cut off from the rest of the country for a month.

June 1997 Landslides in and around Gangtok. Attributed to clogging of drains by plastic waste that lead to water spilling on the roads and causing llandslides.

18 Sept 2011 An earthquake measuring 6.8 on the Reitcher Scale with an eipicentre in North Sikkim triggered landslides and extensive damage to property. 60 lives were lost.The road between Mangan and Lachung was badly damaged.

VISION OF THE STATE GOVERNMENT

- To make Sikkim a 100% literate State by 2015.
- To make Sikkim an organic State by 2015.
- To transform Sikkim into an ideal State with a strong civil society by 2015.
- To generate 5000 MW of power by 2015.
- To make Sikkim strong and prosperous.
- To fulfill the wishes of the people with determination and compassion
- To make Sikkim free from poverty, illiteracy, debt, crime, drugs & AIDS and other diseases.
- To make Sikkim corruption free.
- To make Sikkim another Singapore in the economic sector.
- To transform Sikkim into a State like Cuba and Japan in health services.
- To achieve the status of education of countries like Netherlands, Norway and Singapore.
- To follow the example of Germany, France and Australia in the field of animal husbandry.
- To earn fame at par with Switzerland, Austria, Fiji, Mauritius and Paraguay in eco-tourism.
- To build a strong civil society like that of America, Canada and other European countries.
- To transform Sikkim into the best state of the country and also become a source of inspiration to others.
- To enrich all Sikkimese people mentally, physically and spiritually and to inculcate in them a sense of respect towards elders.
- To make Sikkim into a producer state.
- To make Sikkim the best welfare and happiest state.
- To make Sikkim the ultimate eco-tourism destination.
- To make Sikkim a land of opportunities with zero unemployment zone.

AWARDS WON BY THE GOVERNMENT

- Manav Seva Puraskar, 1994 - to Chief Minister of Sikkim for serving the people with dedication.
- Bharat Shiromani Puraskar, 1997 – to Chief Minister of Sikkim, in recognition of his endeavor to ensure Sikkim's emotional integration with the rest of the country.
- Man of Dedication Award, 1999- to Chief Minister of Sikkim.
- Sarwasrestha Paryawarna Badi Mukhayamantri, 1999-for working towards the preservation of the environment.
- Doctor of Philosophy (Honoris Causa) 2003- to the Chief Minister in recognition of his work towards the development of Sikkim, its education, society and its women.

- International Ambassador of Peace Award, 2008 -to the Chief Minister of Sikkim
- Leadership and Good Governance Award, 2009 -to the Chief Minister of Sikkim
- Highest award in Tourism for many consecutive years.
- The Best Performing State in Education, 2004-05.
- Best State award for progress in primary health sector, its investment friendly environment and its positive budgetary trends, 2006, India Today Group New Delhi.
- Sikkim was declared the best state among 12 Eastern States in the "State of States Conclave" organized by India Today.
- Skoch Challenger Award – 2005, in recognition of commendable work done in the field of information Technology.
- Hospitality India Award, 2006.
- The Highest Eco-Tourism Award to Sikkim.
- 3rd position in best performing states in Panchayati Raj.
- National Award as best performing State in Tourism – 2008.
- Platinum award for Emerging Tourism State of 2008 by Today's Traveller.
- IBN7 Diamond State Award for the best state in the small state category for Citizen Security and Justice.
- Sikkim Nationalised Transport awarded National Trophy for lowest accidents in hilly state category for two consecutive years. i.e. 2005-06 and 2006-07 by the Union Transport Ministry.
- National Tourism Award for the best tourism related programmes for the year 2007-08.
- Sikkim awarded the best in Preserving National Resources and maintaining State's environment.
- Four India Today Awards in the small state category namely; the Best State in Education, Bharat Nirman Award in E-Governance, Bharat Nirman Award in Rural Electrification and Bharat Nirman Award in Rural Roads.
- State Leadership Award 2009 in horticulture.
- Sikkim becomes the first Nirmal Rajya in the country.
- Fourth JRD Tata Memorial Award for Sikkim.
  - CM awarded the Bharat Asmita Jewan Gaurav Purasker
  - Chardham at Namchi bags the Most Innovative and Unique Tourism Project Award 2010

STATE RANKING

- Best State for Adventure Tourism for the year 2009
- IBN7 Diamond State Award for Sikkim in 'Water and Sanitation' category'

1st in Social Sector

1st Total Revenue Receipt as % to GSDP

1st in Contraceptive Prevalence Rate (CPR) (among NE states)

1st in the proportion of households that use the public medical sector as their main source of health care

2nd in Environmental Sustainability Index (ESI)

2nd in Annual Plan as % to GSDP

2nd in % of children born as not- underweight

3rd in women's participation in polls

3rd in Total Budget Expenditure on Education Dept. & other Departments (Rev.) to GSDP

3rd in per capita plan expenditure

4th in Total Budget Expenditure on Education Dept. (Rev.) to GSDP

4th in plan expenditure in social sector

5th in immunization coverage

7th in Wealth Index (above National level)

7th in attaining low Fertility rate

8th in Death Rate (DR)

9th in GSDP Growth Rate at Current Prices

10th in Infant Mortality Rate (IMR)

11th in Birth Rate (BR)

12th in Institutional Delivery

13th in Safe Delivery

13th in per capital NSDP at Current

LIST OF REVENUE BLOCKS

EAST DISTRICT CIRCLE	**REVENUE BLOCK**
Duga	East Pendam, Pachak, Kamarey Bhasmey, Sajong, Central Pendam
West Pendam	Mangthang, Sumin, Lingchey, West Pendam
Gangtok	Arithang, Gangtok, Burtuk, Chandmari, Gnathang
Tadong	Upper Tadong (Old GMC), Tadong, Samdur
Sichey Lingding	Syari, Upper Tathangchen (Old GMC),Tathangchen, Rongyek, Upper sichey (Old GMC), Sichey.
Naitam	Nandok, Naitam,Namong, Bhusuk, Lingzey, Assam
Samdong	Raley Khese, Samdong, Kambal, Rakdong, Tintek
Lingdok	Navey, Shotak, Penlong, Lingdok, Namphong
Sang	Martam, Nazitam, Tirkutam, Sirwani, Sakyong, Chisopani, Tshalumthang, Phengyong, Rapdang, Byang
Sang, Namgeytahng	
Khamdong	Dung Dung, Singbel, Aritar, Budang Thangsing, Beng,
Khamdong	
Tumin	Tumin, Simik, Lingzey, Patuk, Chadey
Ranka	Sangtong, Ranka, Barbing, Lingdum, Luing, Perbing, Reybrok, Rey Mindu
Rumtek	Chinzey, Rawtey rumtek, Sazong Rumtek, Marchak, Namin, Namli, Tumlabung, Chuba
Rongli	Rolep, Lamaten, Chujachen, Rongli Bazar, Changeylakha
Subaneydara	Dalapchand, South Regu, North Regu, Subaneydara, singanebas, Premlakha,Lintgtam, Phadamchen
Rhenock	Rhenock Bazar, rhenock, Tarpin, Mulukey, Sudunglakha,
Aritar	
BeringMachong	Bering, Tareythang, LinkeyLatuk, Chochenpheri, Machong, Parakha, riwa, Thekabong
Pakyong	Pakyong Bazar, Kartok, Namcheybong, Pachey
Dikling(New)	Dikling, Dikling- Pacheykhani, Lossing Pacheykhani,
Chalamthang	
Taza (New)	Taza, Amba
Changey Senti	Changey Senti, Aho, Yangtam

WEST DISTRICT CIRCLE	**REVENUE BLOCK**
Gerethang	Arithang, Chongrong, Gerethang, Labing, Yuksom, Dubdi
Thingling	Thingling-I, Thingling-II, Tsozo, Khechodpalri, Melli, Melli Aching, Singlitam, Timbrong, Topung
Dhupidara	Mangnam, Narkhola, Dhupidara, Labong, Kongri
Tashiding	Tashiding, Lasso, Gangyap
Darap	Sindrangpong, Nambu, Darap, Sindrang, singyang, Naku,
Chumbong	
Gyalshing	Yangtey, Umlok, Bhaluthang, Gyalshing, Omchung, Kyongsa
Lingchom	Yangthang, Linchom, Tikjya, Lungzik, Sardong
Gyaten	Bongten, Srinagi, Sapong, Liching, Karmatar, Gyaten
Dentam	Maneybong, Sopakha, Begha, Mangmoo, Dentam
Radhu Khandu	Sangkhu, Radu Khandu, Hee, Hee Patal
Rinchenpong	Chingthang, Berfok, Meyong, Megyong, Sangdorji, Zeel,
Hathidunga	
Kaluk	Tadong, Rinchenpong, boom, reshi, Bara Samdong, Sribadam
Mangalbaria	Deythang, Pareng-gaon, Takuthang, Chuchen

Kamling Tinzerbong, suldong, Kamling, Mabong, Segeng
Arubotey Khanisherbong, suntaley, Chotasamdong, Arubotey
Chakung Gelling, Samsing, Chakung, Mendogaon
Zoom Chumbong, Zoom
Soreng Malbasey, Soreng, Singling
Dodak Timberbong, Tharpu, Dodak, Karthank, Buriakhop
Sombaria Rumbuk, Buriakhop (Rumbuk), Upper Phambong, Lower Phamdong, Dhallam (Daramdin) Lungchok, Salangdang
Okhrey Siktam, Tikpur, Okhrey, Ribdi, Bhareng.

SOUTH DISTRICT CIRLCLE	**REVENUE BLOCK**
Wak	Tingrithang, Pabong, Pakjer, Wak, Omchu, Chumlok, Sanganath
Tinkitam	Timkitam, rayong, tingmo, Laating, Mangbrue, Hingdam
Tarku	Ben, Deu, Namprik, Tarku, Tanak
Damthang	Damthang, Jaubari, Chemchey, Temi, Aifaltar, Gangchung
Bermiok tokal	Daring, Namphing, Reshep, Pabung (Gangchung)
Rameng	Burul, Rameng, Nizarameng
Sadam	Sadam, suntaley, Sukrabarey, Rabitar
Melli Dara	Melli Dara, Paiyong, Kerabari, Melli, Turuk, Ramabung, Panchgharey
Sumbuk	Sumbuk, Kartikey, Suntaley
Rong	Lungchok, Kamaay, Rong, Bul, Singtam, Palum
Boomtar	Singithang, Boomtar, Gumpa Ghurpisey, Namchi Bazar, Kamrang, Mamley, Tinzir
Kitam	Mickhola, Kitam, Kopchey, Manpur, sorok, Syampani, Gom
Salgahri	Salghari, Dorop, Dhargaon, Jorethang Bazar, Tiniki, Chisopani
Poklok	Assangthang, Sangbung, Poklok, Deenchung
Namthang	Perbing, Phong, Chuba, Karek, Maney Dara, Nalam Kolbong, Kabrey, Kanamtek
Turung	Nagi, Palitam, Kateng, Bokrong, Pamphok, Turung, Mamring, Donok
Maniram	Tangzi, Bikmat, Rabikhola, Rateypani, Passi, Maniram, Phalidara, Salleybong
Ralong	Ralong, Namlung, Lingding, Borong, Phamtam, Polok, Sada
Rabong	Rabong, Sangmo, Rabong Bazar, Berfung, Jarrong, Deytahng
Kewzing	Legship, Kewzing, Bakhim, Lingzo, Dalep
Yangyang	Sripatam, Gagyong, Namphok, Yangyang, Rangang, Satam
Lingi	Lingi, Sokpay, Upper Paiyong, Kau.
Lingmo	Lingmo, Pepthang, Kolthang, Mangzing, Niya Brom, Tokdey

NORTH DISTRICT CIRCLE	**REVENUE BLOCK**
Phensong	Kabi Tingda, Pani Phensong, Labi, G. Phensong, Menrongong, Phamtam, Chawang
Namok/Lungchik	Tumlong, Phodong, rongong, Ramtahng, Tanek, Swyam, Namok, Upper Mangshilla, Lower Mangshilla, Tingchim
Singhik-Mangan	Zimchung, Nampatam, Ringhim, singhik, Kazor, Pakshep, Sentam, Singchit, Meyong
Passingdong	Salim-Pakyel, Lingthem, Lingdem, Tingvong, Pentong, Lingzya
Hee-Gyatahng	Lingdong, Barfok, Hee-Gyathang, Goan- Sangdong
GorChungtahng	Gor, Sangtok SakyongNaga, Toong, Chungthang, Lachung, Lachen, Shipgyer.

GRAM PANCHAYAT UNITS & PANCHAYAT WARDS

NORTH DISTRICT

Kabi-Tingda
Phensong
Men-Rongong
Rongong-Tumlong
Ramthang-Tanek
Namok-Sheyam
Tingchim-Mangshilla
Ringhim-Namapatam
Sentam
Toong-Naga
Chungthang
Ship-Gyer
Lingthem-Lingdem
Passingdang-Saffo
Tingvong
Sakyong-Pentong
Lingdong-Berfok
Hee-Gyathang
Lum-Gor-Sangtok
Lachen Dzumsa
Lachung Dzumsa

EAST DISTRICT

Sumin Lingzey
West Pendam
Central Pendam
East Pendam
Pacheykhani
Taza
Rhenock Tarpin
Aritar
Sudunglakha
Dalapchen
Regoh
Premlakha Subaneydara
Gnathang
Lingtam Phadanchen
Rolep Lamaten
Chujachen
Latuk Chuchenpheri
Thekabong Parkha
Riwa Machong
Linkey Tarey Thang
Amba
Changey Senti
Kartok Namcheybong
Aho Yangtam
Assam Lingzey
Naitam Nandok
Tathangchen Syari
Luing Perbing
Ranka
Rey Mendu
Rawtey Rumtek
Samlik Marchak
Namli
Martam Nazitam
Beng-Phegyong
Sirwani Tshalumthang
Khamdong
Singbel
Simik Lingzey
Tumin
Samdong Kambal
Rakdong Tintek
Lingdok Nampong
Navay Shotak

SOUTH DISTRICT

Lingi
Paiyong
Lingmo Kolthang
Niya Mangzing
Sripatam Gagyong
Yangang Rangang
Rabong Sangmo
Ben Namprik
Temi
Tarku
Namphing
Barnyak Tokal
Rameng Nizrameng
Perbing Dovan
Chuba Phong
Maneydara
Nagi Pamphok
Turung Mamring
Tanji Biktam
Rateypani
Sadam Suntoley
Mellidara Paiyong
Turuk Ramabung
Lungchok Kamarey
Sumbuk Kartikey
Rong Bul
Maniram Singithang
Mikhola Kitam
Sorok Shyampani
Salghari
Assangthang
Poklok Denchung
Tinik Chisopani
Mamley Kamrang
Tingrithang
Damthang
Wak Omchu
Sanganath
Tiniktam Rayong
Lamting Tingmo
Lekship
Kewzing Bakhim
Barfung Zarung
Ralong Namlung
Borong Phamthang

WEST DISTRICT

Karchi Mangam
Dhupidara Narkhola
Kongri Labdang
Tashiding
Arithang Chongrang
Gerethang
Yuksom
Thingle Khachodpalri
Meli
Darap
Singyang Chumbung
Yangten
Gyalshing Omchung
Yangthang
Lingchom Tikjya
Sardung Lungzik
Bongten Sapong
Karmatar Gyaten
Maneybung Sopkha
Dentam
Sangkhu Radukhandu
Hee
Pecherek Martam
Bernyak Barthang
Chingthang
Sangadorji
Tadong Rinchenpong
Samdong
Deythang
Takothang
Suldung Kamling
Mabong Segeng
Khaniserbong Suntoley
Chota Samdong Suntoley
Samsing Gelling
Chakung
Mandogaon berbotey
Chumbung
Zoom
Malbasey
Soreng
Singling
Timburbong
Tharpu
Dodak
Buriakhop
Rumbuk
Upper Fambong
Lower Fambong
Longchok salyangdang
Siktam tikpur
Okhrey
Ribdi Bhareng

SECONDARY AND SENIOR SECONDARY SCHOOLS

East Disrict

Adampool Govt. Sec.
Aho-Shanti Govt. Sec.
Aritar Govt. Sec.
Assam Lingzey Govt. Sr. Sec.
Biraspati Parsai Govt. Sr. Sec.
Bojoghari Govt. Sec.
Central Pendam Govt. Sr. Sec.
Chujachen Govt. Sr. Sec.
Dalapchand Govt. Sec.
Deorali Girls Govt. Sr. Sec.
Dikchu Govt. Sec.
Dikling Govt. Sr. Sec.
Duga Govt. Sec.
Khamdong Govt. Sr. Sec.
Lingdok Govt. Sr. Sec.
Lingtam Govt. Sec.
Lower Samdong Govt. Sec.
Lower Sumin Govt. Sec.
Lower Syari Govt. Sec.
Luing Govt. Sec.
Machong Govt. Sr. Sec.
Makha Govt. Sec.
Mamring Govt. Sec.
Martam Govt. Sec.
Middle Camp Govt. Sec.
Modern Govt. Sec.
Namcheybong Govt.Sec.
Nandok Govt. Sec.
Pabyuik Govt. Sec.
Pacheykhani Govt. Sec.
Padamchey Govt. Sec.
Penlong Govt. Sec.
Phadamchen Govt. Sec.
Rangpo Govt. Sec.
Ranka Govt. Sr. Sec.
Rhenock Govt. Sr.Sec.
Rolep Govt. Sec.
Rumtek Govt. Sr. Sec.
Samdong Govt. Sr. Sec.
Sichey Govt. Sec.
Singtam Govt. Sr. Sec.
Sir Tashi Namgyal Govt. Sr. Sec.
Sirwani Govt. Sec.
Sudunglakha Govt. Sec.
Sumin Lingchey Govt.Sec.
Syaplay Sardaray Govt. Sec.
Tadong Govt. Sr. Sec.
Tarping Govt. Sec.
Tumin Govt. Sec.
West Point Govt. Sr. Sec.

West Disrict

Bariakhop Govt. Sr. Sec.
Bermiok Martam Govt. Sec.
Bongten Govt. Sec.
Central Martam Govt. Sec.
Chakung Govt. Sr. Sec.
Chumbong Govt. Sec.
Daramdin Govt. Sec.
Darap Govt. Sec.
Dentam Govt. Sr. Sec.
Dodak Govt. Sec.
Gelling Govt. Sec.
Gerethang Govt. Sec.
Hee Yangthang Govt. Sr. Sec.
K.B.Limboo Govt. Sec.
Kaluk Govt. Sr. Sec.
Kamling Govt. Sec.
Khandu Govt. Sec.
Khaniserbong Govt. Sec.
Khechuperi Govt. Sec.
Kyongsa Girls Govt. Sr. Sec.
Legship Govt. Sec.
Lingchom Govt. Sec.
Mangalbaria Govt. Sr. Sec.
Mangsari Govt. Sec.
Melli-Aching Govt. Sec.
Middle Geyzing Govt. Sec.
Mukrung Govt. Sec.
Okhrey Govt. Sec.
Pakkigaon Govt. Sec.
Pelling Govt. Sr. Sec.
Pipalay Govt. Sec.
Reshi Govt. Sec.
Ribdi Govt. Sec.
Sakyong Govt. Sec.
Samdong Govt. Sec.
Singling Govt. Sec.
Sombarey Govt. Sr. Sec.
Soreng Govt. Sr. Sec.
Tashiding Govt. Sr. Sec.
Tharpu Govt. Sec.
Tikpur Govt. Sec.
Timburbung Govt. Sec.
Uttarey Govt. Sec.
Yangsum Govt. Sec.
Yuksom Govt. Sec.
Zoom Govt. Sec.

South District

Ben Govt. Sec.
Bermiok Tokal Govt. Sr. Sec.
Bikmat Govt. Sec.
Borong Govt. Sec.
Omchu Govt. Sec.
Jarrong Govt. Sec.
Damthang Govt. Sec.
Denchung Govt. Sec.
Jerman Lepcha Govt. Sec.
Jorethang Govt. Sec.
Kabrey Govt. Sec.
Kamrang Govt. Sec.
Kewzing Govt. Sec.
Kitam Govt. Sec.
Lingee Govt. Sec.
Lingmoo-Kolthang Govt. Sr. Sec.
Maniram Govt. Sec.
Melli Bazar Govt. Sec.
Melli Gumpa Govt. Sec.
N.L.T.Vok Govt. Sec.
Namchi Govt. Sr. Sec.
Namchi Govt. Sr. Sec.
Namchi New Govt. Sec.
Namphok Govt. Sec.
Namthang Govt. Sr. Sec.
Nandugaon Govt. Sec.
Neh Broom Govt. Sec.
Pabong Govt. Sec.
Perbing Govt. Sec.
Ralong Govt. Sec.
Rateypani Govt. Sec.
Rong Govt. Sec.
Sadam Govt. Sr. Sec.
Salghari Govt. Sec.
Sanganath Govt. Sec.
Sumbuk Govt. Sec.
Tarku Govt. Sec.
Temi Govt. Sr. Sec.
Tingley Govt. Sec.
Tingmoo Govt. Sec.
Turuk Govt. Sec.
VCGLRavangla Govt. Sr. Sec.
Yangyang Govt. Sr. Sec.

North Disrict

Gor Govt. Sec.
Hee- gyathang Govt. Sr. Sec.
Kalzang gyatso Govt. Sec.
Lachen Govt. Sec.
Lachung Govt. Sec.
Lingdong Govt. Sec.
Mangan Govt. Sr. Sec.
Mangshila Govt. Sec.
Manul Govt. Sec.
Passingdang Govt. Sec.
Phensong Govt. Sec.
Phodong Govt. Sr. Sec.
Singhik Govt. Sec.
Tasa tengay Govt. Sec.
Tingvong Govt. Sec.

Universities established in Sikkim

Sikkim University

Sikkim Manipal University

Institute of Chartered Finanicial Analysts of India University (ICFAI University) at Gangtok

Eastern Institute for Intergrated Learining in Management University (EIILM University) at Jorethang

Vinayaka Missions Sikkim University at Gangtok

Important educational institutes in Sikkim

1 Rhenock Government College, Rhenock East Sikkim

2 Sikkim Government College, Tadong, East Sikkim

3 I.T.I, Rangpo, East Sikkim **(Under Labour Dept.)**

4 Sikkim Government Law College, Gangtok

5 SHEDA College, Deorali

6 Himalayan Pharmacy Institute, Majhitar, East Sikkim

7 Damber Singh Degree College, Deorali, East Sikkim

8 Namchi Government College, Namchi, South Sikkim

9 Loyala College of Education, Namchi, South Sikkim

10 Sikkim Manipal Institute of Technology (SMIT), Majhitar, East Sikkim

11 Sanskrit College, Gayzing, West Sikkim

12 Advanced Technical Training Centre (ATTC), Bardang(Polytechnic)

13 Centre for Computers and Communication Technology (CCCT), Chisopani, South Sikkim (Polytechnic)

14 Institute of Hotel Mangement Tadong, Gangtok.

15 Sikkim Manipal Institute of Medical Sciences (SMIMS), Gangtok,

16 Harkamaya College of Education, Tadong, East Sikkim

17 Palatine College, Pakyong

18 Bed College Soreng

FACTS AND FIGURES ABOUT SIKKIM

Location:	Approx 27 deg. North 88 deg. East	
Area:	7,096 sq kms (.22% of area of India)	
State Population:	540,493 (Male:288,217; Female: 252,276)	
(As per 2001 Census)	.05 % of the total population of India	
Sex ratio (2001 Census):	875 females/1000 males	
Density of population:	76 per sq. km	
Capital:	Gangtok	
Districts, Areas	East District (954 sq km)	- Gangtok
&District Capitals:	West District (1166 sq km)	- Gyalshing
	South District (750 sq km)	- Namchi
	North District (4226 sq km)	- Mangan
No. of Sub-Divisions:	9 (Gangtok, Pakyong, Rongli, Namchi, Soreng, Gyalshing, Rabongla, Mangan, Chungthang)	
Climate:	Tropical, Temperate and Alpine	

No of Species (rich biodiversity): Sikkim has only 0.2 % area of India but has 26 % of bio-diversity.

There has been a 2% increase in forest coverage(from 43.95% to 46%) in the state during the period 1993-2003 due to to green initiatives of the Government

Mammals 144	*Birds: 550*	*Butterflies: 650*
Flowering plants: over 4000 species		*Orchids: 550*
Rhodendrons: 36	*Ferns: 300*	*Conifers: 9*

State Animal:	Red Panda (Ailurus fulgens)
State Bird:	Blood Pheasant (Ithaginis cruentus)
State Flower:	Nobile Orchid (Dendrobium nobile)
State Tree:	Rhododendron (Rhododendron niveum)
No. of Zilla Panchayat ward: 92	
No. of Gram Panchayat:	166 Units:
No. of Revenue Blocks:	411
Other important towns:	Jorethang, Singtam, Rangpo, Pakyong Rhenock, Melli, Chungthang and Soreng
Official Languages:	English, Nepali, Bhutia, Lepcha, Limboo, Magar, Rai, Gurung, Sherpa, Tamang, Newari, Sunuwar
Main occupations:	Farmers, Cardamom Growers, Government contractors and Government Employees
Per Capita Income:	Rs 9472/- (1995-96, at current prices)
Per capita growth rate:	6.80%
Domestic product:	Rs 446 crores (1995-96, at current prices)
Domestic product Growth rate:10.39% (1995-96, at current prices)	
Plan Allocation:	8th Plan (1992-97): Rs 764 crores

	9th Plan (1997-2002): Rs 1181.24 crores
	10th Plan (2002-2007): Rs 1655.74 crores
Religions:	Hinduism, Buddhism and Christianity
Percentage of : population by religion:	Hindus 67.25%, Buddhists 28.71%, Christians 2.22%, Muslims 1.03%
Percentage of population by caste:	Schedule Caste 5.93%, Schedule Tribe 22%
Urban Population:	9.1%
% below poverty line:	36.55 as against all India 26.1 (in 1999-2000)
Birth rate:	21.9 (in 2001, per 1000)
Death rate:	5.0 (in 2001, per 1000)
Infant Mortality rate:	33 (in 2001, per 1000)
No. of Assembly seats:	32
No. of Lok Sabha seats:	1
No. of Rajya Sabha seats:	1
No. of Police Stations:	26 (as in 2002)
No. of Police Outposts:	38
No. of Police Checkposts:	6
No. of Picket posts:	11
CID/PS	1

Crime Statistics (2010):
Murders:17; Robbery:7;Theft:53; Burglary:72; Rape:18; Kidnapping:6, Cheating: 20; Counterfeiting:3; Arson:7; Molestation:11

Percentage of Electrification:	98%
Cash crops:	Cardmom, Tea, Ginger
Cereal Crops:	Rice, Maize, Millet
Fruits:	Oranges and Apples
Minerals & Metals:	Copper, dolomite, graphite
No. of Doordarsan TV High power Transmitters:	1 at Gangtok
No. of All India Radio: Stations	1, MW & SW at Gangtok

No of Schools and Educational Institutions (2005)

Primary schools-	502	Middle (Junior) schools-	147
Secondary Schools-	92	Senior Sec. Schools-	41
Public Schools-	2		
Degree College-	2	Engineering College-	1
Medical College	1	BEd College-	1
Law College	1	Sheda	1
Monastic Schools	50	Sanskrit patshala	12
Madrasa	1	Teachers Training Inst.	1
Industrial Training Inst.	1		

Pecentage of literacy: 82%

No. of hospitals:	6, including Sir Thutob Namgyal Memorial & Manipal Referral Hospitals
No. of Primary Health Centre	24
No. of Primary Sub Health Centre	147
Population per doctor:	2800
No. of Veterinary Hospitals:	12
No. of Veterinary Dispensaries:	25
No. of food godowns	24

Roads

National Highway -	40 kms	State Highway -	250 kms
Major district roads-	450 kms	Other district roads-	845 kms

Land utilization:

Forest Land	42%	Barren Land	22%
Agriculture Land	16%	Pasture & Grazing Land	17%
Other Land	3%		

Tourist arrivals

Domestic	234394
International	14774

Name of Constituencies(Old):

Soreng, Martam, Daramdin, Damthang, Rumtek, Rhenock, Dentam, Dzongu, Assam Linzey, Gyalshing, Ralang, Bermiok, Pathing, Ranka, Wak, Yoksum, Chakung,Pendam, Regu, Melli, Khamdong, Jorethang, Rakdong, Rateypani, Temi, Tashiding, Sanga, Mangshila, Kabi, Pachekhani, Rinchenpong, Gangtok

NAMES CONSTITUENCIES (AFTER DELIMITATION)

Yoksam-Tashiding	Yangthang	Maneybung-Dentam
Gyalshing-Barnyak	Rinchenpong	Daramdin
Soreong-Chakung	Salgari-Zoom	Barfung
Poklok-Kamrang	Namchi-Singhithang	Melli
Namthang-Rateypani	Temi-Namphing	Rangang-Yangang
Tumen-Lingi	Khamdong-Singtam	West Pendam
Rhenock	Chujachen	Gnathang Machong
Namcheybung	Shyari	Martam-Rumtek
Upper Tadong	Arithang	Gangtok
Upper Burtuk	Kabi Lungchuk	Djongu
Lachen Mangan		

LIST OF BLOCK ADMINISTRATIVE CENTRES: 28

EAST DISTRICT :RHENOCK, KHAMDONG, RANKA, RAKDONG -TINTEK, PAKYONG, GANGTOK, RONGLI, DUGA, PARKHA, NANDOK

WEST DISTRICT :SORENG, GYALSHING, DENTAM, YUKSOM, SANG-DORJEE, HEE-BERMOIK

SOUTH DISTRICT: TEMI, RAVANGLA, SORENG, YANGANG, SUMBUK, SIKIP, NAMCHI, NAMTHANG

NORTH DISTRICT: MANGAN, PASSINGDONG, KABI, CHUNGTHANG

LIST OF HOLIDAYS 2012

New Year's Day	1st January	Sunday
Maghe Sankranti	14th January	Saturday
Sonam Lochar	24th January	Tuesday
Republic Day	26th January	Thursday
Losar	22nd February	Wednesday
Holi	8th March	Thursday
Ramnawami (Chaite Dasain)	1st April	Sunday
Good Friday	6th April	Friday
Dr. B.R. Ambedkar Jayanti	14th April	Saturday
Sakewa	14th May	Monday
State Day	16th May	Wednesday
Saga Dawa	4th June	Monday
Bhanu Jayanti	13th July	Friday
Drukpa Tsheshi	23rd July	Monday
Guru Rimpoche;s Tshechu	28th July	Saturday
Tendong Lho Rum Faat	8th August	Wednesday
Janmastahmi	10th august	Friday
Independence Day	15th August	Wednesday
ID-ul-fitr	20th August	Monday
Pang Lhabsol	31st August	Friday
Indrajatra	29th September	Saturday
Gandhi Jayanti	2nd October	Tuesday
Durga Puja (Dasain)	22nd -26th October	Monday to Friday
Lhabab Duechen	6th November	Tuesday
Laxmi Puja (Diwali)	13th -15th November	Tuesday to Thursday
Kagyed Dance	12th December	Wednesday
Lossong	14th-17th December	Friday to Monday
Nyenpa Gunzom	18th December	Tuesday
Christmas	25th December	Tuesday
Teyongsi Sirijunga Sawan	28th December	Friday
Tamu Lochar	30th December	Sunday

SIKKIM'S CURRENT WHO'S WHO

Name	Designation
MPs	
Mr. Hissey Lachungpa	Member of Parliament, Rajya Sabha
Mr. P.D. Rai	Member of Parliament, Lok Sabha
SPEAKER / DY. SPEAKER	
Mr K. T Gyalsten	Speaker,Sikkim Legislative Assembly
Mr. M.B. Dahal	Dy. Speaker,Sikkim Legislative Assembly
Mr. Ugyen Bhutia	Chief Whip
Name	**Designation / Departments**
MINSTER	
Mr. Pawan Chamling	Chief Minister,Home Deptt.,FRED. Dev.Planning,Eco. Reforms and N-E Council Affairs
Mr. Ran Bahadur Subba	Roads and Bridges and Cooperation
Mr.Thenlay Tshering Bhutia	Water Security and PHE & Transport Deptt.
Mr. Dawa Norbu Takarpa	Health Care, Human Services & Family Welfare, Food Security and Agriculture Dev.and HCC Dev , Parliamentary Affairs Deptt.
Mr. Narendra Kumar Pradhan	HRDD, Sports & Youth Affairs and I.T. Deptt.
Mr. Dil Bahadur Thapa	UDHD, Food, Civil Supplies & Consumer Affairs
Mr. Sonam Gyatso Lepcha	Energy &Power and Cultural Affairs and Heritage Deptt.
Mr. Chandra Bahadur Karki	RMDD , IPR, Printing
Mr. Dawcho Lepcha	AH&,LF &Veterinary Services .and Irrigation and Flood Control Deptt.
Mr. Bhim Prasad Dhungel	Tourism, Forest, Environment and Wildlife Management, Mines, Minerals and Geology, Science &Tec.Deptt.
Mrs. Tilu Gurung	Buildings and Housing Department.
Ms. Neeru Sewa	Commerce and Industries, Excise Deptt and Labour
MLA CHARIMEN/ CHAIRPERSON WITH CABINET RANK	
Mr.Menlom Lepcha	MLA,Chairman,Public Accounts Committee(SLA)
Smt. Tulshi Devi Rai	MLA,Chairperson,Estimate Committee (SLA)
Mr. B.S.Panth	MLA,Chariman,Power Advisory Board,Gangtok
Mr.Prem Singh Tamang	MLA,Chairman,Industries, TCDB
Ms.Chandra Maya Subba	MLA,Chairperson,STCS
Mr.L.M. Lepcha	MLA,Chairman,SBSand SSCB
M LA CHAIRMEN / CHAIRPERSON	
Mr. Puran Kumar Gurung	MLA,Chairman,DACS Ltd.
Mr.Am Prasad Sharma	MLA,Chairman,Sikkim Distilleries Ltd.
Mr.Tshering Wangdi Lepcha	MLA,Chairman,SNT
Mr.Prem Lall Subba	MLA,Chairman,Agriculture / Horticulture Board
Mr.Madan Cintury	MLA,Chairman,SSC,ST& OBC (SAABCO)
Mr.Tenzi Sherpa	MLA,Chairman,Khadi & Village Industries Board
Mr.Bek Bahadur Rai	MLA,Chairman,SIDt & Investment Co.(SIDICO)
Mr.Sonam Gyatso Bhutia	MLA,Chairman,Land Use & Environment Board
Mr.Dorjee Namgyal Bhutia	MLA,Chariman,Sikkim Consumer Cooperative Society
Mr. P.T. Bhutia	MLA, Chairman, Schedule Tribe Welfare Board
Mr.Binod Rai	
NON MLA CHARIMEN/ CHAIRPERSON WITH CABINET RANK	
Shri B.B.Gooroong	Chairman,Welfare Commission
Dr. K.Shreedhar Rao (Retd.)	Chairman, Knowledge Commission
NON M LA CHAIRMEN / CHAIRPERSON	
Mr.N.K.Subba,	Chairman,Sikkim Tourism Development Corporation
Mr.Girish Chandra Rai	Chairman,Sikkim Marketing Federation (SIMFED)
Smt.Malika Rai	Chairperson,STC
ADVISORS	
Mr. R.B. Subba	Legal Advisorto the Chief Minister
Mr. Hishey Lachungpa	Political Advisor to the Chief Minister
Mr. K.N. Rai	Political Secretary to the Chief Minister
OTHERS	
Shri Justice R.K.Patra	Chairman,PoliceComplaint Authority/Law Commission
Shri A.N.Ray	Chairperson,State Human Rights Commission
URBAN LOCAL BODIES	

Municipal Ward	Name of Canditate	Designation
Gangtok Municipal Corporation		
Chandmari	K.N. Topay	Mayor
Upper M.G. Marg	Shakti Singh Chooudhary	Dy. Mayor
Burtuk	Lok Bdr. Bhujel	
Lower Sicehy	Arati Giri	
Upper Sichey	Nell Bdr Chettri	
Development Area	Yodh Bdr Thapa	
Diesel Power House	Srijana Khati	
Arithang	Ashis Hirang Rai	
Lower M.G. Marg	Sandhya Rani Prasad	
Tibet Road	Hissay Doma Bhutia	
Deorali	Udai Lama	
Daragoan	Bhasker Basnett	
Tadong	Prabhat Gurung	
Ranipool	Damber Dahal	
Syari	Lashey Doma Bhutia	
Singtam Nagar Panchayat		
Pipaldara	Meena Kri Chettri	
Daragaon	Sawan Kr. Pradhan	
Mandir Line	Bishnu Maya Sherpa	
Lall Bazar	Ram Naresh Prasad	
Chisopani	Anita Tamang	
Rangpo Nagar Panchayat		
Majhitar	Purna Bdr. Chettri	
Mining	Aita Maya Gurung	
Mandi Bazar	Nirmal Kr.Khati	
Rangpo Upper Bazar	Nikash Kumar Prasad	
Chanatar	Puspa Misra	
Namchi Municipal Council		
Gangyap	Noor Hassan Ansari	Dy. Chairperson
Dambudara	Gita Chettri SDF	
Upper Ghurpisey	Sonam Peden Bhutia	Executive Member
Lower Ghurpisey	Ratna Maya Rai	
Upper Boomtar	Buddha Tamang	Chairperson
Upper Singithang	Tarkeshwar Prasad	
Purano Namchi	Binod Rai	
Jorethang Nagar Panchayat		
Shantinagar	Purushottam Das Agarwal	
Trikaleshwar	Ganesh Chettri	
Daragoan	Prakash Lakandri	
Majhi Goan East	Pema Tamang	
.Majhigaon(West)	Bhanukala Gurung	
Gyalshing Nagar Panchayat		
Tikjuk	Zangmoo Bhutia	
Kyongsa	Roshan Gurung	Vice President
Nayabazar	Sarada Devi Agarwal	
Central Geyzing	Chopel Pintso Bhutia	
New Geyzing	Indra Kumar Neopaney	President
Mangan Nagar Panchayat		
Upper Mangan Bazar	Zangmoo Bhutia	
Pentok	Chewang Dorjee Lepcha	
Power Colony	Nima Doma Lepcha	
Rinzing Namgyal Marg	Karma Jigdal Bhutia	
Lower Mangan Bazar	Prakash Kumar Malu	

LIST OF MAJOR INDUSTRIES IN SIKKIM

1. M/S Sun Pharma SikkimSetipool,East Sikkim
2. M/S STP Pharmaceutical (P) Ltd.Sangkhola,East Sikkim
3. M/S Epitome Petrochemical (P) Ltd.Sangkhola,East Sikkim
4. M/S Zydus Healthcare,Bagheykhola,East Sikkim
5. M/S Sonakshi Pharmaceutical (P) Ltd.Majhitar,East Sikkim
6. M/S Indchemie Health Specialities (P) Ltd.Kumrek,East Sikkim
7. M/S Alkem Laboratories Ltd.Kumrek,East Sikkim
8. M/S JNRT Commercial (p) Ltd.Kumrek,East Sikkim
9. M/S SICPA India Ltd.Mamring,South Sikkim
10. M/S Godrej Consumer Products Ltd.Mamring,South Sikkim
11. M/S Golden Cross Pharma(P) Ltd.Rorathang,East Sikkim
12. M/S Cipla Ltd.Kumrek,East Sikkim
13. M/S PTS Packers & Providers (P) Ltd.Sangkhola,East Sikkim
14. C.G.Foods India (P) Ltd.Near Food Godown,Rangpo,East Sikkim
15. Pristine Life Sciences,Opp.Bhanu Park,Singtam,East Sikkim
16. Sheela Foam (P) Ltd.Bagheykhola,East Sikkim
17. M/S YoksumBreweriesLtd.Melli,South Sikkim
18. M/s Mount Distilleries Ltd.Majhitar,East Sikkim
19. M/S Mayell & Fraser (P) Ltd.Bagheykhola,Singtam,East Sikkim
20. ADS Industries,Manpur,South Sikkim
21. Sikkim Agrochem (P) Ltd.Majhitar,East Sikkim
22. M/S Torrent Pharmaceuticals Ltd.32 Mile , NH 31/A E- Sikkim
23. Sikkim Distilleries Ltd.Majhitar,East Sikkim
24. Intas Pharmaceuticals,Majhitar,East Sikkim
25. Unichem Laboratories,Bagheykhola,East Sikkim
26. Himalaya Distilleries,Majhitar,East Sikkim
27. Sikkim Ispat Udyog (P) Ltd.Majhitar,East Sikkim
28. Greenways (P) Ltd.Samlik Marchak,Industrial Growth Centre,Ranipool
29. Agape Drugs & Pharmaceuticals (P) Ltd.Majhitar,Rangpo,East Sikkim
30. Sikkim Organics,Manpur,East Sikkim
31. Bhawana Paper Industry,Mamring,South Sikkim
32. Nextgen Printers (P) Ltd.Majhitar,Rangpo,East Sikkim
33. Government Fruit Preservation Factory,Singtam,East Sikkim
34. Kailash Roller Flour Mill (P) Ltd.Tadong,East Sikkim
35. M/S Rangeet Associates (P0 Ltd.Sikkim Flour Mill Complex 5th mile, Tadong

NGOs AND COMMUNITY INITIATIVES

Given below are some community initiatives that can be studied and replicated in various areas. Many of the community initiatives have led to local youth getting employed. The major advantages of community participation are shared responsibility, quick resource mobilisation, sustainability and efficient decision making.

Tired of applying for a Government job, landing one is considered as attaining Nirvana, or some contract work, a local unemployed of my locality approached me to ask if I could help him I told him that since jobs in the organised sector were very diffficult to come by, he should explore the possibility of trying out something more innovative. Why not help the community tackle its longstanding problem with parking and garbage. He did just that and is earning his livelihood from the parking fees and the garbage fees. There was also no financial investment involved in this venture: he just capitilised on the demand driven need of the community. He has evenfurther employed six person under him. Garbage may be a waste but by considering it as a resource entreprenuers can make a livelihood out of it.

CREATING JOB OPPORTUNITIES AT THE COLONY LEVEL- PROBLEMS BE SEEN AS OPPORTUNITIES

Rapid development in Sikkim has brought about its concominant problems. For example two issues seem to be directly troubling citizens especially those in the urban areas. These problems can be transformed into opportunities. Garbage disposal and lack of parking space for motor vehicles are two major problems that dog the towns and cities of Sikkim. A system of door to door collection of garbage on a daily basis can be very maeningful. A house hold can easily afford to pay Rs 50 a month for this service.

Because of growing number of vehicles in the towns, car owners are increasingly facing parking problems- inability to find parking space or the car getting immobilised because other parked vehicles have obstructed its way.

Car owners can collectively pay Rs 100 per month each to hire caretaker to take care of their vehicles costing on an average Rs 3 lacs parked on the road side. There are about 30000 vehicles in Sikkim. There is therefore a potential for creating 1000 jobs in Sikkim -nightwatchman and caretakers. The calculation may be simplistic but it shows the potential of opportunities that exist.

The author was a part of an experiment taken up in his locality at Syari - a colony in Gangtok- to solve the parking problem. Working on the above pattern 3 local youth were employed as caretakers by collecting monthly fees from the car owners. The caretakers were also involved for neighbourhood watch- reporting any unsocial activitiy to the police patrol that visits the locality at 10 o'clock in the night. Subsequently, thefts of parts from vehicles and crimes are now negligible. This model is working well since May 2007 and other colonies have evinced interest to replicate it.

MANAGING GARBAGE-THE SYARI MODEL

The author of this book, based on his experience in spearheading various community initiatives suggest how to successfully put in place a mechanism of collection of garbage in your locality

The Sikkim Government and AG Residential Complex at Syari is a rather densely populated locality of Gangtok with almost five hundred households. Proper disposal of garbage was always a problem particularly for the households located far away from the road head which is serviced by the Garbage collection truck of the Local Municipality. Why not begin door to door garbage collection? Besides facilitating the households as well as ensuring a clean environment this arrangement would help in employment generation – a win-win situation for all. Garbage may be a problem for many but it would be an opportunity for others. It was felt that Garbage should be seen as a resource - even as a source of livelihood- and not a waste material

Elucidated below are the steps adopted that made garbage management at Syari a success story. Also spelt out are the benefits that have accrued, the scope for sustainability, replication and augmentation.

Identifying and engaging a committed local unemployed who can take up implementing the programme - at the same time avoiding the programme becoming champion driven

This is the most important cog in the wheel: a person who has the commitment and drive to implement project - a person who is passionate about contributing something for the society and wants to take this up as a sort of occupation. However there is risk of the programme becoming champion-driven: which means that the project fizzles out after the person driving it leaves the scene. A committee consisting of all the stakeholders need to be created.

Involving the local community

Local unemployed youth and the Cheli Morcha were mobilised to spread the word that a proposal for collection of door to collection of garbage was in the offing and all the residents were required to give their acceptance and agree to contribute Rs 50/- per month The Syari Employees Welfare Association and the Neighbourhood Watch Cooperative two community based Organisations got together to implement this scheme.

Formal high profile launch

The door to door to house collection of garbage was formally launched by the Area MLA in the presence of the Councillor, Cheli Morcha, Local Taxi Association, Residents and the unemployed youth. Representatives from the stakeholders were also asked to speak during the inaugural function so that they feel part of the scheme of things. The press both the electronic and print media were called to ensure wide publicity. This anointment of the scheme sent a message across that we were very serious about its implementation and residents felt that they should cooperate.

Glorifying the assignment of Garbage Collector

There seems to be a stigma, very wrong of course, to a job that involves collection of garbage and titles like Sweepers and Safia Karamcharis are considered rather demeaning. We therefore thought of glorifying the job by calling the garbage collectors "Syari Beautifiers". They were given track suits with the words SYARI BEAUTIFIER brightly emblazoned on their jackets.

Garbage is collected from 400 household with each household contributing Rs 50/- per month. Rs 20,000 so collected is used to pay the wages of the supervisor, 3 garbage collector and one bill collector- all unemployed local youth who are proudly going about their important tasks of keeping the environment clean and also making a livelihood out of it.

Collection Mechanism

Carrying garbage bins on their backs and blowing whistles, the Syari Beautifiers go around the residential complex from 7 am to 10 am every morning. The approximately 600 kg of garbage so collected is transferred to huge garbage drums for collection by the Municipality truck at 6 am the next morning.

Sustainability

More and more households are enrolling to have their garbage collected from their doorsteps: the arrangement is therefore demand driven.

Residents do not mind paying a paltry Rs 50 per month. This makes it intrinsically self sustaining. It has a potential for generating more jobs. And that too, without any capital investment.

Corpus Fund

About 5 percent of the money collected goes into a corpus fund to meet unforeseeable and contingent expediture like replacement of garbage bins.

Helpline number, Appraisals and Feedbacks

A helpline number where the residents can lodge complaints if any can be useful. A meeting once in every quarter amongst the stakeholders can provide an opportunity for sorting out any problems.

Scope for replication

It has good scope for being replicated in other densely populated localities. There are about 50,000 households in urban areas in Sikkim: a ball park figure of one garbage collector for every 100 households would mean there is a potential for creation of 500 jobs in Sikkim. Residents would not mind paying Rupees 50 per month to have their garbage collected from their houses. The calculation may be simplistic but it shows the potential of opportunities that exist.

Augmentation

Once should see garbage as a resource and not a waste product. More than fifty percent of the garbage consists of vegetable waste. If this can be disposed off at source, it will considerably reduce the pressure at the Garbage processing plant and the landfills. Similarly 25 percent of the garbage consists of paper waste.

An awareness campaign is being launched to request the residents to use vermicomposting to decompose the vegetable waste and use the compost so generated for manure for their indoor plants. On the anvil is a proposal to begin vermicomposting on a large scale so that the manure can be sold resulting in supplementing income. For the paper waste a mini paper recycling plant is being proposed. The recycled products like paper bags, envelops and file covers can be sold in the local market and government offices resulting in income generation.

Conclusion

If you are troubled by the menace of littering and garbage in your locality, why not take the above measures to combat it? It involves no investments but would pay rich dividends in terms of employment generation and a clean environment.

SOLID WASTE MANAGEMENT - A SUCCESS STORY IN A RURAL AREA

(*How Mr Ganesh Rai, President of Melli Dara Gram Panchayat Unit has succeeded in making his area Solid Waste Free using Organic Composting Technologies - initiatives worth replicating in other localities.*)

22- Melli Dara Paiyong GPU has been making serious strides towards Garbage Management of the GPU. Melli Bazar, a small town falls under our GPU and managing garbage of the town has been a challenging task so far. Initially, responsibility of managing the garbage of the town was with the Urban Development and Housing Department, Government of Sikkiim. Later, the Gram Panchayat decided to take the responsibility of managing the garbage of the town. The Gram Panchayat decided to levy monthly garbage fee and the fee was decided on the basis of residential or the type of enterprise. The Gram Panchayat was supported in this venture by Indo Swiss Project, Sikkim and Rural Management and Development Department by sponsoring a Utility Vehicle. Since then, the Gram Pachayat has been able to manage the garbage of the town very efficiently.

The Gram Panchayat has established a **"Solid Waste Management Unit"** at Lower Paiyong in consultation to Maple Orgitech India Ltd, by South District Zilla Panchayat. The Solid Waste Management Unit has been set up with two purposes in mind. First purpose is to recycle the waste product and produce something useful out of it and to generate revenue. The garbage is separated as degradable and non-degradable at the source itself. The non-degradable such as plastic is be sent to Siliguri for further processing and recycling. In order separate garbage at the source itself, the Gram Panchayat recently launched a very ambitious mission, a mission to make the GPU **"SOLID WASTE FREE BY 2011"**. Under this mission, Lower Paiyong ward has been chosen for Pilot Mode. All the houses were distributed two garbage collecting bins so that degradable and non-degradable garbage is separated at the very source. The pilot mode will run for four months. After four months, the Gram Panchayat shall select another ward for the mission and when all the wards will have been covered, the GPU will be Solid Waste Free. The Gram Panchayat has decided to organize awareness camps in schools as well to make this mission a success.

NGOS AND OTHER ORGANISATION

Although the Government in Sikkim is very proactive and undertaking many welfare measures; there are many NGOs and Community Based Organisations equally making their contributions. Some of the NGOs and Associations working in sectors of health, environment, tourism, social service and sports are listed below

Health

Voluntary Health Association of Sikkim (VHAS) Majong Kothi Complex, Nam Nam Road, Gangtok; Contact Person: Dr. B.B. Rai Ph. No. 206505,200961; Activities: Propagating healthcare at the grass root level

National Association for Blind, C/O Mist Tree Mountain Hotel, Near STNM Hospital, Gangtok; Jayshree Pradhan 231169; Runs a school Jawarlal Nehru Institute for the Handicapped at Namchi

Sikkim Viklang Sahayata Samiti, Zero Point Gangtok Draupadi Ghimirey 201305Rehabilitation of the orthopadeically handicapped

Sikkim Spastic Society Near TNHSS School Development Area Rehabilitation of children suffering from autism, cerebral palsy

Special School for the Hearing Impaired Sichey. Educating and rehabilitating children who are hearing impaired

Sikkim Rehabilitation and Detoxification Centre, Nimitar Working in the field of rehabilitation of the drug abuse

Environment

Green Circle Chumbi Residency Gangtok; Ushal Lachungpa Ph. 205273,Ugyen Choppel Ph: 206618; Rajesh Verma 280672; DR Prodhan,

Sikkim Development Foundation; Tashikhar, Changyal Complex, M.G. Marg, Gangtok; Loday Changyalpa Ph 209276

Ecotourism and Conservation Society of Sikkim (ECOSS), Gangtok; P.D. Rai Ph 209154

Kanchendzonga Conservation Committee (KCC), Yoksum; Pema Gyalsten 03595-241211 or 241216;

Parivarn Samraksah Samiti; Dalapchand Busty; CD Rai, B Poudyal 231141

Tourism

Travel Agents Association of Sikkim;(Ph200842) Changyal Complex; M.G. Marg; Gangtok; Paljor Lachungpa 205113

Sikkim Hostel Associaton, Gangtok

Rotary Club C/O Norkhill Hotel(Ph203186), Near Paljor Stadium, Gangtok; Yogesh Verma 204555 Raj Bangar

Mayalmu Sang Address: Dara Goan, Tadong, East Sikkim Email: Contact No: Contact Person: Activities: Voluntary organization working for the welfare of abandoned children, mentally retarded and homeless persons by providing free food and shelter.

Rotary Club of Gangtok South C/O Hotel Denzong Regency; RC Mangla Bina Sharma, Sunila Verma Ph 280672, Yasoda Chettri

Lions Club Rangpo/Jorethang

Destitute Homes

Kaluk Destitute Home Kaluk run by the Social Welfare Department Government of Sikkim

Atish Dipanker Mission Destitute Home run by Chakung Kripa Buddhist(03595-253326)

Balika Niketan Destitute Home Gangtok run by Arithang Social Welfare Association (03592-203336)

Wangdi Faith Mission Mangan run by Wangdi Faith Mission (03592-234282)

Kingstone Destitute Home run by Rhenock Akhil Sikkim Arahaya Kalyan Samiti(253628)

*There are many other NGOs like Dristi in Namchi and SWRCA in Sadam working in various fields. Their addresses can be obtained from the Law Department, Tashiling, Government of Sikkim. Various communities like the Limbu, Tamang also have their associations to promote their culture. VHAS(*Ph. No. 26505, 20961) *is also compiling a list of all NGOs operating in Sikkim.*

Sports

Besides there are many sports Associations involved in Archery, Amateur Athletic, Tae Kwon Do, Badminton, Basketball, Boxing, Body Building, Cricket, Football, Karate, Table Tennis, Yoga and Mountaineering. The Joint Director,(Ph 203025) Sports and Youths Affair Department at White Hall can be contacted for further details and activities about these Sports Associations.

NGOs in Advocacy

NGOs cannot match the resources and infrastructure that is usually available with the Government: however NGOs can fill the gaps and also play the role of a thinktank and do advocacy like the letter by Green Circle below which prompted the Government after it was vigourslyfollowed up in the Forest, Sikkim Police Checkpost and Transport Department to introduce Garbage bags in vehicles plying in alpine areas. Such type of activities require no funds

To
Secretary cum PCCF
Forest Environment & Wildlife Department, Government of Sikkim, Gangtok

Sub: **Making it mandatory for Taxis going to High Altitude to carry garbage disposal bags**

Sir,

Many tourists have now started visiting ecologically sensitive alpine areas like Tsogmo Lake, Yumthang valley and the Cholhamu plateau

A direct fallout of this been that the roadside leading to these areas is being littered with empty foodstuff packets (Lays, Bingo, Kurkure and the like) thrown out of the vehicles by the tourists. We are aware that such littering can cause immense damage to the alpine areas.

While we cannot prevent tourists from partaking to snacks while travelling we can certainly find a way out for them to conveniently dispose the empty food packets. It is suggested that all taxis, especially those plying to the high altitudes are made to carry at least two small garbage disposal bags located at vantage points within the vehicle where tourists can conveniently dispose the food covers. The taxis could dispose the contents in the garbage bins when they return to their base.

This measure will go a long way in helping us to keep our alpine areas clean and pristine and will be in line with the Government policy for introducing Green Taxis.

Yours faithfully,
Green Circle
The Environment Group of Sikkim

In Sikkim there is no system of having house numbers and addressees are located by landmarks like "the house close to the magnolia tree". This makes it difficult finding out locations. The letter below elucidiates how a community solved this problem and has adivsed the Government to replicate the numbering scheme in other areas.

To
The Chief Secretary,Governmet of Sikkim

Adoption of a simple House number system for Government Residential buildings

Sir,

We would like to bring to your kind notice that at the Government of Sikkim Residential Complex at Syari, we have introduced a very simple system of numbering of the buildings. Class I Quarters are numbered as IA,IB etc. Similarly class 3 Quarters numbered as 3A, 3B etc. It is very easy to remember - no confusing string of numbers with brackets and astericks. These numbers have been prominently emblazoned on the outer of the buildings. The Government may like to adopt this simple schema of numbering the houses for other Government colonies in the sate. This would go a long way in helping the residents to have propoer addresses.

Yours faithfully
Syari Employees Welfare Association

Small idea - big difference

In my locality we were very concerned with a corner of the footpath being used as an open urninal at night. The whole area stank. I suggested installing a light so that the illumination would desist people from easing themselves. But the caretaker of the locality came up with a better idea. A small niche was dug up in the wall adjacent to the place concerned and images of some deities were placed there. And lo and behold the problem vanished with passerbys making a brief stop and paying their obseiencance.

USING INFORMATION TECHNOLOGY TOOLS FOR THE DISABLED

There are quite a number of disabled in the society. However because of social and economic reasons they are left to languish at home. The Government and some NGOs have established institutes like the Special Schools for the Hearing Impaired, The Spastics Society, Sikkim Viklang Sahayata Samiti and the Blind School for rehabiliting them. Various technologies and techniques were adopted to help the disabled children acquire educational and vocational skills to make them employable and useful self dependant citizens of the society not relying on charity and compassion. There is generally fatalistic attitude of the society in Sikkim towards the disabled. The society feels that their disability is due to an act of God and that nothing can be done to rectify it. There is a resigned sort of an attitude towards them: disabled should be kept at home as they do not have that ability to pick up skills- both vocational and educational to make then employable. However the good practices adopted addresses this very issue- using various tools to make them employable and useful citizens of the society.

Case Study I: Using Information Tools to teach the visually challenged children

Here is a case study of the good practices that were adopted for the the Visually challenged by the National Association for the Blind- Sikkim of which the author is a member.

The Challenges

Teaching the visually challenged children is a formidable task because of their disability although most children are mentally alert. Before the introduction of Information Technology tools, the children of the school faced the following problems.

1. Limitation of reading materials in Braille.
2. Whatever material was available in Braille was printed on paper which is prove to degradation because of repetitive use.
3. There was a dearth of audio material available for the children that could help them in their studies.

This resulted in children not being able to cope up with their studies because of which the results were bad and the failure rates were high.

Best Practices adopted

Since 2002 Information Technology tools and assistive technologies for improving and adding value to educating the visually challenged are being used. The action areas addressed are

a. Improving quality in Education
b. Supporting Education in difficult circumstances

The following best practices were adopted.

Establishing a computer centre at the Blind School

Before Information Technology could be used in a meaningful and beneficial manner for the visually impaired children, the basic infrastructure consisting of few computers with internet connectivity, scanner, Braille printers, UPS etc was established in a centrally located room in the school.

Conversion of text to Braille using the services of two hearing impaired computer operators

There is a wealth of information and material available in the electronic format and on the internet. The visually challenged did not have easy access to it all because it was not available in Braille. It was with this in mind that in 2002, two computers were procured along with 4 Perkin Braille printers. As the Perkin Braille printers printed very slowly and could not cope up with the voluminous printing, a faster Juliet Pro printer that could print inter point on both sides of the paper was procured in 2004.

Using Duxbury Braille Translator software whatever content that was available in electronic format was converted to Braille. For books that were not available in the electronic (word format) scanning using OCR (Optical Character Recognition) software was adopted. All books prescribed from Class III to Class VIII were scanned by two deaf and dumb computer operators and converted to text document and thereafter to Braille. In the process we gainfully employed two hearing impaired people who would have it found difficulty in getting jobs elsewhere.

The use of computers has increased manifold with the introduction of the tactile readers because of the ease with which these devices can be used as well as opening a window of information through the internet.

Use of audio medium to read documents and content creation in local language

One effective way to teach the blind children is to read out the material to them. Keeping this in mind, a rich repository of documents in the audio format is being created. Most of it is being collected from various Blind Associations where this material is already available so that we do not re-invent the wheel.

A powerful screen reader software was procured. It enables the user to navigate on the screen by reading out the details of the icons and the text.

A talking library of audio files in MP 3 format as well as Daisy format has been established. Daisy is reading software that makes printed or electronic text accessible to people who are blind in the audio form.

Nepali is the local colloquial language of Sikkim. More than 95 percent of population uses this language. What was lacking is local language content and to meet this requirement we have established a recording studio in which audio content is being created in the local language Nepali.

Story books in local languages are to make school going an interesting experience.

Training for Computer Instructors

The computer instructors of the Blind School are required to undergo a training programme once every year so that they are well equipped to handle and teach the new technologies that are being inducted in the school. So far they have been sent for training in preventive maintenance of the Braille Printers, configuring of the tactile printers and the production of talking libraries.

Measurable outcomes and sustainability

After the IT was adopted, there has been an improvement in the results. There has been a 20 percent increase in the marks scored by the students. The children are able to imbibe the contents of their school books in a better manner.

There has been a 10 percent saving in Braille paper with the induction of the Juliet Pro Printer that prints on both sides of the paper. There are also less printing errors in this printer. The tactile readers have also resulted in the reduction in consumption of Braille paper.

The good practices adopted are also sustainable as they are demand driven. The children have got so used to using the IT tools that they now cannot do without them. Similarly IT tools have been used for the Hearing Impaired, those suffering from autism and cerebral palsy and the orthopedically handiapped. For instance for students who do not have a hand, footswitches have been deployed which have all the functionalties of a mouse thus allowing them to use the keyboard more efficiently.

Case Study II:Using techniques to educate the physically challenged with an aim to make them employable

The project was implemented at the Sikkim Viklang Sahayata Samiti (Institute to aid the orthopedically Handicapped) which deals with the welfare and rehabilitation of the disabled.

The objective of the project was to choose orthopedically disabled and hearing impaired school drop out children from remote areas of the state and put them through a custom-made one year long training programme that would help them to acquire sufficient educational qualification and vocational skills to make them employable.

As there is a big requirement of Computer Operators both in the government and private sector in the state, the project aimed at making them adept, in the use of computers.

Because of the physical disabilities that they were suffering from, special tools and techniques were used to enable them picking up skills as computer operators.

Since the students had dropped out of regular school mid-way, the challenge therefore was also to make them at least Class X (matriculate) which is the minimum requirement for jobs. As it was not possible for them to rejoin formal school, it was decided that they should be tutored to take the Class X Examination directly through the non-formal Open School. Four hours every day were devoted to vocational skills and two hours for teaching them subjects prescribed in the syllabus for the Class X examination. Members of the Rotary Club of Gangtok South volunteered to do the teaching.

Besides imparting computer training on data entry, tabulation and photo editing from Monday to Friday every week using the services of a diabled computer teacher, the candidates were also given classes on essay writing, General Knowledge, Mental mathematics etc. This prepared them for facing various competitive examinations.

The use of various Information Technology Tools were taught to the students with motor disabilities so that they could utilize them to perform functions like typing as efficiently as a normal person. For instance the footswitch help persons who had one hand or loss the use of a hand, to use the foot to navigate the cursor on monitor and has all the functionality of a mouse that a person normally used by hand. The use of voice commands to navigate the icons on the computer monitor was also taught. These allow considerable improvement in the typing skills.

Following a Government circular that the services of these trainees should be used for any data entry work in the Departments, some of the trainees are already being employed on part time basis as data entry operators in various Government organisations and their performace has been found to be better than normal persons. It is found that the loss of use of a faculty by the disabled is amply compensated by sharpening of the other senses. For instance a blind person has an excellent memory, a hearing impaired is not disturbed by external noises and therefore has higher power of concentration and can be more efficient that a normal person.

To
The Chief Secretary
Government of Sikkim
Gangtok

Subject: Hiring of the orthopedically handicapped for data entry work

Sir,

The SIKKIM VIKLANG SAHITYA SAMITI, a local NGO involved in rehabilitating the orthopedically disabled, is endeavoring to make the handicapped employable through the use of various methods and techniques so that they can become useful self dependent citizens of the society not reliant on compassion and charity.

We have trained 20 of these disabled students as data entry operators, Using specialized Information Technology Tools like footswitches and voice commands, these students can operate a computer as efficiently as a normal person if not better.

The Government may kindly like to hire their services for data entry work under various schemes and projects as and when the need arises.

Yours faithfully

Training Consultant SIKKIM VIKLANG SAHITYA SAMITI

SIKKIM QUIZ

(Answers are given in Italics)

GEOGRAPHY

What is the total area of Sikkim in square kms ? *7,096 sq. km*
Name the countries with which Sikkim shares its borders. *Nepal, Bhutan, Tibet*
Name the state with which Sikkim shares its border. *West Bengal*
Name the district headquarters Sikkim? *North -Mangan, South-Namchi, East-Gangtok, West - Gyalshing*
Name the third highest mountain in the world *Kanchendzonga*
Name the major river of Sikkim. *Tista*
Name the place in the Sikkim which has the lowest altitude. *The confluence of Tista and Rangit near Melli at 1100 ft above mean sea level*
Lachung chu is the tributary of which river. *Tista*
Where do the rivers Lachen chu and Lachung chu meet? *Chungthang*
Ramam chu is the tributary of which river? *Rangit*
Besides Tista, name one other river that flows out of Sikkim? This river is located in east Sikkim. *Di-chu or Jaldhaka river*
Name the river that demarcates the boundary between West Bengal and West District of Sikkim. *Ramam river*
There are two rivers that demarcate the boundary between South District and West Bengal. Tista is one. Name the other. *Rangit river*
Name the river that demarcates the boundary between South District and East District. *Tista*
Name three rivers that demarcate the boundary between South and West District. *Rangit, Relli and Rungdung*
Name the river that demarcates the boundary between South and East District. *Tista*
Name the river Rathong chu meets to become Rangit river. *Relli chu*
Name the river that is formed after Tista meets Brahmaputra in Bangladesh. *Jamuna*
Name the river that meets Rangit at Legship. *Kalej Khola*
Name the mountain range between Sikkim and Bhutan. *Pangola range*
Name the mountain range between Nepal and Sikkim. *Singelila range*
Sikkim also has a plateau. In which district is it located? *North District*
Name the place where Tista enters West Bengal fully. *Triveni or Chittrey near Melli. From Rangpo to Melli, Tista flows between West Bengal and Sikkim*
Name the river from which Gangtok derives its drinking water *Ratey chu*
Name the highest mountain in the West District. *Kanchendzonga*
Name the big lake at Kupup. *Bidan Tso*
Name the place where the River Rangit meets River Tista. *Chittrey, Melli*
Name the place where River Tista and River Rongichu meet. *Singtam*
In which district is the Lonak valley located. *North District*
Name the source of River Tista. *Cholamu Lake/Khangchung cho/Tista Khangtse*
Name the river that you cross when entering Singtam from Rangpo. *Rongichu*
Name the river that you cross when you enter Sikkim from West Bengal at Rangpo. *Rangpo Chu*
Name the source of River Rangit. *Dud pokhari/Rathong Glacier/ Omecho*
Name the river that originates from Menmeisto lake. *Rangpo chu*
Nathula and Jelepla are on which border of Sikkim? *Eastern, Tibet-Sikkim Border*
The Chiwabhanjang pass is on which border of Sikkim? *Western, Nepal-Sikkim*
Chorten Nyimala pass is on which border of Sikkim? *Northern, Sikkim-Tibet Border*

Name the largest glacier of Sikkim *Zemu Glacier*
Name the pass that connects the Lashar Valley to the Yumthang valley: *Sebula*
Name the lake on the Gangtok- Nathula highway. *(Tsomgo)Changu Lake*
Phurcha-chu(Reshi) and Yumthang have hotsprings. Name the other hotsprings. *Taramchu, Yumeysamdong, Ralang(Polot) and Borong*
Name the river that flows next to the Yumeysamdong hotspring. *Sebu chu*
Name the river on the banks of which the Phurchachu hotsprings are located. *Rangit river*
Name the nearest railway station to Sikkim. *Ghoom*
Name the four great caves of Sikkim.*Larinvigphu,Kadosanphu,Pephu, Dechhenphu. These are located in the North, South, East and West directions of the holy monastery of Tashiding respectively*
Name the holy cave adjacent to a hotspring. *Kadosangphu*
Name the holy cave near to Mount Narsingh and the Relli chu river. *Larinyingphu*
Name the trijunction of Sikkim, West Bengal & Nepal *Toriphule near Phalut*
Name the trijunction of Bhutan, Sikkim & Tibet *Batangla*
Name the trijunction of Sikkim, West Bengal and Bhutan *Rachela on Pangola range*
Name the trijunction of Sikkim, Nepal and Tibet *Jonsang*
Name the largest district of Sikkim *North District, 4226 sq km*
Name the smallest district of Sikkim *South District,750sqkm*
Name the country with which Sikkim has the longest border.*Tibet,220 kms*
With which country does Sikkim have the shortest border. *Bhutan(approx.33 kms)*
Name the highest peak on the eastern border of Sikkim. *Paunhri(Lopno Kyangzong)*
Name the second highest mountain in Sikkim. *Kabru*
Name the Peak in Bhutan that you see from Nathula: *Chomolhari*
Sikkim has four districts. How many administrative sub-divisions does it have? *9*
How many states including Sikkim constitute the North East Council? *Eight*
What do the following local geographical words stand for
La: *Pass* Tso: *Lake* Chu: *River* Thang: *Flat land* Ri: *Mountain* Cholamu: *The Lake of the Goddess*
Where does the National Highway 31A begin and end? *It begins at Zero Point at Gangtok and ends at Coronation Bridge near Sevoke.*
Which highway does 31A meet at Coronation Brdige near Sevoke? *It meets Highway 31.*
Why is 9th mile in Sikkim famous.? *Because it is a dangerous landslide zone. It is located 9 miles away from Gangtok on the National highway 31A.*
How has the place 32th mile on the National Highway dertived its name? *It is 32 miles from Geil Khola near Tisa. Geil Khola near Tista was the railhead for Sikkim till the early 1950s.*
Why has the B2 landslide area on the North Sikkim Highway been given this name? *The Bridges on the North Sikkim Highway are called Bridge1(B1), Bridge 2(B2) and so on. The land slide is located close to Bridge 2 (B2) on the Ratey chu river. Hence the name B2 slide.*
Name the place in North Sikkim where a massive landslide took place on 11th Sept 1983 killing many.? *Manaul*
Name the places from where you can drive into Sikkim from West Bengal. *Rangpo, Melli, Ramam and Reshi. From Aritar near Rhenock also there is a road that enters a kilometer into West Bengal.*

Name the river that you crossto enter into North District if you take the Kabi route. *Ratey Chu*

Which is the shortest road route between Gangtok and Yoksum? *Gangtok-Ravongla-Tashiding-Yoksum*

What are the three trekking routes that you can take to reach Tendong? *From Damthang, from Parbing and from Samduptse.*

Supposing a landslide blocks the road at Changu, what is alternate route that you can take to reach Nathula. *Gangtok-Rongli-Kupup-Nathula*

If the road between Pelling and Yoksum is blocked because of a landslide, how do you reach Yoksum from Gyalshing? *Go via Legship and Tashiding*

Name the waterfall that you come across while driving from Tashiding to Yoksum. *Fambrong*

Total Bermoik is located in South District. In which District is Hee-bermoik located? *West District.*

Hee-Gyathang is located in Dzongu, North District. Where is Hee-Yangthang located? *West District near Dentam*

Can you see Darjeeling from Gangtok? *Yes you can*

Where are the Kanchendzsonga Waterfalls? *Between Pelling and Yoksum*

Where are the Seven Sister Waterfalls?*Between Phensang and Phodong in North Sikkim*

Name the river that you cross immediately after Kabi on the way to Phensang. Bakcha chu

In which District are the following places located in a) Jorethang b)Nayabazar c) Legship *a)South b)West c) South*

Name the river that you cross when you travel between Rorathang and Rhenock. *Rangpo chu*

Name the river you cross when you travel from East District to North District. *Ratey Chu*

Tista Stage V is located near Singtam, Where is stage III located? *Near Chungtang*

Name the river you cross as soon as you leave Nayabazar for Darjeeling. *Ramam*

Why is it that a temperature of 25 degrees celcius is considered hot in Gangtok wheras cool in Delhi? *Because of the high level of humidity in Sikkim that prevents evaporation of sweat from the skin.*

Give two reasons why it snows heavily in Srinagar which has an altitude of only 5000 ft whereas it hardly snows at altitudes upto 7000 ft in Sikkim. *(a) Srinagar is more towards the North and has a higher latitude b) The Bay of Bengal which is 700 kms away keeps Sikkim relatively warm.*

Name some pairs of places in Sikkim that have the same names

Reshi in East District near Rhenock and Reshi in West District near Legship.
Majitar in East District near Rangpo and Majitar in South South near Jorethang
Martam in East District near Rumtek and Martam in West District near Kaluk
Dhupidara in East District near Singtam and Dhupidara in West District near Labdang

HISTORY, POLITICS AND PERSONALITIES

What does Sukhim in Limbu language mean? *New House*

What does Denjong mean? *Valley of Rice*

What does"Gahn-toh"(Gangtok) mean? *The Hill Top*

In whose memory has the White Hall been built? *Sir James Claude White*

Who was Khye-Bumsa? *Bhutia Chieftan*

Who was Tetong Tek? *Lepcha Chieftan*

Name the place where the treaty between the Tetong Tek and Khye-Bumsa was signed. *Kabi Longstok*

Name the kings of Sikkim with date in chronological order

Name	*Year of accession*	*Important events*
1. Phuntsog Namgyal (1604 -1670)	*1642*	*Consecrated as the first Chogyal of Sikkim. Established capital at Yoksum.*
2. Tensung Namgyal (1644 - 1700)	*1670*	*Capital shifted from Yoksum to Rabdanste*
3. Chakdor Namgyal (1686 - 1717)	*1700*	*Half sister Pendiongmu tried to snatch throne. Chakdor hadto flee to Lhasa but was reinstalledas king with help of the Tibetans.*
4. Gyurmed Namgyal (1707 - 1734)	*1734*	
5. Namgyal Phuntsog (1733 - 1780)	*1734*	*Nepalis make attacks in Sikkim*
6. Tenzing Namgyal1780 (1769 - 1793)		
7. Tsugphud Namgyal (1785 - 1863)	*1793*	*Capital shifted from Rabdantse to Tumlong. Signing of treaty of Titalia in 1817 between Sikkim and British India in which terroteries lost to Nepal are restored to Sikkim Darjeeling gofted to British India in 1835. Two Britishers Dr. Campbell and Dr. Hooker captured by the Sikkinese in 1849. Hostilities between British India and Sikkim and signing of treaty of 1861 in which Darjeeling is formally annexed to British India.*
8. Sidkeong Namgyal (1819 - 1874)	*1863*	
9. Thutob Namgyal (1860 - 1914)	*1874*	*Claude White appointed a the first Political officer of Sikkim in 1889. Capital shifted fromTumlong to Gangtok in 1894.*
10. Sidkeong Tulku (1879 - 5.12. 14)	*02-1914*	*Oxford educated.*
11. Tashi Namgyal (26.10.93- 2.12. 63)	*5.12. 14*	*Many administrative reforms done.Treaty of1950 between Sikkim and India signed.*
12. Palden T.Namgyal (22.5. 23-30.1 82)	*2.12 63*	*Sikkim becomes the twenty second state of India in 1975. Institution of the Chogyal abolished*

What does the term ‘Chogyal’ mean? *King/Maharaja*

Name the first Chogyal of Sikkim? *Phunstok Namgyal*

Where was the first Chogyal of Sikkim crowned and consecrated? *Yoksum*

What did Latsun Chembo, Sempa Chembo, Rinzing Chembo do at Yoksum? *They crowned the first Chogyal of Sikkim*

What does Yuksam mean? *Meeting place of the three superior ones*
Where was the first capital of Sikkim established? *Yoksum*
Name the Chogyal who ruled the longest *Tsudphud Namgyal(1793-1863)*
Name the Chogyal who was murdered by his half sister *Chakdor Namgyal*
Name the Chogyal who shifted the capital from Yoksum to Rabdanste *Tensung*
Name the Chogyal who shifted the capital from Rabdanste to Tumlong *Tsudphud*
Name the Chogyal who shifted the capital from Tumlong to Gangtok *Thutob*
Name the Chogyal who introduced the system of sending one son to the monastery. *Chagdor Namgyal*
Who was Satrajit? *He was Sikkimese General named Chuthup who drove out the Gorkha invaders from Sikkim seventeen times*
Name the Limbu chieftan who gave his daughter in marriage to the Second Chogyal of Sikkim *Yo Yo Hang*
During the almost uninterrupted rule of the Namgyal Dynasty, name the person who self appointed himself as the King of Sikkim. *Chindzod Tamding*
Name the two Britishers who were imprisoned in Tumlong in 1849? *Hooker and Campbell*
During the middle of the last century Hooker visited Sikkim. Who was he? *Botanist*
What were the people who minted coins for the Sikkim Durbar known as? *Taksaris*
Name the Taksari whose statue is installed at Rangpo Bazar? *Chandra bir Taksari*
When was the first treaty between Independent India and Chogyal of Sikkim signed? *1950*
Name the crown prince who was a pilot and died in a plane crash *Paljor Namgyal*
In which year was Palden Thondup Namgyal coronated as the Twelfth Chogyal of Sikkim? *4.4.65*
What was the maiden name of Gyalmo before she got married to Chogyal Palden Thondup Namgyal? *Hope Cooke*
Name the book authored by Gyalmo Hope Cook? *Time Change*
In 1817 a treaty was signed between the British and Nepal by which lands lost by Sikkim to Nepal were restored to Sikkim. Name this Treaty. *Treaty of Titalia.*
When was Darjeeling gifted to British India? *1835*
Who was the first Political officer of Sikkim? *James Claude White*
Who was the first Governor of Sikkim? *B.B. Lal*
Who was the first Chief Minister of Sikkim? *Kazi Lendup Dorjee*
In 1884,Colman Macaulay visited Sikkim to explore the possibility of a trade route between Sikkim and Tibet.Which area did he wish this route to go through ? *The Lachen Valley/Thangu Valley*
When was the Galing Treaty signed ? *It was signed secretly between Sikkim and Tibet in 1886 at Galing in Tibet. It stipulated that Sikkim would be under the control of Tibet and China and that foreigners would not be permitted to cross the Sikkim Tibet border.*
In which year did the British clash with the Tibetans on the Eastern border of Sikkim? *1888*
Name the Viceroy who visited Sikkim. *Lord Linthow*
During the reign of which Chogyal was postal mail attempted to be sent by rockets to Sarmasa, Ranipul and Rumtek? *Tashi Namgyal in the 1930s*
Name the place where a war memorial was constructed by the British in memory of soldiers who died in clashes with the Tibetans. *Gnathang*
What do you understand by the terms Jharlangi, Bhethi, Kuruwa and Khalo Bhari? *Jharlangi was the system of unpaid labour recruited by the Government for the purpose*

of construction of road and bridges. The British expeditions resorted to Jharlangi extensively. Bhethi was the system of each household providing unpaid labour to Mandals and Kazis for a fixed number of days in a year. Kuruwa was again a type of labour conscripted to carry the luggage of Government officials passing through the villages. Khalo Bhari, as its name implies, were goods that were packed in black tarpaulin to be illegally exported to Tibet

What were adhiadars and kutdars? *Adhiadars were engaged to cultivate on condition that they rendered half their produce to the owner; kutdars wee engaged to cultivate on condition that they rendered a stipulated amount of crops to the owner*

Name the first Indian Political Officer of Sikkim. *Harishwar Dayal*

What does Sidlon mean? *Dewan or Prime Minister*

Who was the first Dewan of Sikkim? *John Lall*

When was the Tripartite Agreement between the Government of India,the Chogyal and the political parties aiming at one man one vote signed? *8th May 1973*

When did the first hydel project become operational?

It was located at Ranikhola below present day Sichey Busty. Having a capacity of 50 KW, it became functional on 27th May 1927. It's sub-station was located at STNM Hospital.

Where was Pawan Chamling born? *Yangang*

Name the Sikkimese who was awarded the Victoria Cross during the Second World War for showing exceptional bravery on the Burma Front. *Ganju Lama*

In the erstwhile kingdom of Sikkim, what was the name of the higest medal/award? *Dorjee Pema*

What is the highest civilian award in Sikkim? *Sikkim Ratna*

Who was the Chief Minister of first popular government formed in 1949? *Tashi Tsering*

In which year the Sikkim State Council was constituted?- *In 1953*

What was the total strength of first Sikkim State Council?- *17 members (12 elected and 5 nominated)*

In which year the 2nd Sikkim Council's election was held? – *1958*

What was the the total member of 2nd Sikkim State Council? *20 members.*

In which year the Sangha seats in Sikkim was created?- *In 1958*

Name the Proclamation that created a Sangha seat in Sikkim? – *The Royal Proclamation of 1958*

In which year the 3rd election to Sikkim State Council was held ? *1967*

When the 4th election to Sikkim State Council was held ? *In 1970*

Name the Political Party that won got elected in the Assembly election of 1985 ? *Sikkim Sangram Parishasd.*

Name the only plainsman who got elected in Assembly election of 1985 ? *Balchand Sarda*

When were the general elections during the merger and the post merger period held and name the parties which were returned to power? *1st - 1974 Sikkim Congress, 2nd -1979 - Sikkim Jananta Parisad later renamed Sikkim Pradesh Congress, 3rd - 1984 Sikkim Sangram Parisad, 4th - 1989 Sikkim Sangram Parisad, 5th - 1994 Sikkim Democratic Front 6th-1999 Sikkim Democratic Front 7th - 2004-Sikkim Democratic Front, 8th-2009 Sikkim Democratic Front*

Name the Political Officers of Sikkim in chronological order.

James Claude White 1889

Charles Bell 1905

O'Connor, Bailey, Campbell, Weir, Gould Macdonald, Williamson, Hopkinson, Richardson, Ludlow, Sherrif, Dhondup, Rivett-Carnac, Fletcher, Russell, Hailey, Battye, Sakerr, Kennedy, Vance, Worth, Sinclair, Gloyne, Davis, Mainprice, Flinch, Dark, Thornburgh and Robins served as Political Officers for less than a year each.

Post independence

Harishwar Dayal 1947

Appa B. Pant 1951

Indrajit Bahadur Singh 1960

V.H. Coelho 1966

N.B. Menon 1968

K.S. Bajpai 1971

B. Singh 1972

Gurbachan Singh 1973

What did the 35th Amendment of the Constitution of India passed on 5th Sept. 74 aim at? *It made Sikkim an Associate State of India*

When did Sikkim become an Associate State of India? *4.9.74*

When did Sikkim become a full-fledged State of India? *Sikkim became a full fledged state of India with the passing of the 36th Amendment on 26th April 1975. The formal merger took place on 16th May 1975.*

What did the 36th Amendment of the Constitution of India passed on 26th April 75 aim at? *It made Sikkim the 22nd State of India.The formal merger took place on 16 th May 1975*

When was the referendum seeking the full merger of Sikkim with India held? *14 th Apr'75*

What was the aim of the Representation of the People (Ordinance), 1979? *It withdrew the reservation of seats for the Nepali community*

What was the title given to the person who minted coins for Sikkim? *Taksari*

Name the first Bank that was opened in 1899 at Gangtok. This bank was also the official bank of the Sikkim Durbar. *Jetmull and Bhojraj*

Name the metal that was mined extensively in Pacheykhani and the Rateypani areas of Sikkim during the second half of the 19 th century. *Copper*

What is the importance of the treaty of 1861?

Sikkim resorted to making attacks into British territories and kidnapping British subjects and it was in November 1860 that the British sent an expeditionary force to Sikkim. This force was driven back from Rinchenpong in Sikkim. A stronger force was sent in 1861 under the command of Colonel J.C. Gawler that resulted in a showdown and the signing of a treaty between the British and Sikkimese the same year. This treaty signed by Ashley Eden and Sidekong Namggyal on 28th March 1861 cancelled all the previous treaties signed between Britain and Sikkim and Sikkimese territories in occupation by British India were restored to Sikkim. After the signing of this treaty, the Raja of Sikkim came to be known as Maharajah.

When did Col. Younghusband lead an Expedition to Lhasa? *1903-04*

Name the place where about 500 Tibetans were massacared by the Army led by Younghusband. *Chumik Shenko near Gyanste*

What is the significance of the Anglo Chinese Convention?

Alarmed by the defeat of the Tibetans and apprehending that they would lose influence over Tibet, the Chinese began negotiations with the British that finally resulted in the signing of the Anglo-Chinese convention on 17th March 1890.

What is the Lhasa Convention?
The treaty dictated by Younghusband on Tibet on 7th September 1904. is known as the Lhasa Convention. The treaty secured monopoly trading privileges in Tibet for the British. Tibet agreed to adhere by the Anglo-Chinese Convention of 1890 and to recognise the border between Sikkim and Tibet.

There is a memorial at Nathula pass to honour the approximately 100 Indian soldiers who died fighting a battle with the Chinese. When did this battle take place? *September 1967*

When was trade through Nathula restored after 44 years *6th July 2006*

What does the Nehru stone at Nathula pass signify? *It signifies the visit of Pandit Jawaharlal Nehru to Nathula in 1958*

What was real name of Pagla Dewan the minister of Maharaj Tsugphud Namgyal? *Dunyar Tokhang Namgyal*

Name the Dewans of Sikkim in chronological order.
1. Harishdwar Dayal- He was political officer but later taken into administration as Dewan on 06.06.1941 but was again revereted as political officer.
2. J.S. Lall 11.08.1949
3. Nari Kaikhosru Rustomji 1954.
4. Baleshwar Prasad 22.8.1959 was called the Principal Administrative Officer
5. R.N. Haldipur 1962 was called the Principal Administrative Officer
6. I.S. Chopra 1969 was called the Sidlon

Who was the first Lok Sahba member from Sikkim? *S.K. Rai*

Who was the first Rajya Sabha member from Sikkim? *L. S. Saring*

Who wrote and complied the book " The Gazzetter of Sikkim" *H.H. Risley*

Where did the Gangtok Bazar exist before it was shifted to the present day M.G. Marg? *The Ridge between the Palace Gate and White Hall. It was known as the Sadar Bazar.*

How many members constitute the Sikkim Legislative Assembly? *32*

What number constitutes simple majority in the Sikkim Legislative Assembly? 17

What number consititutes two third majority in the Sikkim Assembly? 23

How many members represent Sikkim in the Lok Sabha and the Rajya Sabha? *1 each*

When was Governor's rule imposed in Sikkim? *From 18th Aug 79 to 17 Oct. 79 and from 25th May 84 to 8th March 85*

List out the names of theGovernors of Sikkim
1. B.B. Lal (15th May 1975- 9th Sept.1981)
2. Homi J.H. Taleyar Khan (10th January 1981 - 17th June 1984)
3. Kona Prabhakara Rao (18th June 1984 - 30th May 1985)
4. Bishma Narayan Singh (31st May 1985 - 20th Nov. 1985)
5. T.V. Rajeshwar (21st Nov.1985 - 1st march 1989)
6. S.K. Bhatnagar (2nd March 1989- 7th Feb 1990)
7. Admiral R.H. Tahiliani (8th Feb 1990 - 20th Sept. 1994)
8. P. Shiva Shanker (21st Sept 1994- 11th Nov. 1995)
9. K.V. Raghunatha Reddy (12th Nov 1995 - 9th March 1996)
10. Chaudhari Randhir Singh (10th March 1996 - 17th May 2001)
11. Kidar Nath Sahani (18th May 2001 - 25.Oct .2002)
12. V. Rama Rao (26.10.2002-25.10.2007)
13R.S. Gaval (13.7.2006-12.8.2006)
14\Sudharsan Agarwal (26.10.2007- 8.07.2007)
15. B.P. Singh (9.07.08-

Give the name of Chief Ministers of Sikkim in chronological order.

1. Kazi L. D. Khangasharpa 23rd July 1974 (under Associate State and then from 16th May 1975 to 18th August 1979

2. N.B. Bhandari (18th October 1979 - 11th May 1984).

3. B.B. Gurung (11th May 1984 - 25th May 1984)

4. N.B. Bhandari (8th March 1985 to 1990)

5 N.B. Bhandari (1989 to 17th May 1994)

5. Sancha Man Limboo (18th May 1994 - 13th December 1994)

6. Pawan Chamling (14th December 1994 - 11th October 1999)

7. Pawan Chamling (12th October 1999 - March 2004).

8.Pawan Chamling (15th May 2004 - till date)

Give the names of MPs of Lok Sabha and Rajya Sabha from Sikkim

Lok Sabha

1. Son Kumar Rai (4th Dec1975- 5th Lok Sabha, nominated)

2. Chatra Bahadur Katwal (22nd Feb 77- 6th Lok Sabha, uncontested).

3. Pahal Man Subba (1st Mar 1980-7th Lok Sabha).

4. Nar Bahadur Bhandari (23rd Dec 1984- 8th Lok Sabha).

5. Dil Kumari Bhandari (1st Apr 1985- 8th Lok Sabha)

6. Nandu Thapa (26th Nov. 1989- 9th Lok sabha)

7. Dil Kumari Bhandari (20th May 1991- 10th Lok Sabha).

8. Bhim Dahal (16th Feb 1996- 12th Lok Sabha).

9. Bhim Dahal (16th Feb 1998- 12th Lok Sabha).

10. Bhim Dahal (3rd Oct 1999- 13th Lok sabha).

11.Nakul Rai (20th May 2004 -14th Lok Sabha

12 P.D. Rai (22nd May 2009 - 15th Lok Sabha

Rajya Sabha

1. Leonard Solomon Saring (29th Nov. 1975)

2. Leonard Solomon Saring (22nd Sept 1981).

3. Kesang Namgyal Paljor (26th Sept 1987).

4. Karma Tenzing Tobden (23rd March 1988).

5. Karma Tenzing Tobden (17th Feb 1994).

6. Kalzang Gyatsho Bhutia (13th Jan 2000).

7. Palden T. Gyamtso (11th Sept. 2000).

8 OT Lepcha 2006-Jan 2012

9. Hisey Lacchungpa Jan 2012-

When was Nepali recognised as an official language and included in the Eight Schedule of the Constitution? *20th August 1992 with the 71st constitution amendment Bill*

What is Revenue Order No 1.?*Under this order of 1917, land belonging to Bhutias and Lepchas cannot be sold to other communities.*

Name the first woman MLA of Sikkim. *Hem Lata Chettri*

Name the first speaker of Sikkim. *Chatur Singh Rai*

Name the first woman speaker of Sikkim. *Kalawati Subba*

What does Mintogang mean? *Blossomed crowned hill-top*

Which Department of the Government of Sikkim is concerned with Monasteries and religious affairs? *Ecclesiastical Department. This Department is unique to Sikkim*

Who wrote the book 'The Sikkim Saga' ? *B.S. Das*

Name the great Nepali writer who translated the Ramayana to Nepali *Bhanu Bhakta*

Who was the first Chief Secretary of Sikkim? *T.D. Densepa*

Name the author who wrote "Sikkim- A Himalayan Tragedy" *Nari K Rustomji*
Who was Fakir Chand Jali? *He was the first Chief Engineer of Sikkim and built roads, bridges, buildings and power stations in Sikkim. He was conferred the title of Rai Bahadur Sahib. He came to Sikkim in 1911 as a draughtsman and rose to the rank of Chief Engineer.*

Name the 12 ST/BL reserved constituencies of SLA. – *Yoksam- Tashiding / Rinchenpong / Daramdin / Barfung / Tumen – Lingi/ Gyathang –Machong / Martam- Rumtek/ Gangtok/ Syari/ Kabi – Lungchok / Dzongu / Lachen-Mangan.*
Who was the Chief Minister of first popular government formed in 1949? – *Tashi Tsering*

Name the Panchyat Act that had abolishes the Chhodu System of Dzongu. – *Sikkim Panchayat Act 1965*
In which year the first Panchayat election was held? – *In 1951*
When were the second and third panchayat elections held before ?- *In 1966 and 1968*
When were the panchayat elections held after merger to India ? – *In 1976,1983,19988,1993,1997,2002 and 2007.*
The reservation of seats to women, SC and ST in pachayats were provided by which Act. – *Sikkim Panchayat Act 1993.*
Which Panchayat Act has raised the reservation of seats of women from 33 to 40 per cent ? – *Sikkim Panchayat (Amendment) Act 2007.*
Which Panchayat Act has allowed the Limbu and Tamang communities to contest the panchayat election from ST reserved seats ? – *Sikkim Panchayat (Amendment) Act 2007.*
When was the State Planning Commission set up in Sikkim? *On 8th May 2001.*
Who is the Chairman State Planning Commission of Sikkim ? *Chief Minister of Sikkim.*
When was the reserved and khasmal forest in Sikkim demarcated ? *In 1902 and 1905.*
In which year the Sikkim State Council was constituted? *In 1953*
What was the total strength of first Sikkim State Council?- *17 members (12 elected and 5 nominated)*
Name the Proclamation and the year that created a Sangha seat in Sikkim? – *The Royal Proclamation of 1958*
In which year the Sikkim State Congress was formed? *In 1947*
The Sikkim state congress was formed by merging three political organizations. Give the name of organizations? *Parja Sudharak Samaj, praja sammelan and praja Mandal*
Who were the founders of Praja Sudharak Samaj? *Tashi Tsering & Sonam Tsering*
Name the founders of Praja Sammelan. *Gobardhan Pradhan & Dhan Bahadur Tewari*
Who were the founders of Praja Mandal? *Kazi Lhendup Dorji Khangsarpa*

Who was the president of Sikkim state Congress? *Tashi Tsering*
When was Sikkim National party formed? *In 1948*
When was Swatantra Dal formed? *In 1958*
In which year the scheduled caste Leagus was formed? *In 1958*
When was Sikkim National Congress formed? *In 1960*
Who was the president of Sikkim National Congress? *Kazi Lhendup Dorji Khangsarpa*
In which year the Sikkim Independent front was formed? *In 1966*
Who was the founder of Sikkim Independent front? *Mrs Ruth Karthak Lepchani*
When was Sikkim Janta Party formed? *In 1970*
Who was the founder of Sikkim janta party? *L.B. Basnet*
When was Sikkim janta congress formed? *October 1972*
When was Sikkim congress formed? *February 1973*
In which year the Sikkim congress merged with Indian National congress? *In December 1975*
When Sikkim party, later renamed as Sikkim Janta parished was formed? *On 22nd March 1977*
Who was the founder of Sikkim Janta Parished? *N.B. Bhandari*
When was Sikkim Congress (Revolutionary) formed? *In September 1979*
Who was the founder of Sikkim congress (Revolutionary) party? *R.C. Poudyal*
In which year the Himali Congress was formed? *In 1983*
When was Sikkim United Council formed? *In June 1983*
Who was the President of Sikkim United Council? *Kazi Lhendup Dorji Khangsarpa*
When was the Gorkha League formed? *In 1984*
Who was the founder of the Gorkha League? *N.B. Khatiwada*
In which year the Sikkim Sangram Parished was formed? *In 1984*
Who was the president of Sikkim Sangram parsihed? *N.B. Bhandari*
When was Sikkim Democratic front formed? *In 1992*
When was Sikkim Himali Rajya parsihed formed? *In 2002*
How may languages in Sikkim are declard as State Languages? – *11 Languages.*
Name the Act that made the Rai, Newar, Gurung , Manger, Sherpa, Sunuwar and Tamang languages as the state language of Sikkim. – *Sikkim Offical Languages (Amendment) Act 1995.*
Name the Municipality Act that created three – tier municipality in Sikkim. – *Sikkim the Municipality Act,2007.*
Name the three-tier municipality established in Sikkim ? - *Municipal Corporation, Municipal Council and Nagar Panchayat.*
Name the only Municipal Corportaion of Sikkim.- *Gangtok Municipal Corporation.*
Name the only Municipal Council of Sikkim. – *Namchi Municipal Council.*
Name the five Nagare Panchayats created recently in Sikkim. *Singtam Nagar Panchayat, Rangpoo Nagar Panchayat, Jorethang Nagar Panchayat, Geyzing Nagar Panchayat and Mangan Nagar Panchayat.*
When was first election of three-tier municipality in Sikkim was held on …… *-27.04.2010*

Where will you find the Tibetan words Kham Sum Wangdi meaning "Conqueror of Three worlds" written? *Official emblem of the Government of Sikkim*
Name the oldest school in Sikkim. *Sang Senior Secondary School initially established as a Missionary school in 1880*
The Statues of Unity installed at MG Marg, Gangtok depicts the figures of three historical figures. Two of them are Thetong Tek and his wife Ngo-kong-ngol. Who is the third figure? *Khye Bumsa*
Whose statue exists in the lawn of the Sikkim Legislative AssemblyBuilding? *Dr Ambedkar*
Whose statue was installed at the Chintan Bhawan on 16th May 2008? *L.D. Kazi*
Opposite Hanuman Tok is a cremation ground. What is it known as? *Royal Cremation Ground, Lukshyama*
Name the Department that looks after Disaster Management. *The Land Revenue and Disaster Management Department.*
Name the Department unique to Sikkim that looks after the religious affairs. *Ecclesiastical Department*
What is the erstwhile Lal Bazar known as presently? *Kanchendzonga Shopping Complex*
Name the French explorer and writer who was gifted a bronze statue by Chogyal Sidkeong Tulku. The statue was later returned to Phodong Monastery. *Madame Alexandra David Neel.*
Victoria Cross Ganju Lama's name was mis-spelt during his enlistment. What was his real name? *Gyamtso Shandarpa*
What is the original name of Danny Denzongpa? *Tshering Phinstog Denzongpa.*
In 1967 a superhit Hindi movie starring Dev Anand was shot in Sikkim. Name it. *Jewel Thief*
Who is the author of the book 'Perennial Dreams'? *Pawan Chamling*
Name the university which conferred the honorary doctorate degree to Pawan Chamling. *Manipal University*
In 1999, Pawan Chamling was awarded the Best Environmental CM by which presitigous organisation? *Centre for Science and Environment*
In the late 1950s a ropeway was built between Gangok and which place? *Thegu Before Nathula*
The Sikkim Police was born after the first Police station was established at Aritar, near Rhenock. When was this? *27th Nov 1897*
Name three Sikkimese who have been awarded the Arjuna award. *Sonam Sonam Gyatso for mountaineering, Baichung Bhutia for football and Jaslall Pradhan for boxing, Tarun Deep Rai for archery*
Name the first Sikkimese to reach the summit of Everest? *Sonam Gyatso in 1965*
Name the first women to climb Mount Everest. *Phul Maya Tamang and Yangdi Sherpa. They reached the summit on 22 May 2008*
Name the various expeditions to the Mount Kanchendzonga
First Attempt led by Crowley 1905 from the Nepal side; Second Attempt by E.F. Farmer Solo attempt 1929 Nepal side; Third Attempt Paul Bauer 1929 from Sikkim Side;Fourth attempt Dyrenfurth 1930 Nepal side; Fifth attempt Paul Bauer 1931 from Sikkim side; Sixth attempt first successful attempt Charles Evan (team leader and climbed by George Band and Joe Brown1955 from Nepal Side; Seventh attempt (successful) led by Col Kumar and climbed by Prem Chand 1977 from Sikkim side
How did Frey Peak in West Sikkim get its name? *After George Frey Mountaineer*

who fell and died on this peak during a pre-Everest Expedition in 1950. Tenzing Norgay was also on this expedition

Name the Sikkimese who represented India in archery in the Athens Olympics 2004 *Mandeep Rai*

Name the Sikkimese who was awarded the Arjuna Award in 2006?
Tarun Deep Rai for Archery

Name Sikkimese who have be awarded the second highest civilian award of India the Padma Vibhusan. *Chogyal Palden Thondup Namgyal(1954) Kazi Lendup Dorejee*

Name the Sikkimese who have been awarded the Padma Bhusan? *Sonam Gyasto, the mountaineer;*

Name the Sikkimese who have been awarded the Padma Shree? *Sonam Gyasto, the mountaineer; G.S. Lama the poet, Danny Denzongpa the actor, Bhaichung the footballer, Sonam Tshering Lepcha, Keepu Lepcha, Norden Tshering Bhutia,Kedar Gurung.*

Name the recceipt of the Ashok Chakra from Sikkim.*Sahid Sanjog Chettri*

Who is known as the Tinkitam Express?*Bhaichung Bhutia*

What was the old name of Sonam Gyasto Road in Gangtok? *Tibet Road*

Who coined the slogan "Apno Gaon Afia banao"? *Pawan Chamling*

What was the old name of Sonam Tshering Road in Gangtok? *Kazi Road*

Name the organisation that first introduced computers in Sikkim? *Sikkim Police. Paybill software was implemented for the entire organisation in 1988.*

What is the finger of Sikkim and why is it famous. *It is fiinger like area of Sikkim that juts into China. In 2008, it was a lot in the news because of incursions by the Chinese.*

In 2006, the 27th Nov commmittee was constituted by Government employees. Which rule was it concerned with? *Rule 4(4) of Establishment Department*

CULTURE AND TRADITIONS

Lepchas

What do Lepchas call Sikkim?
Ney-Mel-Renjyong-Lyang which means sacred place inhabited by honest and peace loving people

What does Boongthing mean? *Boong means mouth and Athing means good orator. They are Lepcha priests.*

Who are Muns? *Muns are Lepcha priestresses.*

Where was the Sikkim's equivalent of the Tower of Babel built by the Lepchas? *Daramdin near Sombaria*

Rom, Itbumoo & Tamsang Thing are the dieties of which community? *Lepcha*

Where is the Lepcha museum located? *Daramdin*

In Lepcha what is the naming cermony of newly born babies known as? *It is known as Tungbong Faat*

What is the name of the traditional Lepcha Panchayat? *Chhodu*

Who is said to have invented the Lepchas script ? *Lord Tamsang Thing*

What is the Lepcha festival marking the New Year known as? *Namsoong*

What does "Tendong Lho Rum Faat" mean? *Worship of Tendong*

Which mountain is worshipped during the "CHYU RUM FAT" ceremony of the Lepchas? *Kanchendzonga*

Kirats (Rais, Limboos etc.)

What does Kirat mean?
Kirat Means Hunter of pigs or boars (Kir stands for pig or boar)

Name some Kirat communities*Rai, Limboo*

What are the Rai witch doctors known as? *Mangpas*

To which Community is the occasion of 'Sakewa' associated with? *Rai*
What does the Rai festival Sakewa mean? *It means whole hearted offering to invoke the blessing of goddess Chandi during the planting season.*
What are the dances performed during Sakewa known as?*Silis*
Name the 3 stones which are placed in front of the hearth called Samkha?*Suptulang, Taralung and Shankalung*
What is Mundum?
Mundum are the traditional folklores and unwritten holy scriptures of the Kirats chanted in the poetic form.
What is the pot used to make offering during Sakewa known as? *Wabuk or Salawa made of fruit of a dried plant*
What is Hongken?*Drum popularly used during Sakewa festival*
What is the Omadar or Dhulay Puja?
Omadar Puja is a week long puja performed by Rais during full moon (Vaishakhi Purnima)
What dish is prepared out of chicken feathers by the Rai Community? *Wachipa*
What is a more common name for the Yakthumbas ? *Limbus*
What is a Subba Limbu witch doctor known as? *Yehba*
Why is Teyongsi Sirijunga Sawan Tongnam celebrated? *To mark the birth anniversary of the Limbu god Sirijunga*
What is the animist religion of the Limboos known as?
It is known as Yumasa Myoor Yumaism.
Who wrote the Limboo script? *Srijunga*
What are the Cymbals and Bells used by the Limboo priests known as?
They are known as Soyeng and Ponghe
Chyap Brung or Kongsing Kay is a traditional musical instrument in the shape of large Dholak(Drum). Which Nepali community is it associated with? *Limbu/Subba*
Yuma Shamma, Sri Janga and Tagyera Powa are the dieties of which community? *Limbu*
What is a Tungeba?*It is a single stringed musical insturment and made of a piece of bamboo and a large dried hollow gourd.*
What is Udung? *It is a Sarangi or violin*
What is Binayo? *It is musical instrument made of bamboo chips*
What is Murchuynga? *Murchunga is a musical instrumentis made of iron piece played by keeping it between the teeth.*
What is Soya Matchi? *It is a type of pickle*
What is Thi? *It is a home made intoxicating beverage.*
Who is a Yuma Sam? *Yuma Sam is a Lemboo female priestess*
The Lepchases during the old days used the root of which plant for poisoning the arrowhead for hunting purpose? *Aconite (Aconitum spicatum to be more specific.)*
What is Sang Sang?
Sang Sang is a combination of Millet beer in a wooden container with a pipe and eight pieces of meat that is kept on the altar during Puja.
Where is the Siri Junga Manghim located? *Hee Bermoik*
Where is the Rodhu Khim of the Kirat Khamu Rai located? *At Baiguney*
What is Palam?
Palam is an introductory song sung by the Limmboos before a dance.
According to the Limboo religion what are the eighteen worlds or Loks?
They are Sangram Pedang Den, Sang-Sang Den, Mang Khoma Den, Sey-sywa Den, Sunaing Tong Den, Muthang Khara Den, Torong Tangson Den, Samyukna Den,

Iksading Khamdek Den, Khambongba Lungbongba Yukna Den, Muroplung Kheroplung Den, Muguplung Theguplung Den, Murupli Kherupli Den, Mujingna Kheyonna Den, Musekha Sekhana Den, Tungutlung Haralung Den, Sumbadoma Lekwadoma Den, and Khemding Yogsong Den

Bhutias and Buddhism

What are "Thankas"? *Religious scrolls*

"Saga Dawa" signifies three important incidents that occured in the life of Lord Buddha. One was his birth, the other attainment of Nirvana. What was the third one? *Gaining Enlightment*

What are roadside holy walls with mantras engraved on them known as? *Medangs*

What is ceremony of airing and sunning of the belongings and relics of the Latsun Chembo at Tholung Monastery known as? *Kamsel*

What does Dalai Lama Mean? *Ocean of Wisdom*

What does the festival "Losar" signify? *Tibetan New Year*

Name the Buddhist festival that symbolises the Descent of Buddha from the heaven of the thirty three gods after visiting his mother. *Lhabab Dhuechen*

What does the festival "Phang Labsol" signify? *Worship of the Snowy Range to.mark the signing of the treaty of brotherhood between Lepchas and Bhutias*

What are "Chaams"? *Religious masked dances*

What are Gyalsten, Sernya, Pema, Palbheu & Choekyi Khorlo also popularly known as in English? *Eight Lucky signs*

What do the eight spokes in the Wheel of Dharma stand for? *Eight fold paths*

What does "Bodhisattvas" mean? *Buddha in the making*

What does Shambhala mean? *Shangrila,paradise in the North*

Where is the festival of "Bhumchu" held? *Tashiding Monastery*

From which river is the water for the Bhumchu used? *Rathong Chu*

What does festival of "Drukpa Teshi" signify? *The first preaching of Buddha to his five disciples*

Who was the founder of the Nyingmapa Sect? *Guru Padmasambva*

Name the Buddhist Diety of Knowledge. *Manjushri*

Who was the founder of the Gelugpa Sect? *Tsongkhapa*

Four of the five parts of a Chorten are Earth, water, air, ether. Which is the fifth one? *Fire*

What dance is performed annually in honour of the Eight Buddhist Dieties? *Kagyet Dance*

In the Lachen and Lachung valleys of North Sikkim a unique traditional system of administration is still operational. In this, the village headman is called the *"Pipon".*

What is this system known as? *Dzomsa*

How does the Dzumsa system differ from the Panchayat? *Dzumsa has a tenure of one to two years whereas Panchayat a tenure of four to five years. In the Dzumsa the Pipon is always a male.*

Name the five treasures that are housed in the Kanchendzonga

The Five Treasures are said to be Chai Dzu (Salt), Shar-Dhan-Ngul-ki-Dzu (Gold and Silver), Du-Dhan-MenkiDzue (Medicine and grain), Kokchen-Ki-Dzu (Weapons) and Chue-Ki-Dzu (Scriptures).

What is Shanag? *Black hat dance*

What is Hdur chaam? *The skeleton dance*

What is Shawa Chaam? *Stag Dance*

What does Shanag (Black Hat dance) signify? *It celebrates the killing of the*

antiBuddhist King Langdarma of the Yarlung dynasty by a monk.
Who was the monk who killed King Langdarma? *Pelkyi Dorjee*
Who is Dorjee Lopen? *Head Lama of a monastery*
Who is Rolpon? *Music conductor directing the Chaam*
What are four Noble Truths?
1. Existence of Sorrow2. Cause of Sorrow 3. Cessationof Sorrow 4. Ways which lead to the cessationof sorrow
What are the Eight Fold Paths of Buddhism?
1. Right Understanding 2. Right Thought 3. Right Speech 4. Right Actions 5.Right livelihood 6.Right Effort 7. Right Mindfulness 8. Right Concentration
Why is Guru Rinpoche's Trungkar Tsechu celebrated? *To mark the birth anniversary of Guru Rinpoche*
Where was Gurupadmasambva born? *Swat Valley in Pakistan*
What are rolmos and silnyen? *Cymbals*
What are nga chen? *Drums*
What is phurpa? *Dagger*
What is chaamgo? *Dress worn by the dancers during chaams*
What is Lham? *Boots made of colourful cloth*
Gutor and Kagyed precedes which Sikkimese festival? *Losoong*
What is the first day of the eleventh month marking the beginning of Losoong known as?*Tseche Tchi*
What are the sixth or seventh day of Losoong known as? *Nyempa Guxzom*
What is the significance of Nyempa Guzom? *It is considered as the day on which the nine bad spirits met.*
What is the difference between Losoong and Losar? *Losoong marks the end of the harvest eason and hapens during the end of the Tibetan Year. Losar is the beginning of the Tibetan New Year.*
What is Kutse Shegu? *49th day death ceremony of the Buddhists*
What is the traditional name for the jester who also controls the crowd during Buddhist “Chaams”? *Atchar*
The Bhutia horoscope is named after animals and unlike other horoscopes it is based upon a cycle of years rather than months. How many years does it take to complete one cycle? *Twelve*
Name the 3 animals at the centre of the Wheel of Life. *Pig, Cock and Snake*
What does the the intermediate circle of the Wheel of Life represent? *It represents the five worlds after death*
What does the outermost circle of the Wheel of life represent? *It represents the 12 phases of life.*
What are “Kagyur” and “Tangur” of Buddhists? *They are the sacred, holy books*
Name the monastery in North Sikkim where the relics belonging to Latsun Chembo are shown to the public once in three years. *Tholoung Gompa. The next time this will be done will be in March-April 2009.*
HH the Dalai Lama performed an important religious ceremony at Gangtok in March/April 1993. What was this ceremony? *Kalchakra puja*
What is the English translation of the mantra ‘Om Mani Padme Hum’? *Hail Lotus in the Jewel*
What is Rolchaam? *Dance of Cymbals*
What is Tshamche chaam? *Animal headed mask dance*
What is Shyak? *Dance of horned animals*
What is Namding? *Dance of the winged animals*

What is a Sheda? *It is a monastic college. Nygnimpa Institute of Higher Studies in Gangtok is one Sheda in Sikkim. It is affliated to a university in Banaras.*
The Government has banned Sherbung for other than religious personalities? What is it? *Sherbung is religious reception given to high ranking monk. It had started being misused for political leaders and others*
Name the Rimpoche under whose supervision the Phurba Chorten near Tibetology was built? *Trul-shi Rimpoche*
In November 2008 a Thai delegation of monks handed over Buddha's Relics for which project in Sikkim? *The Sakya Muni Project at Rabong*

Miscellenaeous

What is the nine instrument orchestra of the Nepalis locally known as? *Naumati Baja*
Name the nine instruments of the Naumati Baja?
They are 1.Sahanai 2. Doholki 3.Jhiyali 4.Damaka(Big Drum) 5.Tinamko(two sticks) 6.Bhaley(Additional Sahanai) 7.Pothi Damaka 8.Narshingha(Longish trumpet 9.Karnal
What is Kaneyma?*Kaneyma is fermented soya beans*
What is Gundrook?*Fermented leaves of vegetables*
Why is Janamastami celebrated? *To mark the birth anniversary of Lord Krishna*
What does Chaite Dasain or Ramnami signify? *Birth of Lord Ram*
What does Shivratri signify? *Marriage of Lord Shiva to Parvati*
In the Hindu religion name the Nau Gharas (Nine Planets)
Surya(Sun) Chandra(Moon) Mangal(Mars) Biraspati (Jupiter), Budh(Mercury), Shukar(Venus), Shani (Saturn), And the imaginary (shadow planets) of Rahu and Ketu
In Gurung terminology what is Rodhi? *Rodhi means a resting place. In fact it is kind of a community house of a tribe in which young boys and girls are taught about the traditions. They are also taught singing and dancing.*
In Gurung culture, what is Falki and Paigo? *Falki traditional food made of boiled green maize and head or legs of sheep. Paigo is food made of millet and maize with dal.*
What is the language and script of the Gurungs known as? *Tamu Kye and Khema Prhi*
What is the first hair cutting ceremony of a male Nepali child called? *Chewar*
In Sherpa culture what is Somar? *It is Cheese curry.*
What is the traditional name for the jester during a "Maruni Naach"? *Dhatuwarey*
What is dungri? *It is a nose ring worn by Nepali womenfolk*
What is the day of flowers known as in Dasain? *Fulpati*
During the festival of Tihar, the Ghai Tihar and Kukoor Tihar is preceeded by _________? *Kak Tihar*
What is the carol singing tradition of the Nepalis during Tihar or Diwali called? *Bhailo or Deusi*
Which fesitival is celebrated in the month of September to honour the 'God of Machines? *Vishwa Karma Puja*
With which community is Barahimijong associated ? *Magar*
Who is worshipped during the Magar ceremony of Barahimijong? *The forefathers*
Which festival is celebrated by the Newars to honour the God of the Rains? *Indra Jatra.*
The Lakhey Dance is associated with which community? *Newar*
What is the dialect and script of the Sunuwar Community known as? *Koicha*

Bimsen Puja and Buri Boju are associated with which community? *The Sunuwars*
Which community derives its name from the word Drum? *Damai*
With whom are folk songs of Juari and dance of Madale Naach associaed with? *Kami*
With which community is the question and answer song of Dohori associated with? *Gurung*
Which Hindu festival is celebrated in the month of February to honour the 'Goddess of Knowledge? *Saraswati Puja*
There is memorial in memory of some missionaries who died in a flood in a village near Lachung in the 1930s. Which country did they belong to? *Finlamd*
The missionaries who set up the first schools in Sikkim at Sang, Khamdong and Mangan belonged which country. *Finland.*
What is the Tamang New Year known as? *Lochar*
Where is Rangey Mela celebrated? *Namchi*
Where is the Pilgrimage cum Culture Centre also known at Siddeshvera (Char Dham) with a 108 ft high tall state of Lord Shiva located? *At Solophok near Namchi*
Name the four Dhams depicted in the Siddeshvera (Char Dham) temple at Solophok Namchi? *Badrinath Uttarakhand, Rameswaram Tamil Nadu, Jaganath Orissa, Dwarka Gujrat.*
Name the 12 original Jyotilingas that have been have been depicted at Siddeshvera temple Solophok Namchi
Somnath in Saurashtra (Guj) ,Mallikarjun in Srisailam (A.P.) ,Mahakaleshwar in Ujjain (M.P.) ,Omkareshwar in Shivpuri / Amaleswara (M.P.) ,Vaidyanath in Parali (Mah) ,Nageswar in Darukavanam ,Kedareswar in Kedarnath / Himalayas (Utt) Tryambakeswar in Nasik (Mah) ,Rameshwar in Setubandanam / Rameshwaram (T.N.) ,Bhimashankar in Dakini (Mah) ,Visweswar in Varanasi (U.P.) and Ghrishneswar in Devasrovar (Mah).
There is a smaller statue of a manifestationat Lord Shiva at Siddeshvera. Name it *Kirateshwar*
Name the saint who consecrated the Siddeshevera Dham at Namchi on 8th Nov 2011. *Jagadguru Sankarcharya Swami Swarupananda Saraswati*
Where in Sikkim did Rabrinath Tagore visit in 1920s? *Rinchenpong and stayed in the now named Smriti Van. He wrote a few verses of his poems while staying here.*
Name the famous 19th century poet who translated Ramayan into Nepali? *Bhanu Bhakta*
When is Bhanu Bhakta's birthday celebrated in Sikkim? *13th July*
In 1997 the Government scrapped and abandoned a major Power Project because of environment and religious considerations. Name the project? *Rathong Power Project*
Who was the first Chief Justice of Sikkim? *Rajendra Sacher*
Sikkim has a few institutes for the physically handicapped. Name them. *Jawharilala Nehru Memorial Institute for the Handicapped (JNMIH) for the Blind at Namchi; Special school for the Hearing impaired at Gangtok; Sikkim Viklang Society for orthopaedically handicapped; Sikkim Spastic Society for children suffering from Cerebral Palsy and Austism*
The Limca Book of Records 2007 Edition has declared a Cyber Cafe in Sikkim as the highest in the world. Where is it located.?*The Community Information Centre at the Sherathang Trade MART at 13600 ft run by the Department of Information Technology*
Name the first Vice Chancellor of Sikkim University. *Mahendra P Lama*

What is the concrete bridge at Jorethang known as? *Akkar Bridge*
In Sikkim where is the product Alpine Chees made? *At Dentam, West Sikkim*
Where is Ashirwad Bhawan? *At Raj Bhawan used for official functions*
Where is Samman Bhawan? *At the Mintogang Complex. Chief Minister meets the public here.*
When was the Governor's Gold Cup football tournament first held? *1978*
Where is Bhaichung Stadium? *Namchi. It was known as Youth Ground earlier*
Where is the Chief Minister's Gold cup football tournament normally played? *Namchi*
What is Bidawa Punaribhaha Yojna? *It is a scheme in which a cash incentive of Rs 10000/- is given to those persons who marry widows.*
What are Sukambasis? *They are Landless Sikkimese*
What is CM Annapurna Programme? *Old people of 65 and above are provided 10 kg of rice permonth*
Why was Saramsa Garden earlier called Ipecac garden? *Because of the medicinal plant called Ipecac that was grown here till 1970*
What is the difference between Inner Line Permit and Restricted/Protected Area Permit?*An Inner Line permit is issued to foreigners who want to visit Sikkim by Indian Embassies, Tourism Department and other designated agencies whereas a Restricted Area Permit is issued by the Sikkim Police to anyone wanting to visit restricted areas like Changu lake*
Who headed the Commission to Review Environment and Social Policies? *Roy Burman*
What is the signifance of National Education Day 11th Nov?
To commemorate the birth anniversary of India's First Education Minister, Maulana Abul Kalam Azad. The nation re-dedicates itself to the cause of Universal Education during this day.

FLORA AND FAUNA

What is the Green Mission? *It is an environment related initiative launched by Pawan Chamling on 27th Feb 2006. It aims at making Sikkimn a garden state by extensive afforestation programmes.*
Name the State animal of Sikkim. *Red Panda/Ailurus fulgens*
Name the State bird of Sikkim. *Blood Pheasant*
Name the State flower of Sikkim. *Nobile Orchid/ Dendrobium nobile*
Name the State tree of Sikkim. *Rhododendron nevium*
Name the most popular cash crop of Sikkim. *Cardamom*
Name the most important fruit produce of Sikkim. *Orange*
What is the Tibetan Wildass found in Sikkim known as? *Kiang*
Name a riverine mammal of low altitude Sikkim *Otter/ Lutra lutra*
Which is the biggest bird of Sikkim? *Griffon Vulture/ Gyps himalayanus*
Name the biggest lizard of Sikkim *Monitor Lizard/ Varanus sp.*
Which is the biggest moth of Sikkim? *Atlas moth*
Which is the largest snake of Sikkim? *Python/ Python molurus*
What is the biological name for the high altitude poisonous plant Bikh or Monkshood? *Aconite.*
What is the scientific name of Large Cardamom? *Amomum Subulatum*
Name the German who discovered the Shapi in Sikkim?*Ernest Schalfer*
Name the rhododendron sanctuary near Yumthang, North Sikkim . *Shingba*
Name the Sanctuary adjacent to Tsomgo lake, East Sikkim. *Kyongnosla Sanctuary*
Name the Sanctuary in East Sikkim opposite Gangtok on the Rumtek hill.

Fambong Lho Wildlife Sanctuary

Where is the Sidekong Tulku Bird Park located? Rabdentse near Pelling Gyalsing

Name the plant from which hand made paper is made. *Argali*

Name the plant used extensively for making brooms in Sikkim. *Amliso*

What is the biological and local name of theTibetan Wolf? *Canis lupus chanco or Chonku*

What is the biological and local name for the Sikkim Snow Toad? *Scutiger boulengeri or Baepo*

What is the English name of the animal Zimo found on the Cholamu plateau? *Siberian Weasel*

Name the biological and local name of Tibetan Gazelle?*Procapra picticaudata , Raakon*

Name the biological and local name of Bharal (Blue Sheep)?*Pseudois nayaur, Nao*

Name the biological and local name of Eurasian Lynx?*Lynx lynx, lh*

Name the biological and local name of Tibetan Fox.?*Vulpes ferrilatus, Dezey*

Name the biological and local name of Red Fox? *Vulpes vulpes, Wamo*

Name the biological and local name of Siberian Weasel? *Mustela sibirica, Zimo*

Name the biological and local name of Kiang (Tibetan Wild Ass)?*Equus kiang, Kyang*

Name the biological and local name of Himalayan Marmot?*Marmota himalayana, Kaagey-phieu, phae, Chipik*

Name the biological and local name of Long- Eared Bat?*Plecotes auritus, Pholon-thhaa*

Name the biological and local name of Woolly Hare? *Lepus oiostolus, Regon*

Name the biological and local name of Pika (Mouse-Hare)? *Ochotona thibetana, Abra*

Name the biological and local name of Yak?*Domesticated in Sikkim, Dong*

Name the biological and local name of Snow Leopard? *Panthera uncial, Saagey*

Name the biological and local name of Nayan (Great Tibetan Sheep, Argali)? *Ovis ammon hodgsoni, Nyen.*

Name the highest National Park in the country. *Kanchendzonga National park*

Name the Wildlife Sanctuary adjacent to Rabongla, South Sikkim *Maenam Wildlife Sanctuary*

Name the Sanctuary near Hilley in West Sikim *Varsey Rhododendron Sanctuary*

Name two rare animals found in the Cold Desert plateau of Sikkim. *Marmots and Kiangs.*

Name the largest cat of Sikkim. *Leopard or Panther/Panthera pardus*

Name the largest rat of Sikkim *Him Marmot (Marmota bobak).*

Name the largest bat of Sikkim *Flying fox (Pteropus giganteus)*

Shingba Sanctuary is famous for Rhododendrons; name the other Sanctuary in Sikkim also famous for Rhododendrons. *Barsey Rhododendron Sanctuary*

A rare and highly endangered relative of the Bighorn Sheep of America is found in the high cold desert of Sikkim. What is its name? *Nayan or Great Tibetan Sheep*

Name the famous ornithologist who wrote the book"Birds of Sikkim". *Salim Ali*

What is Pangolin? *It is an ant eater animal found in the area below Namchi*

What is the botanical name of Argali used for making handmade peper? *Edgeworthia gardneri*

What is the difference between a National park and Sanctuary? *There is a basic difference between National park and Sanctuary, A national park is an area which is sstrictly dedicated to conserve the wild flora fauna and natural habitat whereas a sanctuary is an area for the conservation for only one type of species.In National park all private ownership rights are nonexistent and all forestry grazing, cultivation activities are prohibited whereas in a sanctuarythese are permitted provided they do not interfere with well being of the ecosystem.*

What is a biosphere? A biosphere is a reserve around a park or sanctuary where scientific research and envoronment training and education is carried out.

What is Gaucharan land? *It is Grazing land "Gau" meaning cow Charan meaning pasture*

What is khasmahal? *A community forest land kept for meeting immediate fuel and fodder needs of a society.*

What are Tibi Beans and where are they grown? *These are very large protein rich beans grown in North Sikkim especially the Lachung area. Attempts are being made to begin large scale commercial cultivation of these beans.*

What is the local and botanical name of the rare Caterpillar fungu?

Yarchagumba(Cordyceps sinensis) *It grows wild in high altitudes in Sikkim between 3000 m and 5000 m and is used in Chinese and Tibetan traditional medicine. It sells at about 5000 US dollars in the international market. It is called catterpillar fungus as it grows on the back of the catterpillar of a moth.*

Why do radishes and potatos grow very big in high altitudes? *Because of high level of Ultra violet radiation and good sunshine.*

ABBREVIATIONS

There are many abbreviations that are widely used in official correspondences, government documents, news items and press reports in Sikkim. These are listed below:

SNT *Sikkim Nationalised Transport*
SITCO *Sikkim Time Corporation*
UD&HD *Urban Development & Housing Department*
DESM&E *Directorate of Economics Statistics Monitoring and Evaluation*
IPR *Information and Public Relations*
VC *Victoria Cross*
SIDICO *Sikkim Industrial Development and Investment Corporation Ltd.*
DIET *District Institute of Education and Training*
CIC *Community Information Centre/Chief Information Commisionar*
RTI *Right to Information*
PIO *Public Information Officer*
SBS State Bank of Sikkim
SISCO Sikkim State Cooperative Bank Limited
STDC *Sikkim Tourism Development Corporation*
SLA *Sikkim Legislative Assembly*
TTI *Teachers Training Institute*
SIE *State Institute of Education*
SIMFED *Sikkim Marketing Federation*
SBS *State Bank of Sikkim*
SPSC *Sikkim Public Service Commission*
SBI *State Bank of India*
STCS *State Trading Corporation of Sikkim*
FCI *Food Corporation of India*
IAS *Indian Administrative Service*
IFS *Indian Forest Service*
IPS *Indian Police Service*
SCS *Sikkim Civil Service*
IRB *India Reserve Battalion*
SAP *Sikkim Armed Police*
VLW *Village Level Worker*
MR *Muster Roll*
PSU *Public Sector Undertaking*
MOU *Memorandum of Understanding*
PAC Public Accounts Committee
NGO *Non Government Organisation*
PHC *Public Health Centre*
PHSC *Public Health Sub Centre*

CBO *Community Based Organisation* GCI *Galvanised Corrugated Iron*
BPL *Below Poverty Line* ACT *Affected Citizens of Tista*
CAT *Central Administrative Tribunal* MHA *Ministry of Home Affairs*
AIDs *Acquired Immuno Deficiency* TB *Tuberculosis*
NSV Non Scapel Vasectormy RCT Root Canal Tunneling
OPD *Out Patient Department* GDP *Gross Domestic Product*
SGMI *Sonam Gyasto Mountaineering Institute* *MBC Most Backward Class*
TRYSEM *Training of Rural Youth for Self-Employment*
IRDP *Integrated Rural Development Programme*
DWCRA *Development of Women and Children in Rural Areas*
NC *Natural Calamity* LPG *Liquefied Petroleum Gas*
NRSE *New and Renewal Sources of Energy* UD Unnatural Death
KNP *Kanchendzonga National Park*
SSA *Sarva Siksha Abiyan* AG *Advocate General or Accountant General*
SC/ST *Schedule Caste/ Sched. Tribe* PAN Permanent Account Number
GPF *General Provident Fund* CMO *Chief Medical Officer*
GIS *Geographical Information System/General Insurance Scheme*
GPS Global Positioning System OBC *Other Backward Classes*
ICAR *Indian Council for Agricultural Research*
CPWD *Central Public Works Department*
SIB *Subsidary Intelligence Bureau* LIC *Life Insurance Corporation*
AIR *All India Radio* PTI *Press Trust of India*
PIB *Press Information Bureau* UNI *United News of India*
CWC *Central Water Commission* BSI *Botanical Survey of India*
GREF *General Reserve Engineering Force* GSI *Geological Survey of India*
NJP *New Jalpaiguri* NEC *North East Council*
DA *Dearness Allowance/ Daily Allowance* TA *Travel Allowance*
HRA *House Rent Allownace* HCA *Hill Compensatory Allowance*
/NTACH Indian National Trust for Art and Cultural Heritage
NIC *National Informatics Centre* EC *Election Commission*
SMIT *Sikkim Manipal Institute of Technololgy*
DPR *Detailed Project Report* EOI *Expression of Interest*
PPP *Public Private Parternship* BOOT *Build Operate Own Transfer*
SSB *Sashastra Suraksa Bal*
BO *Block Officer* RO *Revenue Officer*
OSD *Officer on Special Duty NREGA National rural Employment Guarantee Act*
DGHC *Darjeeling Gorkha Hill Council* SRS *System Requirement Study*
RFP *Request for Proposal* EOI *Expression of Interest*
POL *Petrol oil Lubricants* HSD *High speed Diesel*
MS *MotorSpirit* SKO Superior kerosene oil
LS Rice *Long Sela Rice* MRP Maximum Retail Price
ICU *Intensive Care unit* MPCS *Multi purpose Cooperative Society*
AI I M S *All India Institute of Medical sciences*
I IT *Indian Institute Of Technology* TAR Tibetan Autonomous Region
CAT Scan *Computerised axial Tomography* MRI *Magnetic Resonant Imaging*
JEE *Joint entrance Examination* CET *Common Entrance test*
ZIP *Zone Improvement plan* SUV S*ports Utility Vehicle*
STPI *Software Technology Park of India* ITBP *Indo Tibet Border Police*
ATM *Automatic teller Machine* EP *European plan*
NABARD National Bank for Agriculture and Rural Development

UGC University Grants Commission
VAT *Value Added tax* WWW *World wide Web*
SMS *Short Message Service* SIM *Subsriber Identification Module*
GSM *Global system for mobile Communication*
GPRS *General Packet Radio Service* RoR *Right of Records*
BP0 *Business process Outsourcing* RCC Reinforced Cement Concrete
ITES *Information Technology Enabled Services*
OEM *Original Equipment Manufact urer*
PNR *Passenger Name Record* FAQ *Frequently Asked Questions*
MNC *Multi National Company* UTI *Unit Trust of India*
ICICl *Industrial Credit and Investment Corporation of India*
SAARC *South asia association for Regional Cooperation*
IDBI *Industrial Development Bank of India*
RBI *Reserve Bank of India* RoR *Right of Record*
EMI *Equated Monthly Instalment* NAV *Net Asset Value*
ROI *Return on investment* UV *Ultra Violet*
IR Infra Red qs Quantity sufficient NSS *National service* Scheme
NCC *National cadet Corp* PIL *Public Interest Litigation*
JCO *Junior Commissioned Officer*
WTO *World Trade organisation* PGT *Post graduate teacher*
TGT *Trained graduate Teacher* PRI *Panchayat Raj Institution*
Cp *Copy page* Nsp *note sheet page*
PUC *Put up for Consideration* Pp *Previous pages*
GATE *Graduate Aptitude Test in Engineering*
IL&FS *Infrasture Leasing and Financial Services*
WWF *World Wide Fund* ISRO *Indian Space Research Organisation*
DC *District Collector/DevCommisionar* SDM *Sub Divisional Magistrate*
DGP *Director General of Police* SP *Superintendent of Police*
DDO *District Development Officer*
BDO Block Development Officer BAC Block Development Centre
SDF *Sikkim Democratic Front* SSP *Sikkim Sangram Parishad*
TAAS Travel Agents Association of Sikkim ILP *Inner Line Permit*
SIBLAC *Sikkim Bhutia Lepcha Apex Committee*
SHRPP *Sikkim Himali Rajya Parisad Party*
GJMM Gorkha Jan Mukti Morcha
ANM *Auxiliary Nurse & Midwife* *JRY Jawahar Rojghar Yojna*
STNM *Sir Thondup Namgyal Memorial* GICI *Govt. Inst. of Cottage In*
NHPC *National Hydroelectric Power Corporation*
NBCC *National Building and Construction Corporation*
CBSE *Central Board of Secondary Education*
DAV *Dayananda Anglo Vedic* CTC Tea Crush Turn and curl
JNV *Jawarlal Nehru Vidhyalaya*
AISSE *All India Secondary School Examination*
AISSC *All India Senior Secondary Certificate* GST *Goods and Services Tax*
FRO *Foreigners' Registration Office*
PDS *Public Distribution System* PMGY Pradhan Mantri Gramin Yojna
IT *Income Tax or Information Technology*
BSNL *Bharat Sanchar Nigam Limited* NRHM *National Rural Health Mission*
IGNOU *Indra Gandhi National Open University*
SIRD State Institute of Rural Development

JFM Joint Forest Management JGSY Jawahar Gram Samidri Yojana
AUSAID *Austrailian Agency for International Development*
UNDP *United Nations Development Programme*
ADB *Asian Development Bank* APO Army Post Office
VHAS *Voluntary Health Associaton of Sikkim*
HUDCO *Housing and Urban Development Corporation*
STDC *Sikkim Tourism Develolpment Corporation*
SPDC *Sikkim Power Development Corporation*
SREDA *Sikkim Rural Energy Develolpment Agency*
SFA *Sikkim Football Association* DD *Doorsharshan*
SISI *Sikkim Industries Service Institute*
VLO *Village Level Officer* CB *Contingent Bill*
VLW Village Levbel Worker
NAB *National Association for the Blind*
JNMIH *Jawahar Lal Nehru Memorial Institute for the Handicapped*
IEC *Information Education and Communication*
ICT *Information Communication Technology*
SWOT *Strength Weaknesses Opportunity and Threats*
DONER *Ministry of Development of North Eastern Region*
NLPCR *Non Lapsable pool of Central Resources*
HRDD *Human Resource Development Department*
EM Technology *Effective Micro-organism Technology*
MPLADP *Member of Parliament Local Area Development Programme*
DTH *Direct to Home TV* TAR Tibetan Autonomous Region
SAARC *South Asia Association for Regional Cooperation* DOTs *Direct Observation Treatment* short
RTO *Regional Transport Office* *GLOF Glacial lake Outburst Flood*
RITES *Rail India Technical and Economic Services*
HDFC *Housing Development Finance Corporation*
HSBC *Honkong Shangai Bank Corporation*
JNV *Jawharlal Navodya Vidhyalaya* *OFC Optical Fibre Cable*
CAPART *Council for Advancement of People's action &Rural Technology*
PGCIL *Power Grid Corporation of Inida Limited*
CAPEX Capital Expenditure OPEX Operating Expenditure
UID Unique Identification Number ULB Urban Local Bodies
AIFF All India Football Federation KYC Know your Customer
CATCH Comprehensive Annual and Total Checkup
JNNURM Jawharlala Nehru National Urban Renewal Mission
When driving in army areas one comes across signs like 200 m AGE and MAP. What are these terms?*AGE is the hindi word for ahead. MAP is Medical Aid Post*

IMPORTANT EVENTS OBSERVED IN SIKKIKM

Republic Day	26th January
Gandhi Assasination Day	30th January
National Science Day	28th February
World Forestry Day	21st March
World Water Day	22nd March
Earth Day	22nd April
State Day(Sikkim)	16th May
Anti Terrorism Day	21st May
Kargil Diwas	26th July

Independence Day	15th August
Sadbhawana Diwas (Rajiv gandhi Assasination)	20th August
Gandhi Jayanti	2nd October
Rastriya Sankalp Diwas(Indira Gandhi assasination)	31st October
Children's Day (Birthday of Nehru)	14th November
National Integration Day	19th November
Teacher's Day (Birthday of Radha Krishna)	5th Sept
World Environment Day	5th. June
World Population Day	11th July
World Tourism Day	27th5ept
World Labour Day	1st May
World Wildlife week	1 to 7 October
World Habitat day	3rd October
International day for Natural Disaster Reduction	13 October
Anti Leprosy Day	3oth Jan
International Water Day	23rdMarch
World tuberculosis Day	24thMarch
World Health Day	7th April
Safe Motherhood Day	11thApril
World No Tobacco Day	31stMay
World Environment Day	5th June
International Day against Drug Abuse & Illicit Trafficking	26th June
World Population Day	11th July
Breast Feeding Week	1st to 7th Aug
National Education Day	11th Nov
World Ozone Day	16th Sept
nternational Day of Peace	17th Sept;
National Day of Peace	17th Sept
National Voluntary Blood Donation Day	1stOct
National No Tobacco Day	11th Oct'
World Food Day	16th Oct
Diabetes Day	15th Nov
World AIDs Day	1stDec
National Pollution & Prevention Day	2nd Dec.
International Volunteer Day	5thDec.
World Human Rights Day	10thDec

Name the roads in Sikkim that have been renamed after personalities?

Ravongla-Tarku Marg,	Late Ganju Lama V.C. MArg
Soreng-sombaria Marg,	Late Dharmadutta Sharma Marg
Kazi Marg,	Sonam Tshering Marg
Tibet Marg,	Sonam Gyatso Marg
Nam Nam Deorali Marg,	Kashi Raj Pradhan Marg
Paljor Stadium-Zilla Adalat Marg,	Dr. B.R. Ambedkar Marg
Rongli-Chujachen Marg,	Tulshiram Kashyap Marg
Namchi-Maniram Marg,	Late Agam Singh Tamang Marg
Arithang Marg,	Rahmi Prasad Alley Marg
Namchi-Manpur Marg,	C.D. Rai Marg
Chakung-Khaniserbung Kamling	B.B. Gurung Marg
Rangpo-Duga Marg,	Nakul Pradhan Marg
Dzongtempa Hotel Rinzing Mangan	Namgyal Kazi Marg

P.W.D. – D.A.C. (Mangan) Marg,	Dr. Lobzang Tenzing Marg
Secretariat to Zero Point	Bhanu Path
Community Hall -TNHSS School	Jeewan Thing Marg
Soreng to 8th Mile Budang	Padam Singh Apatan Road

Name the schools in Sikkim that have been renamed after various personalities.?

Ravangla Secondary School,	V.C. Ganju Lama Sr. Secondary School
Wok Secondary School,	Nayan Tshering Lepcha Secondary School
Kabi-Tingda High School,	Kalzang Gyatso High School
Omechu Jr. High School ,	Chhatraman Rai Jr. High School
Central Pendam Sr Sec School	Tikala Nirola Sr Sec School
Turung Secondary School	German Lepcha Secondary School
Daramdin Sr Secondary school	Kripasalyan Sr Secondary School
Sribadam Secondary School,	K.B. Limboo Sr. Secondary School
Ranipool Sr. Secondary School,	Brishaspati Prasai Sr. Secondary School
Chungthang Secondary School,	Tasa Tengay Lepcha Secondary School
Arithang Jr. High School,	Chatursing Rai Jr. High School
Okrey Secondary School	Padam Bahadur Gurung School

OTHERS

Allay Maidan, Namchi, Bhaichung Stadium

Rustamji Deer Park, Rustamji Park

The Government of Sikkim designated various years in which specific focus was to be made. Which were these?

2008: Year of Responsibility
2005 Year of the Youth (Yuva Kranti Varsh)
2002: Year of the Cooperative
1996 Green Revolution Year

SOME MILESTONES SINCE 1975

April 1975	-	The erstwhile Himalayan Kingdom Sikkim became the twenty - second State of India
May 16th, 1975	-	Mr. Bipin Bihari Lal, ICS, sworn-in as the first Governor of the state of Sikkim.
May 16th, 1975	-	Kazi Lhendup Dorjee Khangsarpa, sworn-in as the first Chief Minister of Sikkim State with his Council of Ministers.
May 16th, 1975	-	First State Day observed all over the State.
May 29th, 1975	-	Anti-Corruption branch set up in Gangtok.
June 29th, 1975	-	Special Session of Sikkim Legislative Assembly held to ratify the Constitution (Thirty four Amendment) Bill, 1975.
November 11th, 1975	-	Mrs. Indira Gandhi, Prime Minister of India visited Sikkim.
December 21st,197	-	Chief Minister, Mr. L.D. Kazi, laid the foundation stone of Temi Tea Factory in South Sikkim.
February 17th, 1976	-	Mother Teresa visited Sikkim.
October 18th, 1979	-	Mr. N.B. Bhandari sworn in as the second Chief Minister of Sikkim.
October 28th, *1979*	-	President of India, Mr.Neelam Sanjeeva Reddy visited Sikkim.
January 9th, 1981	-	Mr.Homi J.H. Taleyarkhan appointed as the 2nd Governor of Sikkim.
April 13th, 1981	-	The Union Finance Minister, Mr.R. Venkataraman inaugurated the Central Blood Bank of Sikkim.
November 6th, 198	-	His Holiness the 16th Gyalwa Karmapa passed away.
January 30th, 1982	-	Chogyal Palden Thondup Namgyal passed away at the age of 59.

May 1st, 1982 - First Helicopter service between Bagdogra and Gangtok inaugurated.

May 23rd, 1983 - The Eighth Finance Commission headed by Mr. Y.R Chavan visited Gangtok.

June 13th, 1983 - The 691 ft. long concrete bridge over the river Teesta at Melli inaugurated. The bridge was named after Pandit Jawaharlal Nehru.

1983 - Olympian Boxer, Mr.Jaslal Pradhan conferred the prestigious Arjuna Award.

May 11th,1984 - Mr.B.B. Gooroog sworn in as the third Chief Minister of Sikkim.

May 25th, 1984 - President Rule imposed in Sikkim.

June 17th,1984 - Mr.Kona Prabhakar Rao appointed as the third Governor of Sikkim.

March 8th, 1985 - Mr.N. B. Bhandari re-elected and sworn in as the Chief Minister of Sikkim for the second consecutive term.

May 31st, 1985 - Mr.Bhisma Narain Singh sworn in as the fourth Governor of Sikkim.

November 21st, 1985 - Mr.T.V.Rajeswar sworn in as the Governor of Sikkim

October 7th, 1987 - President of India, Mr. R. Venkataraman inaugurated G.B. Pant Leprosy Hospital at Sajong, East Sikkim.

October 9th, 1988 - New Sikkim House inaugurated at New Delhi.

March 2nd, 1989 - Mr.S.K.Bhatnagar sworn in as the Governor of Sikkim.

February 8th, 1990 - Mr.R.H.Tahiliani sworn in as the Governor of Sikkim.

August 1992 - Nepali language included in the Eighth Schedule of Indian Constitution

May 17th,1994 - Bhandari Government lost vote of confidence in the Sikkim Legislative Assembly.

May 18th, 1994 - Mr.Sanchaman Limboo sworn in as the Chief Minister of Sikkim.

July 1994 - The Prime Minister Employment Assurance Scheme implemented.

July, 1994 - Loyola B.Ed College inaugurated at Namchi.

September 21st, 1994 - Mr.P.Shiv Shankar sworn in as the Governor of Sikkim.

October 29th, 1994 - Sikkim Nationalised Transport receives National Productivity Award from the President of India.

December 12th, 1994 - Mr.Pawan Chamling sworn in as the fifth Chief Minister of Sikkim.

June 1st, 1995 - Grazing in forest land by cattles banned.

August 8th, 1995 - Degree College inaugurated at Namchi.

November 13th, 1995 - Mr.K.V.Raghunath Reddy sworn in as the Governor of Sikkim

March 10th, 1996 - Chaudhary Randhir Singh sworn in as the new Governor of Sikkim.

1997 - Establishment of Mahavidyalaya of Sanskrit at Gyalshing in West Sikkim

March 4th, 1997 - 500 bedded Central Referral Hospital inaugurated.

March 5th, 1997 - Chief Minister, Dr.Pawan Chamling conferred with Bharat Shiromani Award by the President of India, Mr. K. R. Narayanan.

March, 1997 - Sikkim becomes the first State to ban the use of non-biodegradable items like plastic bags

April 1997 - "Small Family Scheme" launched to encourage the education of girl child and Savings Accounts in the name of the school-going girl child also opened.

August 20th, 1997 - Scrapping of controversial Rathong-Chu Hydel Project in reverence to religious sentiments of the people of the region.

May 8th, 1998 - Successful inclusion of Sikkim as an eighth member of the North Eastern Council.

1999	-	Mr.Danny Denzongpa conferred with Padma Shri
May 6th, 1999	-	Vice-President of India, Mr.Krishan Kant laid the foundation stone of airport at a Pakyong.
May 20th, 1999	-	Centre for Science and Environment (CSE) conferred Chief Minister, Mr.Pawan Chamling with the Greenest Chief Minister of India Award.
September 1st, 1999	-	Ace Footballer, Mr.Bhaichung Bhutia conferred with the prestigious Arjuna Award
October 11th, 1999	-	Dr.Pawan Chamling and his council of Ministers sworn in for the second consecutive term.
November 12th, 1999	-	Mr.Pawan Chamling felicitated with Man of Dedication Award 1999 in recognition of his services to the people of the state and the country.
December,1999	-	Janata Mela - Biggest ever welfare package for Sikkimese poor launched.
January 25th, 2000	-	Sikkim recieves National Tourism Award for the best performing state in the North East region.
April 22nd, 2000	-	Union Home Minister, Mr.L.K.Advani visited Sikkim.
June 20th, 2000	-	Thami, Jogis and Dewan declared as OBCs.
July, 2000	-	Bhutia, Lepcha, Limbu languages included in North Bengal University.
September, 2000	-	First Community Information Centre inaugurated in Gangtok
January 2001	-	Rice at subsidized rate of Rs.4/- per kilogram to the BPL families and 35 kilograms of rice free of cost to the poorest of the poor.
February 2001	-	Sikkim awarded the Best Tourism performing state in the North East for 1999-2000 for the second consecutive year.
May 1st, 2001	-	Mr.K.N.Sahani sworn in as the new Governor of Sikkim
August 14th, 2001	-	Free Hepatitis B vaccine programme for children launched.
September 5th, 2001	-	Two historic Documents: Sikkim Human Development Report 2001 and Sikkim: The People's Vision were published and released by the Prime Minister in Delhi
September 6th, 2001	-	Computerised Ration Card programme launched
January 2002	-	Old age pension of ex-servicemen enhanced from Rs. 150 to Rs. 200 p.m.
February 1st, 2002	-	Governor, Mr.Kidar Nath Sahani inaugurated Head Race Tunnel of Teesta (Stage V) Hydroelectric Project at Dhupidara.
October 25th, 2002	-	Mr.V.Rama Rao sworn in as the 12th Governor of Sikkim.
December 18th, 2002	-	Lok Sabha clears deck for tribal status to Tamang and Limboo communities.
2002 & 2003	-	Sikkim bags Tourism National Award for the best performing state for the fourth consecutive year.
April 11th, 2003	-	Prime Minister, Mr.Atal Behari Vajpayee visited Sikkim for four days.
April 29th, 2003	-	First Bio-Diversity park inaugurated at South Sikkim.
May 27th, 2003	-	Sikkim's first Chief Minister, Kazi Lhendup Dorji Khangsarpa awarded Padma Vibhusan.
August 21st, 2003	-	Samman Bhawan inaugurated.
September 8th, 2003	-	Chintan Bhawan inaugurated.
September 10th, 2003	-	Confederation of Indian Industry CEOs conclave with the Governor's and Chief Ministers of North East States held.
October 11th, 2003	-	Chief Minister, conferred Degree of Doctor of Philosophy (Honoris Causa) by Manipal University
December 6th, 2003	-	Bicable Jigback Ropeway inaugurated at Deorali.
December 2003	-	Reservation in all Government jobs revised with 33% of seats for Scheduled Tribe, 6% to SC and 21 % to OBCs. 30% reservations for women in Government jobs, 33 percent in

		Panchayats for women, 3% for Ex-Servicemen and persons with disabilities and 2% for Sportsperson and artisans of excellence.
January 26th, 2004	-	Late Sanjog Chhetri was posthumously conferred the prestigious Ashok Chakra by the President of India.
February18th, 2004	-	Chief Minister, Dr.Pawan Chamling formally inaugurated 135 feet tall statue of Sikkim's Patron Saint, Guru Padmasambhava at Samdruptse in South Sikkim.
February 28th, 2004	-	Chief Justice of India, Justice V.N.Khare inaugurated new High Court Building at Sichey.
May 21th, 2004	-	Dr.Chamling and his Council of Ministers sworn in for the third consecutive term.
June, 2004	-	Mr.Nakul Das Rai took oath in Nepali as Sikkim's lone Lok Sabha M.P.
July 14th, 2004	-	Eminent Nepali speaking Indian felicitated during Sikkim Samman Sammilan.
August 2004	-	M.G.Marg declared as litter and spit free zone.
August 6th, 2004	-	Sikkim ranks first among the smaller states in the field of Education and among the first three best performing states in the field of Law and Order, Health and Investment scenario at a conclave of Chief Minister organized by India Today Group.
August 12th, 2004	-	Janata Bhawan inaugurated in Gangtok.
August 15th, 2004	-	Former Chief Minister, Kazi Lhendup Dorji Khangsarpa conferred Sikkim's highest civilian award, Sikkim Ratna.
January, 2005	-	Mr. G.S.Lama conferred with Padma Shri
April 21st, 2005	-	His Holiness the Dalai Lama visited Sikkim.
April, 2005	-	Union Minister for Home Affairs, Mr.Shivraj Patil visits
May, 2005	-	Union Minister for Finance, Mr .P. Chidambaram inaugurated Security Ink Plant of SICPA India Limited in Mamring.
July 22, 2005	-	Sikkim Renewal Energy Development Agency (SREDA) Bhawan inaugurated.
August 6, 2005	-	Sikkim awarded Best Small State for Investment Environment and Best Small State for Education.
September 18th, 2005	-	Summiteers of Mt.Khangchendzonga felicitated.
September 22nd, 2005	-	The President of India, Dr.A.P.J.Abdul Kalam inaugurated ultra modern Paljor Stadium.
October 5th, 2005		Sang Sr School, the oldest school in Sikkim celebrates its 125th Anniversary
December, 2005	-	Mr.O.T.Lepcha elected as the Member of Rajya Sabha from Sikkim
March 2nd, 2006	-	Kanchenjunga Shopping Plaza inaugurated.
March 28th, 2006	-	Sikkim receives Skoch Challenger Award for best usage of Information Technology.
February 27th, 2006	-	State Green Mission launched.
March 2006	-	Chief Minister, Dr.Pawan Chamling visits 6 European Nations for study tour.
April, 2006	-	Sikkim stood third in best performing state in Panchayati Raj in India.
April 2006		Chief Secretary inaugurates the Community Information Centre at Sherathang, the Higest Cyber Cafte in the world (Limca Book of Records-2007 edition)
July 6th, 2006	-	Nathula Trade Route reopens after 44 years and a Trade Mart inaugurated at Sherathang.
August 1st, 2006	-	Dr.D.K.Gazmer sworn in as the first State Chief Information Commissioner of Sikkim.
August 18th, 2006	-	Vice-President of India, Mr.Bhairon Singh Shekawat visits Sikkim.

August 29th, 2006	- Archer Tarundeep Rai conferred the prestigious Arjuna Award by the President of India.
September 1st, 2006	- Sikkim ranks first among the twelve eastern states of India in overall performance, sectors of primary health, investment environment and budget and prosperity at the 4th State of the States Conclave in New Delhi organized by the India Today.
September 8th, 2006	- Indoor Stadium/Multipurpose Community Centre inaugurated at Namchi.
November 18th, 2006	- Lepchas accorded Primitive Tribe status.
November 18th, 2006	- First Block Administration Centre inaugurated at Yuksom
December 13th, 2006	- Rajya Sabha passes Sikkim University Bill 2006.
December 20th, 2007	- Chief Minister lays foundation stone for Bhutia Literary Centre.
December 27th, 2006	- President of India, Dr.A.P.J.Abdul Kalam inaugurated 14th National Children's Science Congress at Sikkim Manipal Institute of Technology.
January 25th, 2007	- Sikkim awarded the Best performing state in Tourism in North East for the year 2005-06.
February 24th, 2007	- Sikkim hosts 21st North East Sports Festival.
April 15th, 2007	- CM inaugurated Sri Satya Sai Sarva Dharma Kendra at Daramdin.
April 27th, 2007	- Sikkim hosts 4th Sectoral Summit on Tourism and Hospitality of North Eastern Council.
Jan 10th 2008	- Thai trade delegation visists Sikkim
Feb 2008	- Baichung Bhutia conferred the Padma Shree
March 14th-16th 2008	- International Florishow 2008 held at Saramsa Garden Inaugurated by Montek Singh Aluwalia Dy Chairman Planning commission Remodelled MG Marg inaugurated Remodelled Ridge Road inaugurated
April 9th-10th 08	- Workshop on E-Governance at Chintan Bhawan
April 19th 2008	- Water Shed Memorial inaugurated at Sherathang in memory of the soldiers who laid their lives f
June12th -14th 08	- Kharif Kisan Mela at Saramsa
May 22th 08	- Mountaineer, including two women from Sikkim scale Mount Everest
June 15th 08	- Foundation stone of Tista Urja Stage III Hydel Project laid at Chungthang by Dr Pawan Chamling
June 16th, 2008	- Sikkim Income Tax Manual of 1948 revoked by theFinance Act 2008 exempting Sikkimese people from being assessed under the Indian Income Tax Act
July 9th, 2008	- B.P. Singh sworn as the Governor of Sikkim Inauguration of the Regional Administrative Centre at Karfectar (Jorethang)
Sept 29th, 2008	- Sikkim Bandh to protest against CM effigy burning incident
Nov 10th, 2008	- Meeting with Thirteenth Finance commission
Nov 18th, 2008	- CM addresses Global Climate change Summit at California
April 20th, 2009	- Sikkim Assembly and Parliamentary elections held New SDF Government installed
July 15th, 2009	- 10 minutes to earth programme held all over Sikkim in which 6 lac tree saplings planted as part of the State Government's Green Mission
Sept17th &18th, 2009	- SIKITEX 2009National level Exhibition and Conference organised by Information Technology Department in Chintan Bhawan

Oct 30th, 2009	-	Laying Foundation Stone of 52.70 km long railway line between Sevok and Sikkim at Rangpo Mining Ground by Vice President of India H. Ansari and Union Railway Minister Ms Mamta Banerjee
Dec 5th, 2009	-	Kumari Selaja Union Minister lays foundation stone of Basic Services to Urban Poor (BSUP) at Rangpo
Jan 25th, 2010	-	Sub Office of Reserve Bank of India established in Gangtok
Feb 10th, 2010	-	Foundation stone of 575 bedded Multi speciality STNM Hospital laid at Suchak gang
Feb 23rd, 2010	-	The Headquarters of India Reserve Battalion inaugurated at Piplay Jorethang
April 15th, 2010	-	President visits Sikkim inaugurates 'Khangchendzonga Tourist Villa' at Ranka Municipal Elections to urban local bodies held
April 27th, 2010	-	International Rhododendron Festival held at Lachung/Singba Rhododendron Forest Reserve
June 15th, 2010	-	5th Phase of Green Mission and 2nd Phase of 10 minutes to Earth unveiled at Chintan Bhawan by Chief Minister
June 25th, 2010	-	10 minutes to Earth programme held all over Sikkim
July 16th, 2010	-	Common Wealth Games Queen's Baton arrives in Sikkim
August 7th, 2010	-	National Seminar on Mountain regions and climate change at Gangtok
August 26th, 2010	-	CM launches Comprehensive Annual and Total Check up for Healthy Sikkim
Sept 18th, 2010	-	Governor inaugurates Sikkim Guest House at Salt Lake Kolkata
Oct 7th, 2010	-	CM inaugurates SIKITEX 2010 an IT exhibition at Chintan Bhawan
Nov 3rd, 2010	-	CM inaugurates Shridi Sai Baba Mandir at Assangthang
Dec15th, 2010	-	HH Dalai Lama visits Sikkim
Jan 14th,2011	-	CM lays foundation stone of Green Park Project and ingurates newly constructed parking Plaza at Jorethang
Jan 21st, 2011	-	CM inaugurates District Library cum Museum and Car Parking cum Shopping Plaza in Namchi
Feb 09th	-	Horticulture show 2011 inaugurated at Gyalshing
Feb 16th	-	Sikkim participates in World Organic Trade Fair in Germany
Feb 26 th	-	Sikkim conferred IBN 7 Award as best small state in citizen security
May 17th	-	CM embarks on a month long tour around Sikkim
June 28th	-	CM inaugurates Government Degree College at Gyalshing
Sept 18th	-	Sikkim hit by 6.8 magnitude earthquake
Sept 29th	-	Prime Minister visits Sikkim
Oct 25th	-	CM lays foundation stone for underground tunnel at Theng North Sikkim
Nov 2nd	-	Kanchendzonga Amusement Park at Rank opens
Nov 8th	-	Shrideshwar Dham (Char Cham) in Namchi inaugurated.
Nov 11th	-	National Education Day observed
Nov 24th & 25th	-	3rd IT Exhibition and Conference SIKITEX held
Feb 4th, 2012	-	CM awarded the Bharat Asmita Jewan Gaurav Purasker
Feb 29th 2012	-	Chardham at Namchi bags the Most Innovative and Unique Tourism Project Award 2010

VISITING SIKKIM AND ITS PLACES OF INTEREST

BEST SEASON TO VISIT

The best season to visit Sikkim will to a great extent depend on what you are really interested in.

If you want to be assured of a clear sight of the snowy ranges as well as clear skies, then the best months to visit this region would be mid-October to mid of January (over the last three to four years it has been noticed that the monsoons even extend to the third week of October). It does however tend to get cold in December and January. For trekking, I feel the months of October and November are the most suitable; March and April are also fine for trekking at altitudes less than 4000 metres but can be hampered by occasional heavy showers and hail. The sky is hazy in the month of March and April but this is amply compensated by the rhododendrons and other flowers in bloom. Snow at high altitudes -4000 metres to 6000 metres- persists till May and therefore it is not possible to trek at these altitudes from December to May. If you are interested in alpine plants at altitudes above 3000 metres the best months to see them are August and September. If Buddhism holds your interest, then a visit in December is appropriate as the month is full of Buddhist festivals.

PERMITS AND GENERAL INFORMATION

Indian nationals do not require any permit to visit unrestricted areas in Sikkim, like Gangtok, Rumtek, Pemayanste, Yoksum, Phodong etc. However to visit restricted areas under army control, like Changu, Nathula and Yumthang, Indian Nationals are required to obtain an Restricted Area Permit from the Sikkim Police at Gangtok. The travel agent can arrange thepermit for you within a few hours. Besides Changu, Nathula and Yumthang, Indian Nationals are not normally permitted to visit other restricted places in Sikkim. Only under special circumstances visits to other restricted places in Sikkim is permitted but permission is required to be sought from the Home Department, Government of Sikkim. Although the Dzongu area of Sikkim does not fall in the restricted area, a permit from the Home Secretary, Government of Sikkim is required to visit it.

The Government has also levied Environmental Fees and Entry Fees for trekkers, the details of which have been spelt out in a different chapter.

Foreign nationals would require an Inner Line Permit besides their visa to visit any part of Sikkim. Indian Embassies abroad, representatives of Government of Sikkim at Delhi, Calcutta and Siliguri and some other offices have been authorised to issue these permits to foreigners. Foreign nationals are permitted to visit Gangtok, Rumtek, Phodong and Pemayanste and other specified areas on the basis of their visas for a period totalling fifteen days that can further be extended till sixty days. Foreigners are also permitted to trek to many areas in Sikkim provided they are in a group of two or more. They are also permitted to visit the Changu Lake and the Yumthang valley provided they are in groups. Foreigners are not permitted to visit Nathula pass. For details of entry formalities and the trekking routes that have been opened to foreigners, the relevant section towards the end of this book may be referred to.

The Tourist Information Centre (☎ 03592-205277) can always be contacted for any clarifications.

GETTING TO SIKKIM AND OTHER PLACES FROM SILIGURI

The primary means of communication within Sikkim is by road: there is no railway and therefore it is not surprising that many people in Sikkim have never travelled by train. However Sikkim is well connected to rest of the country by rail and air through Siliguri in West Bengal which is about 115 kilometres from Gangtok and forms the railhead of Sikkim. To get to Sikkim you must reach Siliguri first. Siliguri incidentally is an important nerve centre also for Bhutan, the eastern part of Nepal and Darjeeling, another picturesque hill station 80 kms away. There are no direct routes from Sikkim to Nepal or Bhutan by road: one has to travel via Siliguri. Kathmandu is an overnight journey from Siliguri through Kakribitta on the Nepal border and Dhulabari, which is famous as a market for foreign goods and is a one hour drive away. One has to reach Kakribitta first by local bus from where long distance buses for Kathmandu are available. Phunsoling on the Bhutan border is about four hours away enroute to Thimphu the capital of Bhutan.

Siliguri has two railway stations: the New Jalpaiguri Railway station on the Broad Gauge and the Siliguri Junction on the Meter Gauge Railway line. New Jalpaiguri Railway station in Siliguri is connected to almost all parts of India by train. There are four daily trains to Delhi which cover the distance in about 30 hours. These trains originate from Guwahati. Many daily trains are also available for Calcutta covering the distance in about 10 hours. South-bound trains to Cochin, Trivandrum, Madras, Banglore and Bombay are also available althought these are not daily

The airport of Siliguri is known as Bagdogra. Daily Indian Airline and Jet Airways flights for Delhi, Calcutta, Guwahati are available. There is a daily Helicopter Service between Bagdogra and Gangtok. The railway and the air timetable towards the end of this book may be consulted for details.

Many buses both State Government and Private and shared taxis (Tata Sumos, Commander Jeeps etc that acccommodate 10-12 passengers) ply the route between Siliguri/New Jalpaiguri and Gangtok and some other important places in Sikkim. Buses to Gangtok are available from 6.30 am to 3.30 pm from bus stands of the Sikkim Nationalised Transport (SNT), opposite the Siliguri Junction and the Tenzing Norgay Bus Terminal also opposite the Siliguri Railway Junction. Private taxis can also be hired to travel to Sikkim. From Siliguri, buses to Darjeeling (80 kilometres), Kalimpong (70 kilometres), Phunsoling (150 kilometres), Guwahati (480 kilometres), Calcutta (600 kilometres) and some other important places in Bihar, West Bengal and Assam are available.

From Siliguri, Darjeeling falls on a different route than Gangtok. From

Darjeeling the usual two routes to Gangtok are the shorter and steep road via Peshoke and the longer one via Mongpoo. The shorter route can only be negotiated by small vehicles. For reaching Kalimpong from Siliguri the usual route is to take the road for Gangtok till Tista from where a bifurcation branches to that town. As can be seen from the road maps, these places can also be reached by other routes which are used only when the shorter routes are blocked due to landslides or some reason or the other.

Buses of the Sikkim Nationalised Transport (SNT) ply within various places in Sikkim. The Tourism Department of the Government of Sikkim and many travel agencies organise conducted tours to the Yumthang hot springs in North Sikkim and the Changu Lake. Private taxis can also be hired to all the places of tourist interest at rates that have been fixed by the Tourism Department. As distances are small, travelling within Sikkim is not expensive specially if it is done in groups. Tourists are permitted to take their private vehicles to all parts of Sikkim. During the monsoons, due to heavy rainfall, road communication is frequently disrupted because of landslides and it is always safe to first check up with the Tourist Information Centre or Sikkim Nationalised Transport about the condition of the road before making a move. Taxis abound in Gangtok although distances within the town are rather short. Unfortunately, Gangtok does not have a city bus service worth the name.

PLACES OF INTEREST

There is more to Sikkim than just natural beauty. Sikkim does provide a wide potential in tourism that has yet largely remained unexploited. The perennially snow-capped mountains, lush green tropical and temperate forests, gurgling streams and the rich flora and fauna are all there for the tourist to savour.

Sikkimese hospitality tangibly manifests itself in the intricately designed welcome gates with pagoda type roofs that are normally located at the entrances of monasteries and important public buildings. Wayside resting sheds which Sikkim abounds in also have curved roofs and pillars around which painted dragons curl themselves. So much so that even public buildings, powerhouses and other structures tend to look like huge pagodas in a true blend of typical Tibetan and modern architectures.

Besides the natural beauty that one continuously beholds while in Sikkim, there are many places that deserve a special mention. These are given below.

GANGTOK

Straddling a ridge, Gangtok has a cosmopolitian flavour with a lively mix of cultures and has undergone rapid modernization in the last two decades or so. Being the capital of a state, Gangtok contains all modern facilities. There are good schools, a railway outagency, an Indian Airlines Counter, cinema halls, a well-equipped hospital, fast food centres and telephone booths for making outstation calls and sending faxes.

With expansion, Gangtok town is literally spilling downwards with huge buildings precariously clinging to the hillside. It is infact becoming a concrete jungle with trees vying for space in the town area. Where is the wooden shop that was there yesterday or that beautiful tree that adorned the corner of the road?

Big hoardings advertise products, including some exhorting "Practise of Safe Sex and Use of Condoms to prevent Aids" . A banner elsewhere trumpets the opening of an Internet Cafe and another put up by a local environment group Green Circle exhorts the public not to use plastic carry bags and keep Gangtok clean.

The Government Bus Terminus is located about 5 minutes walk away from the M.G. Marg. The M.G Marg is out of bounds for vehicles. Gangtok has a few Taxi and Bus Stands. If you are coming by bus or shared taxi from Siliguri, you will be dropped at the Taxi Stand at Deorali which is two kilometers short of Gangtok town. If you are leaving for South and West District, then you will catch your shared taxi from the Taxi stand near M.G. Marg. If going to North Sikkim, you can catch your taxi from the Stand near Vajra Cinema Hall.

An imposing manmade landmark of Gangtok is the 60 metres high TV tower which overlooks the town and is situated near the Enchey Monastery below Ganesh Tok. The Main Market which has hotels, restaurants, curio, garment, footwear and grocery shops lines the flat Mahatma Gandhi Marg.All buildings on M.G.; Marg have been painted green in line with the green initiatives taken by the state. The Government is exhorting house owners in other areas and towns to also paint their buildings green.

GETTING AROUND AT GANGTOK (☎Country Code-0091, Area Code-3592)

Staying and Eating

Gangtok offers an excellent range of places to stay from expensive hotels to cheap and comfortable lodges all within walking distance from the bus stands. Hotel Denzong Regency(☎201565) is very upclass having rich rooms offering a good view of Gangtok Town and the Kanchendzonga Range. Hotel Royal Plaza also has well appointed rooms in the range of Rs 6000/-. Chumbi Residency (☎226618) on Tibet Road charges about Rs 1900 for a standard room. But for a real hotel experience try Mayfair 10 kms away from Gangtok beginning Rs 12000/-

For traditional paying guest accommodation, Netuk House (202374) on Tibet Road charges Rs 3700 for double bed inclusive of meals.

For a full course meal, the restaurant at Hotel Tibet should be visited. Although expensive you can be assured of the quality of the food. It is neat, hygenic and comfortable with crockery that is impeccable. Unique Sweets and Metro's Fast Food Centre both on the MG Marg and National Highway intersection are good placs to taste Indian snacks. Baker's Cafe again on the M.G. Marg has an European ambience and is a great place to relax while sipping coffee and relishing the pizzas, cakes, pastries and salads. The Rasoi Fast Food Centre and restaurant just adjacent to the Tourist Information Centre is another good eating joint. For good North Indian fare try Apna Dhaba and Masala on M.G. Marg. Masala can be tried for vegetarian dishes. Domino pizzas, Subway, Coffee Day Cafe, Tripitis and Cacao can be tried for bakery and confectionary items.

Ticketing Agencies and Travel Agents

Gangtok has a computerised Railway Outagency at the SNT Government Bus Stand Terminus (☎ 202016) where one can book railway tickets for any train in India. The Outagency is open from 8 am to 2 pm everday and 8 am to 12 noon on holidays and Sundays. Very often the out-agency is not able to issue tickets because of technical problems specially bad connectivity. Therefore avoid making last minute changes/ booking of your railway journey. For cancellations, go only after 10 am as refund is paid from the money that has been collected till that time: the outagency does not have any money early in the morning.

Silk Route Tours and Travel & Coxs & King(☎203354) on first floor of Green Hotel on M.G. Marg issues tickets for all airliness on any sector and a few buildings further away is Josse & Josse (☎205534).The Tourist Information Centre (☎222064) can be contacted for Helicopter tickets.

For arranging your travel within Sikkim some of the travel agents you could contact are: Yoksum Tours and Treks (☎206822) Near Telephone Exchange There are many other travel agents as well.

Casinos

Sikkim is fast emerging as a new destination for tourists who want to experience the thrills of gambling. Royal Plaza Hotel (☎281570) at Syari Gangtok boasts of the first land based Casino in India and offers Roulettes, Blackjack and electronic slot machines. Casino Majong in Hotel Mayfair(☎250128) also offers similar gambling options.

Discos and Night Clubs

As of now Gangtok does not have much of a night life, but there are a few Night Clubs where people can unwind. X- Cape (☎209887)at Vajra Cinema Hall Complex is one popular discoteque. Code Oranage near Ranipu about 8 kms from Gangtok is another popular joint.

Language

The language used for communication in Sikkim is Nepali. However everybody seems to know a smattering of Hindi thanks to the Cable TV. In major towns most people can communicate in English. Written official correspondences in Sikkim take place in English.

Business Hours

All Sikkim Government Offices and banks follow a six day week. While the Government offices have 10 am to 4 pm working hours with Second Saturdays off, banks are open from 10 am to 2 pm (on Saturdays 10 am to 12 noon). Both the banks and Sikkim Government Offices follow the Government of Sikkim Almanac which has many holidays. The Central Government Offices like the Central Public Works Department have a five day week (10 am to 5 pm). Restaurants open as early as 7 am but also close early: by 8 pm. The markets open by 7 am and close by 7 pm. The Tourism Department Information Counter (☎ 222064) is open from 8 am to 7 pm during the season (April to June & October to November)

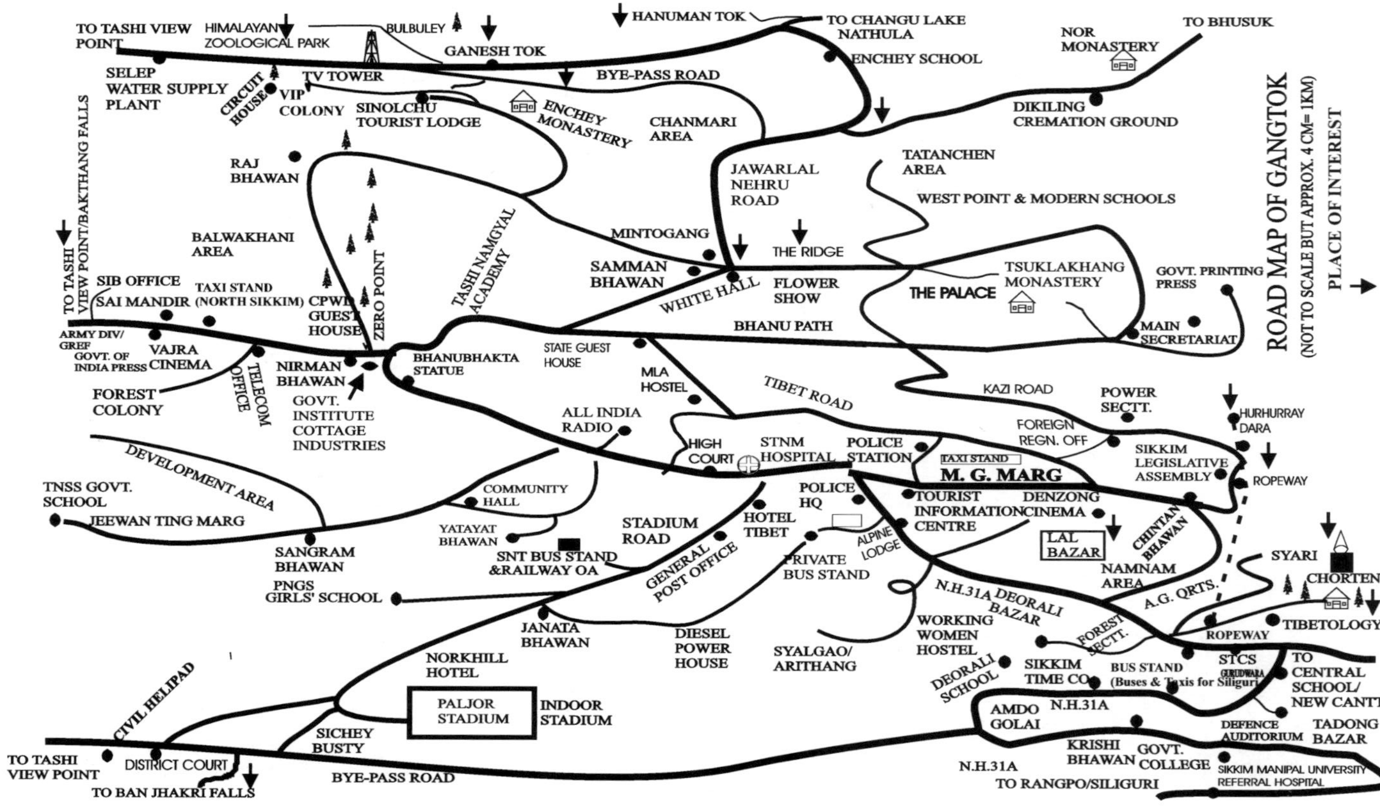
ROAD MAP OF GANGTOK
(NOT TO SCALE BUT APPROX. 4 CM= 1KM)
PLACE OF INTEREST
TO TASHI VIEW POINT
HIMALAYAN ZOOLOGICAL PARK
BULBULEY
GANESH TOK
HANUMAN TOK
TO CHANGU LAKE NATHULA
ENCHEY SCHOOL
NOR MONASTERY
TO BHUSUK
SELEP WATER SUPPLY PLANT
CIRCUIT HOUSE
VIP COLONY
TV TOWER
SINOLCHU TOURIST LODGE
ENCHEY MONASTERY
BYE-PASS ROAD
CHANMARI AREA
DIKILING CREMATION GROUND
RAJ BHAWAN
JAWARLAL NEHRU ROAD
TATANCHEN AREA
WEST POINT & MODERN SCHOOLS
BALWAKHANI AREA
MINTOGANG
THE RIDGE
TO TASHI VIEW POINT/BAKTHANG FALLS
SIB OFFICE
SAI MANDIR
TAXI STAND (NORTH SIKKIM)
CPWD GUEST HOUSE
ZERO POINT
TASHI NAMGYAL ACADEMY
SAMMAN BHAWAN
WHITE HALL
FLOWER SHOW
THE PALACE
TSUKLAKHANG MONASTERY
GOVT. PRINTING PRESS
BHANU PATH
MAIN SECRETARIAT
ARMY DIV/ GREF
GOVT. OF INDIA PRESS
VAJRA CINEMA
TELECOM OFFICE
NIRMAN BHAWAN
BHANUBHAKTA STATUE
STATE GUEST HOUSE
MLA HOSTEL
TIBET ROAD
KAZI ROAD
POWER SECTT.
FOREST COLONY
GOVT. INSTITUTE COTTAGE INDUSTRIES
ALL INDIA RADIO
FOREIGN REGN. OFF
HURHURRAY DARA
HIGH COURT
STNM HOSPITAL
POLICE STATION
TAXI STAND
M. G. MARG
SIKKIM LEGISLATIVE ASSEMBLY
ROPEWAY
DEVELOPMENT AREA
TNSS GOVT. SCHOOL
JEEWAN TING MARG
COMMUNITY HALL
POLICE HQ
TOURIST INFORMATION CENTRE
DENZONG CINEMA
YATAYAT BHAWAN
STADIUM ROAD
HOTEL TIBET
ALPINE LODGE
LAL BAZAR
CHINTAN BHAWAN
SANGRAM BHAWAN
SNT BUS STAND &RAILWAY OA
GENERAL POST OFFICE
PRIVATE BUS STAND
NAMNAM AREA
SYARI
CHORTEN
PNGS GIRLS' SCHOOL
N.H.31A DEORALI BAZAR
A.G. QRTS.
TIBETOLOGY
JANATA BHAWAN
DIESEL POWER HOUSE
SYALGAO/ ARITHANG
WORKING WOMEN HOSTEL
FOREST SECTT.
ROPEWAY
NORKHILL HOTEL
DEORALI SCHOOL
SIKKIM TIME CO
BUS STAND (Buses & Taxis for Siliguri)
STCS
GURUDWARA
TO CENTRAL SCHOOL/ NEW CANTT.
CIVIL HELIPAD
PALJOR STADIUM
INDOOR STADIUM
AMDO GOLAI
N.H.31A
SICHEY BUSTY
DEFENCE AUDITORIUM
TADONG BAZAR
TO TASHI VIEW POINT
DISTRICT COURT
TO BAN JHAKRI FALLS
BYE-PASS ROAD
N.H.31A
KRISHI BHAWAN
GOVT. COLLEGE
SIKKIM MANIPAL UNIVERSITY REFERRAL HOSPITAL
TO RANGPO/SILIGURI

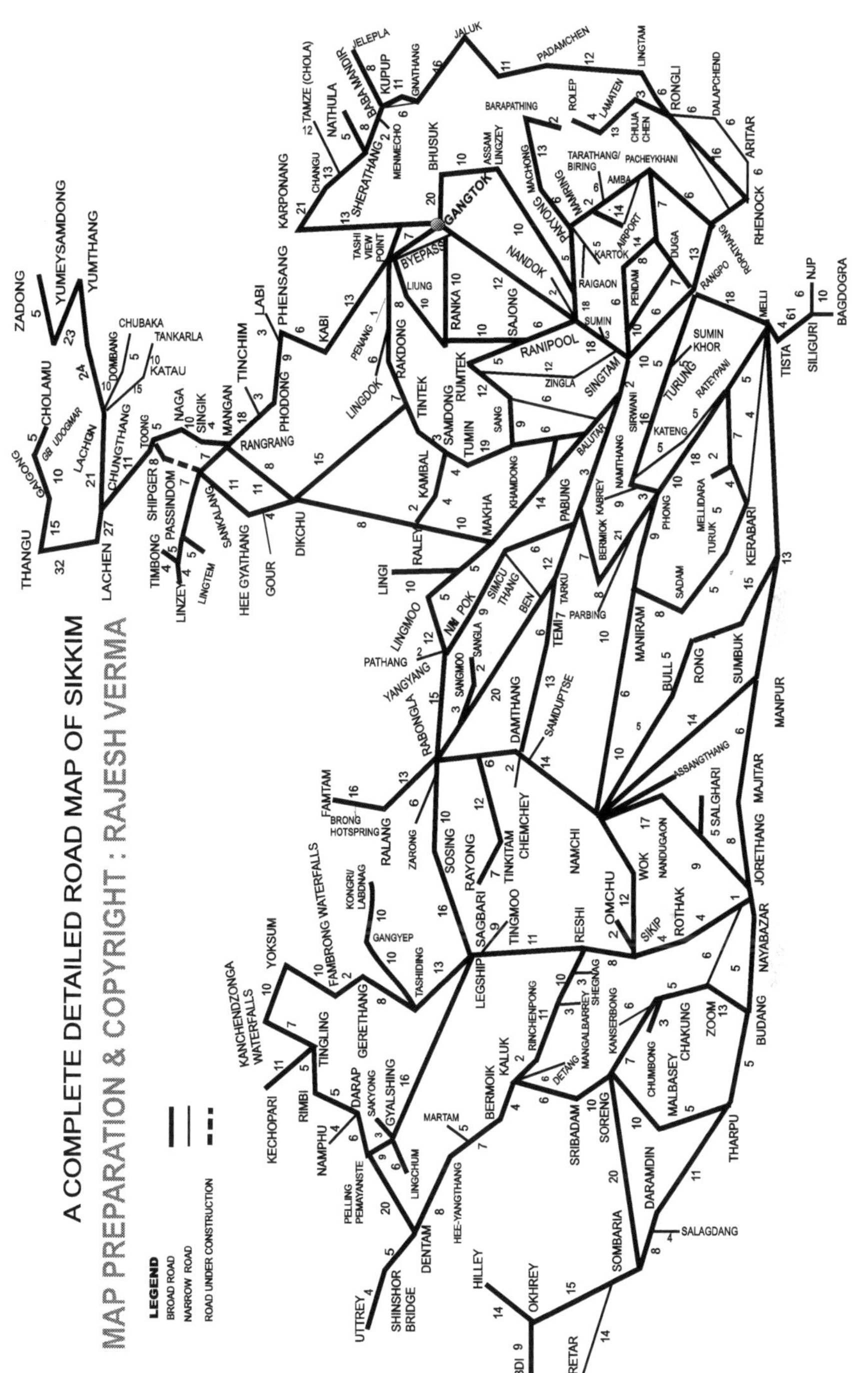
A COMPLETE DETAILED ROAD MAP OF SIKKIM
MAP PREPARATION & COPYRIGHT : RAJESH VERMA
LEGEND
BROAD ROAD
NARROW ROAD
ROAD UNDER CONSTRUCTION
THANGU
ZADONG
YUMEYSAMDONG
YUMTHANG
GAGONG
CHOLAMU
LACHUNG
CHUBAKA
TANKARLA
KATAU
DOMBANG
LACHEN
CHUNGTHANG
TOONG
NAGA
SINGIK
MANGAN
TINCHIM
LABI
PHENSANG
KARPONANG
CHANGU
TAMZE (CHOLA)
NATHULA
BABA MANDIR
JELEPLA
KUPUP
GNATHANG
MENMECHO
SHERATHANG
JALUK
PADAMCHEN
LINGTAM
RONGLI
DALAPCHEND
ARITAR
RHENOCK
ROLEP
LAMATEN
CHUJA CHEN
BARAPATHING
BHUSUK
GANGTOK
ASSAM LINGZEY
TASHI VIEW POINT
BYEPASS
LIUNG
RANKA
SAJONG
NANDOK
MACHONG
PAKYONG
MAMRING
TARATHANG/ BIRING
PACHEYKHANI
AMBA
AIRPORT
KARTOK
RAIGAON
PENDAM
DUGA
RANGPO
RORATHANG
MELLI
TISTA
SILIGURI
NJP
BAGDOGRA
SUMIN
RANIPOOL
ZINGLA
SINGTAM
SUMIN KHOR
TURUNG
RATEYPANI
KATENG
SIRWANI
RUMTEK
SANG
SAMDONG
TINTEK
RAKDONG
PENANG
LINGDOK
PHODONG
KABI
RANGRANG
SHIPGER
PASSINDOM
SANKALANG
TIMBONG
LINZEY
LINGTEM
HEE GYATHANG
GOUR
DIKCHU
TUMIN
KAMBAL
MAKHA
KHAMDONG
BALUTAR
PABUNG
NAMTHANG
KABREY
BERMIOK
PHONG
MELLIDARA
TURUK
KERABARI
LINGI
RALEY
LINGMOO
SIMCU THANG
POK
BEN
TARKU
PARBING
TEMI
PATHANG
YANGYANG
RABONGLA
SANGMOO
SANGLA
DAMTHANG
SAMDUPTSE
MANIRAM
SADAM
BULL
RONG
SUMBUK
MANPUR
FAMTAM
BRONG HOTSPRING
RALANG
ZARONG
SOSING
RAYONG
TINKITAM
CHEMCHEY
NAMCHI
ASSANGTHANG
SALGHARI
MAJITAR
JORETHANG
NANDUGAON
WOK
OMCHU
RESHI
SIKIP
ROTHAK
NAYABAZAR
YOKSUM
FAMBRONG WATERFALLS
KONGRI/ LABDNAG
GANGYEP
TASHIDING
SAGBARI
TINGMOO
LEGSHIP
KANCHENDZONGA WATERFALLS
TINGLING
GERETHANG
KECHOPARI
RIMBI
DARAP
SAKYONG
GYALSHING
NAMPHU
PELLING PEMAYANGTSE
LINGCHUM
MARTAM
BERMOIK
KALUK
RINCHENPONG
DETANG
MANGALBARREY
SHEGNAG
KANSERBONG
CHUMBONG
CHAKUNG
ZOOM
BUDANG
SRIBADAM
SORENG
MALBASEY
THARPU
DARAMDIN
SALAGDANG
SOMBARIA
HEE-YANGTHANG
DENTAM
UTTREY
SHINSHOR BRIDGE
HILLEY
OKHREY
RIBDI
PURETAR

Postal Service and Courier

The Post Offices in Sikkim follow a six day week (10 am to 3 pm) with only four or five public holidays in a year. The Head Post Office (☎ 225442) at Gangtok is well equipped. There are many reputed courier in Gangtok as well. They areBlue Dart (205790) DTDC (281985), Gati (281401) Overnight Express (203813)

Telecommunication

Gangtok and the district headquarters have many telephone booths from where you can make international calls. Some of them are also equipped with fax machines. Most of these booths open by 6 am but close by 9 pm. Gangtok also has good mobile coverage provided by BSNL, Reliance and Airtel.

Banks and ATMs

Gangtok has all the major banks . Listed below are the banks in Gangtok and some surrounding areas. Most of the banks have their ATM. (See Chapter on Travel for the telephone numbers of the Banks in the state)

Money Transfers

Western Union has an officein the General Post Office.Tourists can have their remittances from abroad collected here.

Internet Cafes

There are many internet cafes on the M.G. Marg and can be used for sending and receiving e-mail messages and browsing the internet. The Government run Community Information Centre, at t the Main Secretariat charges only Rs 20 per hour of browsing.

Money Changing

Branches of State Bank of India are to be found at all the major towns here and they readily convert foreign hard currency to local currency. However these banks follow the local holiday calender and they are sometimes closed for days together with frequent strikes: so carry sufficient local currency before coming here. Notes of Rs 500 denominations should be preferred as they can be carried easily. However when visiting places that are remote, carry a sufficient assortment of Rs 50, Rs 10 and Rs 5 notes as getting change for higher denomination notes can be a problem. Some of the big hotels are authorised to change money and many also accept credit cards.

Bookshops

In Gangtok, Jainco (☎ 203774) , Citinews (☎225660) and Goodbooks on M.G. Marg, Pasupati Nath (☎228212) on the Lal Bazar Road and Alphabets(☎ 222973) Opp. Hotel Tibet are all well stocked with books and magazines. Rachna(☎204336, www.rachnabooks.com, mail@rachnabooks.com) near Community Hall is a quiet place just 5 minutes walk away from the hustle and bustle of MG Marg and stocks wide range of books especially on Sikkim. M/S D.K. Pandey(☎207096) on Tibet road also stocks books.

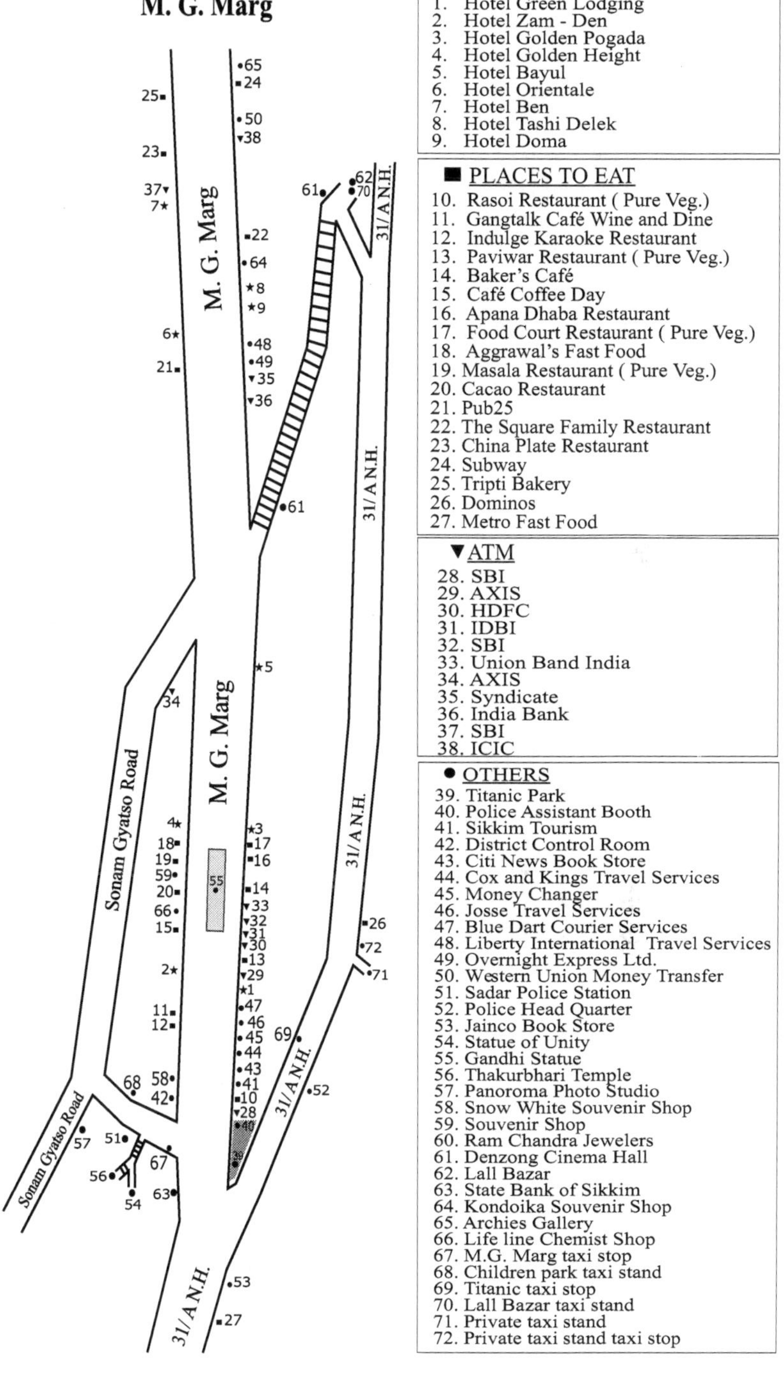
M. G. Marg
M. G. Marg
M. G. Marg
Sonam Gyatso Road
Sonam Gyatso Road
31/A N.H.
31/A N.H.
31/A N.H.
31/A N.H.
31/A N.H.
★ PLACES TO STAY
1. Hotel Green Lodging
2. Hotel Zam - Den
3. Hotel Golden Pogada
4. Hotel Golden Height
5. Hotel Bayul
6. Hotel Orientale
7. Hotel Ben
8. Hotel Tashi Delek
9. Hotel Doma
■ PLACES TO EAT
10. Rasoi Restaurant (Pure Veg.)
11. Gangtalk Café Wine and Dine
12. Indulge Karaoke Restaurant
13. Paviwar Restaurant (Pure Veg.)
14. Baker's Café
15. Café Coffee Day
16. Apana Dhaba Restaurant
17. Food Court Restaurant (Pure Veg.)
18. Aggrawal's Fast Food
19. Masala Restaurant (Pure Veg.)
20. Cacao Restaurant
21. Pub25
22. The Square Family Restaurant
23. China Plate Restaurant
24. Subway
25. Tripti Bakery
26. Dominos
27. Metro Fast Food
▼ATM
28. SBI
29. AXIS
30. HDFC
31. IDBI
32. SBI
33. Union Band India
34. AXIS
35. Syndicate
36. India Bank
37. SBI
38. ICIC
● OTHERS
39. Titanic Park
40. Police Assistant Booth
41. Sikkim Tourism
42. District Control Room
43. Citi News Book Store
44. Cox and Kings Travel Services
45. Money Changer
46. Josse Travel Services
47. Blue Dart Courier Services
48. Liberty International Travel Services
49. Overnight Express Ltd.
50. Western Union Money Transfer
51. Sadar Police Station
52. Police Head Quarter
53. Jainco Book Store
54. Statue of Unity
55. Gandhi Statue
56. Thakurbhari Temple
57. Panoroma Photo Studio
58. Snow White Souvenir Shop
59. Souvenir Shop
60. Ram Chandra Jewelers
61. Denzong Cinema Hall
62. Lall Bazar
63. State Bank of Sikkim
64. Kondoika Souvenir Shop
65. Archies Gallery
66. Life line Chemist Shop
67. M.G. Marg taxi stop
68. Children park taxi stand
69. Titanic taxi stop
70. Lall Bazar taxi stand
71. Private taxi stand
72. Private taxi stand taxi stop

Local periodicals

The dailies "NOW" and "Sikim Express" are good newspapers that are packed with information on what is happening locally. The weekly official bulletin of the Government, the Sikkim Herald also has a lot of local news.

Public Library

The Community Hall Library (☎ 222029) has good books on Sikkim. The reading room is comfortable and well stocked with newspapers and magazines. The Library is open from 11.30 am to 5 pm daily (even on Sundays) but remains closed on Wednesdays and public holidays.

Public Toilets

Gangtok has quite a few pay and use toilets run by Saulab International.

Cinema Halls and video parlours

Denzong Cinema (☎202692), Near Lal Bazar and Vajra (☎202861) with 70 mm screen at Balwakhani show the latest Hindi and English movies. There are three shows: 11.30 am, 2.30 pm and 5.30 pm. There are many video parlours in town as well.

Flower Nurseries

Hidden Forest (☎225197), Himalayan Flora (☎222223) and Wayside Gardens and Nurseries(☎250706) in and around Gangtok can be visited for those interested in plants. The Flower Show venue on Ridge Road also stocks plants for sale.

Photography

Films and batteries are available in all major towns in this region. However you may have problems finding films for slides. Orient Studio (☎ 224114) and Panorama Studio (☎ 225098) can process your films within 24 hours. Panorama also processes slide films but the delivery period is about a week.

Medical facilities and Chemists

Chiranjilal Lalchand (☎203762), Life Line Medicos (☎222864) and Sree Krishna Medical Store (☎224807) all on M.G. Marg are well stocked with all types of medicines. Care Diagnostics (☎203870, 204555) Opp. Private Bus Stand, can be contacted for various pathological tests.The Government run STNM Hospital (☎222944) and Central Referral Hospital(☎231137) are well equipped to cater all sorts of emergencies. Besides, there are many private doctors in town as well.

Places of Worship

The Thakurbari complex near the Tourist Information Centre has small temples of the main Gods and goddesses of the Hindus. Sia Baba (Putaparti) Mandir is located at Balwakhani near the Vajra Cinema. There is a Protestant Church (CNI) and a Catholic Church both near the main town. A mosque is located next to the Private Bus Stand.

There are many religious organsiations in Sikkim which organise regular prayer meetings. Tourists affliated to these organisations may like to visit them if time permits. Some of them are Brahma Kumaris, The Art of Living, Vipasana, Chinmaya Mission, Sahaj Marg.

The towering Statue of Guru Padmasambva at Sadumupste near Namchi

A lama dancer at Pemayanste Monastery

Rumtek Monastery

A panoramic view of Gangtok town from Ganesh Tok showing some landmarks

Temple at Hanuman Tok, Gangtok

A resthouse on the Ridge Road

Institute of Tibetology, Gangtok

The Chorten, Gangtok

Ropeway at Gangtok

Enchey Monastery

M.G. Marg, Gangtok

A busy road in Gangtok

PLACES OF INTEREST IN GANGTOK

The Government has fixed the taxi rates (Van with capacity for 4 passengers) for the following sightseeing points

3 point(Tashiview point, Gangesh Tox Hanuman Tok: Rs 387

5point(Chorten, Tibetology, Cottage Industries, Enchey Monastery Hurhuray Dara: Rs 363

7 point Chorten, Tibetology, Cottage Industries, Enchey Monastery, Hururay Dara, Saramsa Garden, Rumtek Monastery: Rs 762.

However I would personally recommend the following itinerary:

Early morning (6am-8 am): Visit Enchey Monastery, Ganesh Tok, Hanuman Tok, Tashi View Point and Bakthang Waterfalls and be back in the hotel for breakfast at 8 am.

After breakfast

9.00 am- 9.15 am Gangtok to Ban Jhakri Falls (6km)

9.15 am - 9.40 am Halt at Ban Jhakri Falls (Open from 9 am to 5 pm on all days, Entry Rs 10/-)

9.40 am - 9.50 am Ban Jhakri Falls to Kanchendzonga Tourist Complex (3km)

9.50 am - 10.30 am Halt at Kanchendzonga Amusement Park Entry fees Rs 100

10.30 am - 10.40 am Kanchendzonga Tourist Complex to Lingdum Monastery (4 km)

10.40 am-11am Halt at Lingdum Monastery

11 am - 11.20 am Lingdum Monastery to Rumtek Monastery (18 km)

11.20 am - 12.00 noon Halt at Rumtek Monastery

12.00 noon - 1.15 pm Rumtek Monastery to Tibetology/Chorten (Gangtok) with a 20 minutes halt at Rumtek Monastery or Shanti View Point for light lunch (22km)

1.15 pm - 2.00 pm Visit Tibetology Museum and Chorten (Chorten Stupa can be visited any part of the day any day. However the Tibetology is open from 10 am to 4 pm on working days only. Entry fee to museum Rs 5/-)

2.00 pm - 2.15 pm Tibetology to Government Cottage Industry(3km)

2.15 pm -3.00 pm Shopping for souvenir at the Govt. Cottage Industry. Pay a shsort vist to the Weaving and Thanka painting Centres

3.00 pm-3.10 pm Government Cottage Industry to Flower Show on the Ridge(1 km)

3.10 pm - 3.30pm Visit the Flower Show on the Ridge

3.30 pm-3.40 Flower Show to Hururay Dara/Ropeway Middle Terminus at Nam Nam (1km)

3.40 pm - 4.30 pm A two minute walk to Hurhuray Dara gives you a breataking viw of the deep valley. Then take a Ropeway ride to Terminus at Deorali and back. (Ropeway ride Rs 60/- both way. Same price charged if the ride is taken one way, Open from 9 am to 5 pm)

4.30 pmTake Five minutes walk from Nam Nam to M.G. Marg where you can spend about half an hour for momos or Pizzas at Baker's Cafe. Shop for

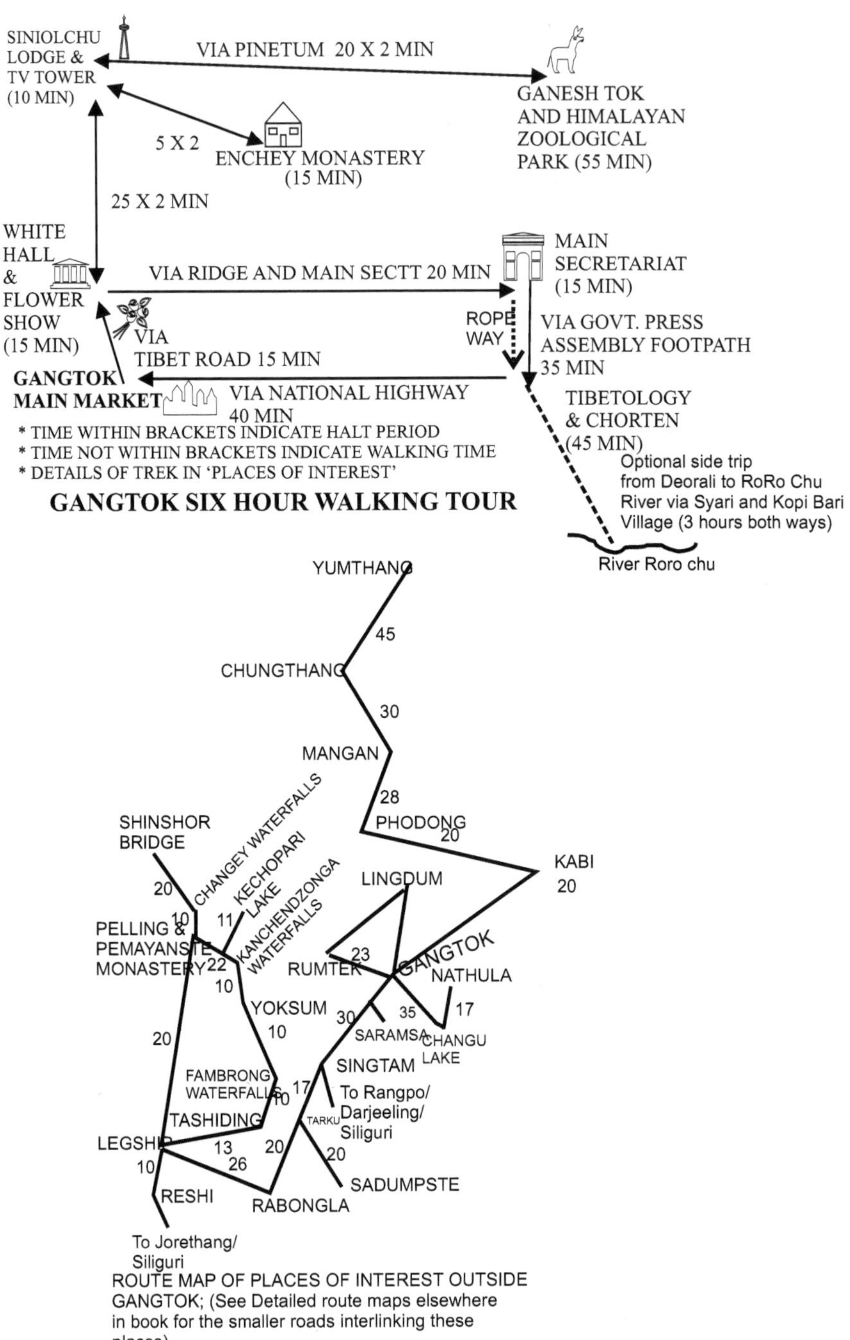

ROUTE MAP OF PLACES OF INTEREST OUTSIDE GANGTOK; (See Detailed route maps elsewhere in book for the smaller roads interlinking these places)

Sikkim Tea and Cardamom and other souvenir . Visit Lal Bazar close by and return to your hotel by 6.30 pmTry Hotel Tibet for Dinner.

The above itinerary would be hectic but it can be done if you are short of time. A visit to Himalayan Zoological Park opp. Ganesh Tok requires almost one and a half hour and therefore you may like to split your visit to two days.

If you are visiting Changu and Nathula, Hanuman Tok can be visited on the wauy back. Similarly if you are visiting Yumthang, Bakthang Waterfall and TashiView Point can be visited on the way. You may also try to squeeze in a 20 minute Helicopter Mountain flight (costing Rs 1200/- per person)

For those who are interested in walking and saving money, the Gangtok six hour walking tour described elsewhere in this chapter can be undertaken and would cover all the points mentioned above except the Tashi View Point, Hanuman Tok and the Government Institute of Cottage Industry.

These places of interest and some others have been described below.

Research Institute of Tibetology

About a kilometre downhill from the main market of Gangtok, amidst a small forest of oak, magnolia and birch trees stands the Institute of Tibetology. The building accommodating the Institute is an example of Tibetan architecture. It is world renowned and is one of the few of its kind. Its library is well stocked with rare books and documents on Buddhism. There are about 30 thousand volumes, mostly xylographs,(xylographs are documents that are printed using wooden slabs that have the matter embossed on them in the reverse) translations of the original teachings of the Lord Buddha, and treatises by distinguished Buddhist scholars from different parts of the world. The museum at the Institute consists of rare collection of antiques like statues, coins and Thankas which are scrolls with paintings on them. This institute is a premier institute in the world that conducts research in the language and culture of Tibet. It has on its faculty eminent scholars. The library and museum of the Institute are open to the public 10 am to 4 pm on all days excluding holidays and Sundays. An entry fees of Rs 5 is charged.

The foundation stone of the Institute was laid in February 1957 by the Dalai Lama and it was inaugurated by Pandit Jawaharlal Nehru in October 1958.

Phurba-Chorten

Just adjacent to the Research Institute of Tibetology, a few hundred feet away, on a small hillock is located this huge and towering religious monument which is in the form of a stupa. The periphery of the chorten is surrounded by 113 small prayer wheels with the mystic mantra "Om Mane Padme Hum" in Tibetan inscribed on them. The Chorten was built by Late Trul Shik Rimpoche, who was the head of the Nyingma Order, and late Chogyal of Sikkim Tashi Namgyal in the mid forties to invoke the Gods to keep peace and tranquility in the state. Placed inside the Chorten are a complete set of Kanjur holy books, relics, complete mantras and other religious objects. A small chorten known as Jhang Chub Chorten was built besides the Phurba Chorten in the memory of Trul Shik Rimpoche who passed away in 1962.

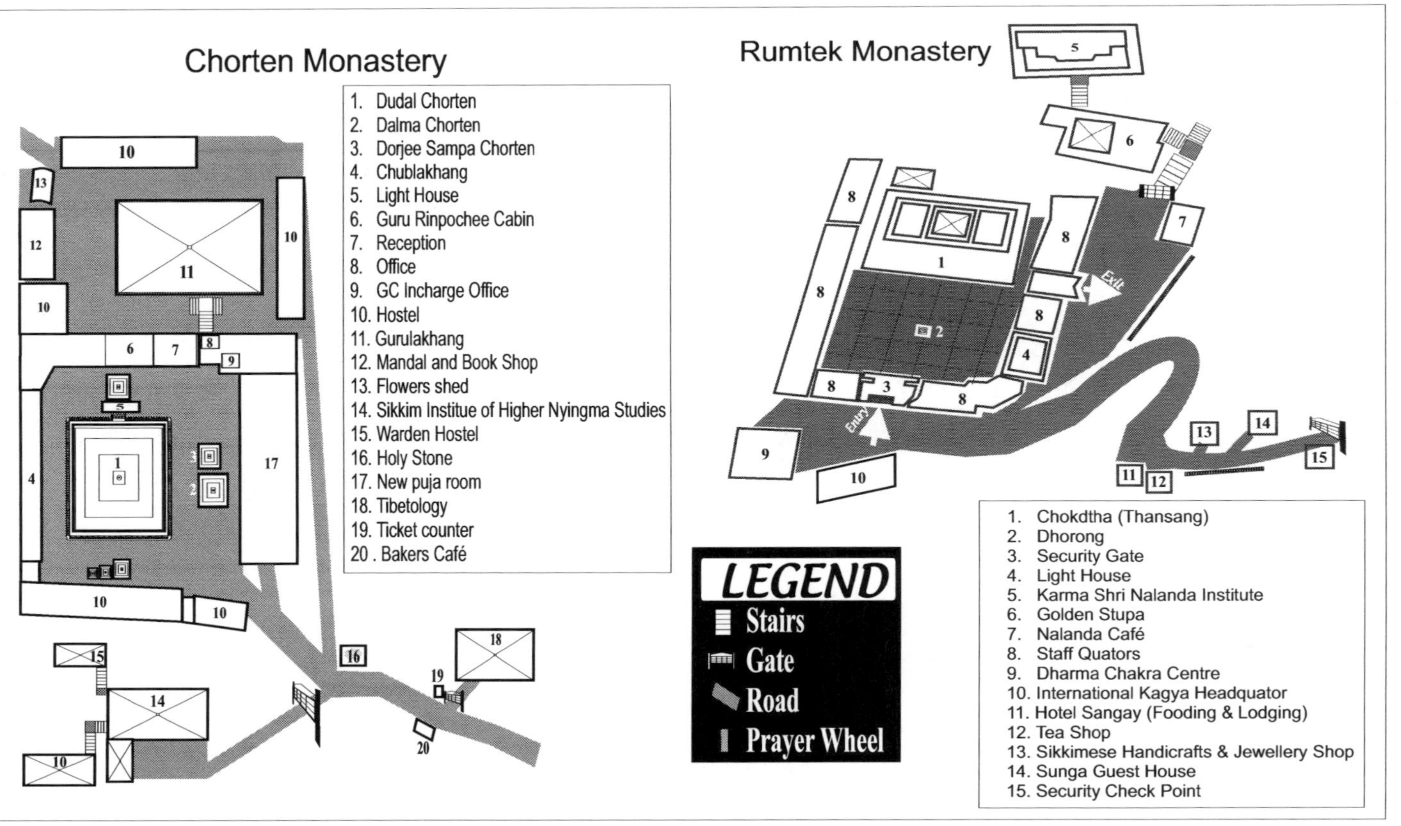
Chorten Monastery
1. Dudal Chorten
2. Dalma Chorten
3. Dorjee Sampa Chorten
4. Chublakhang
5. Light House
6. Guru Rinpochee Cabin
7. Reception
8. Office
9. GC Incharge Office
10. Hostel
11. Gurulakhang
12. Mandal and Book Shop
13. Flowers shed
14. Sikkim Institue of Higher Nyingma Studies
15. Warden Hostel
16. Holy Stone
17. New puja room
18. Tibetology
19. Ticket counter
20 . Bakers Café
Rumtek Monastery
Exit
Entry
LEGEND
Stairs
Gate
Road
Prayer Wheel
1. Chokdtha (Thansang)
2. Dhorong
3. Security Gate
4. Light House
5. Karma Shri Nalanda Institute
6. Golden Stupa
7. Nalanda Café
8. Staff Quators
9. Dharma Chakra Centre
10. International Kagya Headquator
11. Hotel Sangay (Fooding & Lodging)
12. Tea Shop
13. Sikkimese Handicrafts & Jewellery Shop
14. Sunga Guest House
15. Security Check Point

Government Institute of Cottage Industries (GICI)

This institute is located at about a kilometre uphill from the main market of Gangtok. It was established, in 1957 with the purpose of promoting the manufacture and sale of local handicrafts, carpets and furniture. An emporium at the institute sells handicrafts, Thankas which are scrolls with paintings, hand carved foldable wooden tables known as Choksees and exquisitively woven woollen carpets, masks and dolls. Hand made paper is another unique novelty of the Institute and is made from the bark of a tree Argali. The paper is used extensively for invitation cards and letter-pads. It is open from 10 am to 4 pm and closed on government holidays.

Flower Show, The Ridge and The White Hall

The Ridge is a small stretch of plain and flat road above the town of Gangtok. It is just about fifteen minutes walk from the main market. The Ridge has the White Hall and the Chief Minister's official residence, known as the Mintogang, meaning "blossomed crowned hilltop" on one end and the beautifully designed Palace Gate with a pagoda rooftop on the other end. A statue of Nehru, the late Prime Minister of India, adorns the roundabout above White Hall. Situated on the Ridge is also a resting shed using Tibetan architecture. The ridge is lined with plants and trees which when in bloom are a riot of colours. Flower shows which attract tourists from all over the world are held just below the Ridge.

The White Hall only has historical value and is situated on the Ridge. It is a two storeyed structure and has typical British architecture and was built in 1932. Till the nineteen sixties, all important functions used to be held in this hall in memory of the first Political Officer Claude White.

Enchey Monastery

This monastery is located just adjacent to the Tourist Lodge (Siniolchu Lodge) and the TV Tower about a kilometre uphill from the White Hall. The monastery is located in a dense wood and one can see the Kanchendzonga range over the crown of trees.

Lama Druptob Karpo is supposed to have built a small hermitage at this spot after he flew here from Maenam Hill more than two hundred years ago. During the reign of Sidkeong Tulku, a monastery was built here in 1901 in the form of a Chinese Pagoda. The monastery follows the Nyingma Order and the main puja and dances are held here on the 18th and 19th of the twelfth month of the Tibetan calendar which normally corresponds to the month of December.

Hurhurray Dara

Located just next to the Sikkim Legislative Assembly and the ropeway terminus, this view-point offers an excellent view of the deep valley below with the river Ro-ro chu snaking through it.

Jig Back Ropeway

Inaugurated on 7th Dec 2003, the ropeway operates between the Main Secretariat Deer Park , Sikkim Legislative Assembly and the Tibetology at Deorali. The two cable cars have a capacity of accommodating 25 passengers each. A one way trip taking about 10 minutes costs Rs 60/- :it is worth the money as the ride gives a breathtaking view of the river about 1000 metres below as well as the Deorali Bazar.

Tashi View Point

Situated about six kilometres away from Gangtok on the North Sikkim Highway, this place offers an astounding view of the Kanchendzonga snowy range. On the opposite hill, the Phodong and the Labrang monasteries can be seen. A resting shed and a small cafeteria situated at Tashi View Point provides shelter and other amenities to the tourists. A park above the View Point is a good place to enjoy a picnic.

Ganesh Tok & Pinetum

Ganesh Tok is located on the hill adjoining the TV Tower. A small temple of God Ganesh nests on the hilltop at an altitude of 2000 metres (6500 ft). The temple is so small in size that it can hardly accommodate one person and one has to crawl to get inside it. A panoramic view of Gangtok town and the Raj Bhawan Complex can be obtained from here. All the snowy peaks on the western border including the mighty Kanchendzonga are visible from here and present a breathtaking scene. During the tourist season, a small cafeteria is opened for the convenience of the visitors. Just adjoining the Ganesh Tok is a pinetum garden containing pine trees. A walk on the footpath amongst the pine trees is refreshing.

Himalayan Zoological Park

The park is located exactly across the road opposite Ganesh Tok and covers an area of 205 hectares. This area is also known as Bulbuley and extends almost upto Hanuman Tok. Although a 3 kilometres long jeepable road runs right through the park, vehicles are not allowed in. There is a paved cement path that passes by fenced open air enclosures housing the red pandas, barking deer, bears and other animals of Sikkim in a semi natural habitat. As the enclosures encompass a huge area the animals are sometimes not easily visible and one has to be patient to get a sight of them.

Hanuman Tok

Situated about five kilometres uphill from White Hall on a bifurcation road of the Gangtok Nathula Highway, is a temple of God Hanuman at an altitude of 2195 m (7200 ft). From the temple, the snowy peaks of Kanchendzonga present a panoramic picture. As you offer your prayers, the statue of Lord Hanuman gazes down at you. The temple of Hanuman is flanked by a small temple of Shirdi Saibaba.

A short distance before the stair case leading to the Hanuman Temple is the cremation ground of the erstwhile royal family of Sikkim. The cremation ground has stupas and chortens each marking the place where the mortal remains of the departed souls were consigned to the flames.

Bakthang Waterfall

Bakthang waterfall is located three kilometers away from Gangtok on the North Sikkim Highway towards Tashi View Point. Though the waterfall is not vry high, it is picturesque with the water falling over a canopy of green creepers. A good place to stop for a few minutes on the way to Tashi View Point.

M.G. Marg Main Market

Every major town in India has a Mahatma Gandhi Road and Gangtok is no exception. Slightly less than a kilometre in length, this impeccable "Litter & Spit Free" boulevard road is flat and is lined with shops which constitute the Main Market and downtown of Gangtok. All buildings on the M.G Marg are painted green. Overlooking the M.G. Marg is the Statue of Unity which depicts the meeting of the Bhutia Chieftan Khye Bumsa with the Lepcha leader Thetong Tek and his wife Ngo-kong-ngol. Almost midway, is the bust statue of Mahatma Gandhi. The market has hotels, restaurants and shops selling all types of consumer goods. There are many liquor shops and bars too: literally Bacchus' backyard! The shops are open by 8 am and close by 7 pm. This market is closed on Tuesdays.

Lal Bazar (Kanchendzonga Shopping Complex)

Located just below the Main Market a few minutes walk away is the Lal Bazar which has renamed to Kanchendzonga Shopping Complex. It used to be an open space market encircled with shops This market was built in 1956 and named thus in honour of J. Lal, a Dewan of the Chogyal. In 2004-05 it was demolished and a multistoried complex vegetable shopping complex built in its place. If you are interested in seeing how different cultures - old and new as well as diverse - blend together here in Sikkim, then a visit to the Lal Bazar on Hat Day that is Sunday is a must. Villagers in bakhus(Bhutia dress), daura-saurals(Nepali dress) and Bihari businessmen in dhotis brush shoulders with urbanites sporting jeans and chic fashions communicating with each other in Bhutia, Lepcha, Nepali and Hindi over the blare of both Indian and Western songs - a seemingly Tower of Babel! The wares on sale are equally diverse - from local cottage-cheese, incense sticks to the latest electronic gadgets. The smell of fish, spices, cheese and vegetables permeates the air. For me and many others in Gangtok, a visit to the Lal-Bazar on Sundays is almost a weekly ritual, carrying a couple of bags and purchasing vegetables and fruits in the jostling crowd. Even persons holding high positions have no qualms about carrying their own vegetable bags once they are in the Lal-Bazar which transcends all classes and distinctions.

This market along with the market on the Lal Bazar road that connects it to M.G. Road is closed on Thursdays.

GANGTOK SIX HOUR WALKING TOUR(with option for an extra 3 hour rural trek to river side)

If you are fond of a little walking, it is suggested that you see Gangtok on foot: the city itself a trekking trail waiting to be explored. And the distances are not much that calls for artificial mode of transport. It will enable you to feel the contemporary life of the town. Most of the important places of interest in Gangtok can be seen on foot at a leisurely pace within six hours. You can start after having an early breakfast and be back in time for lunch.

The unpredictable showers may be a hindrance but what is a visit to Gangtok without getting a little drenched.

From Gangtok Bazar a walk of about fifteen minutes through the Tibet Road takes you to the Nehru Point just above White Hall which is at four crossroads. Before reaching the White Hall the claustrophobic assemblage of buildings - urban canyons - start breaking apart and is replaced by tall trees and gardens. You take the road that passes below the Chief Minister's Official residence also called Mintogang and reach the Tashi Namgyal Academy Upper Gate. A walk up the steep road on the right takes you to the Siniolchu Tourist Lodge. Catch your breath and enjoy the panoramic view of Gangtok far down below you. The walk from White hall till here has taken about half an hour. In another ten minutes you are ready to move again. A walk of another five minutes takes you to the Enchey Monastery. Spend about fifteen minutes seeing the Monastery which is itself situated in a thick forest. From the Enchey Monastery you take the track uphill just below the TV Tower, through the Pinetum under the shadow of beautiful pine trees and reach the Bye-Pass Road. A walk of a few more minutes and you are at Ganesh Tok. The walk between the Monastery and Ganesh Tok takes about twenty minutes. At the Ganesh Tok, it is like floating high up in the air. The TV tower and the Enchey Monastery lie just below your foot and the town of Gangtok further down. The whole Kanchendzonga range in front presents a heavenly sight and serenely gazes back at you. Enjoy the scenery for about ten minutes and you are ready to walk down.Spend about forty-five minutes watching wild animals in the Himalayan Zoological Park just opposite Ganesh Tok. Follow the same route back to the White Hall and take fifteen minutes to watch the Flower show. If you feel, rest a while at the traditionally designed resting shed on the Ridge and enjoy the fragrance of the flowers around.

Another walk of about twenty minutes on the Ridge and around the Palace area takes you to the Main Secretariat Complex and the Rustomji Park through the Pagoda gate. Walkinn the ridge and around the palace, you are reminded that this area used to be once the seat of power of the Chogyals - bubbling with activity and visited by many dignitaries. The palace now stands forlorn and desolate - a far cry from the good old days. Spend 10 minutes strolling around the Main Secretariat which is now the seat of power and the Rustomji Park which has a statue of Buddha . Far below, the glistening white Chorten with its yellow crown seems to peep out from the forest and beckon you. From the Main Secretariat you move further down and take the well paved foot-path connecting the Government Press and the Legislative Assembly Building. From this footpath the view of the river Roro-chu, which flows almost a thousand metres below, is breathtaking. On reaching the imposing Sikkim Legislative Assembly Building you move downwards to Nam Nam. The steep road down from Nam Nam reaches you to Deorali and further down to Tibetology and the Chorten. The walk down from the Main Secretariat to the Chorten takes just over half an hour at a leisurely pace. Alternatively you can take the ropeway from the Assembly Building to the Chorten. Walk around the Chorten and spin the prayer wheels on which are inscribed the mantra "Om Mane Padme Hum" and also visit the monastery with the towering statue of Guru Padmasambva in it. Spend about twenty minutes at the Tibetology and walk back to Gangtok Bazar in about forty five minutes.

This trek has taken you only about six hours and has given you a real feel of the town and its way of life. The afternoon can be kept for a visit to the Government Institute of Cottage Industries for souvenir purchasing and the evening for going around the market. A route map of the trek is also shown elsewhere in the book.

If you have a a few more hours to spare then a trek through the countryside to the river is an interesting addition. From close to the lower terminus at Deorali walk ten minutes down to the Syari Cooperative Store past the Hotel Royal Plaza. Take the Concrete Foothpath down to Kopibari village a further fifteen minutes away.

Kopibari has all the ingredients of a pastrol way of life. Cowsheds, small maize and ricefields and huts made of wood and tin sheets. And there is even a small village school. It is difficult to comprehend that 15 minutes away from town and you are in a different world. Take the steep footpath down to the riverside through a thick forest punctuated here and there by huts with thatchwed roots. Within half an hour you are at the river Roro Chu. Explore the river and its surrounding and walk across the supension bridge across it. Partake to the packeed lunch that you surely will be caryying with you. The walk back to the Main road would take about an hour and fifteen minutes.

PLACES OF INTEREST OUTSIDE GANGTOK IN EAST DISTRICT

The Saramsa Garden

This garden,established in 1922, is located at a distance of about 14 kilometres downhill from Gangtok, 2 kilometres from Ranipool. The area covered by this garden is six acres. This garden was earlier known as the Ipecac garden because of the medicinal plant(used ofr treating emetine) by that name grown here from 1940 till 1970 when its cultivation became commercially unviable. This garden contains a wide variety of other flora including numerous types of orchids and medicinal plants. A large green house also accommodates many other species. The garden is a very popular picnic spot. In March 2008, the International Flori Show was held here. One has to take a taxi to reach this place.

Rumtek Monastery

The monastery is at a distance of 23 kilometres from Gangtok. In fact it is located on the hill facing Gangtok.

The present monastery was constructed by His Holiness, the Gyalwa Karmapa in 1960s. Gyalwa Karmapa was the sixteenth Karmapa and came to settle in Sikkim in the late fifties when the Chinese invaded Tibet. He passed away in 1981.

The Kargyugpa Sect of Buddhism has its origins in Tibet in the twelfth century. It is said that after the first Karmapa spent many years meditating in a cave, ten thousand fairies came to congratulate him and each offered a strand of hair. These strand of hair were woven into a black hat. This black hat came to be passed down and is still at the Rumtek Monastery. It is said that unless held with the hand, or kept in a box, it will fly away. It was worn by the Karmapas on ceremonial occasions.

The monastery is certainly the largest in Sikkim and is an example of fine Tibetan architecture. The Main Monastery is three storied and has a large prayerhall on the ground floor lined with small tables which the monks use to keep their religious books to read during prayers. The prayer hall is intricately decorated with Statues, wall paintings, thankas and tubular silk banners. On the first floor are the living quarters of the last Karmapa. The top floor has a terrace and a small stupa. The monastery is surrounded by a courtyard and the living quarters of the lamas. A flight of stairs from just outside the Main Monastery Complex takes you to the Nalanda Institute for Higher Buddhist studies. You are greeted by a huge painting of Lord Buddha just outside the Nalanda Institute: for the Buddhists gods loom large in art as they do in belief.

Just adjacent to it is a small hall that has a stupa that contains the bone and ashes of the Sixteenth Karmapa. The stupa is surrounded by small statues of all the earlier Karmapas. On the same level as the Nalanda Institute is a small two storied building, in which the Gyalwa Karmapa used to reside during the summers. A few metres ahead is an aviary containing the most exotic birds. The Gyalwa Karmapa had a special liking for birds and dogs and I have fond memories, as a child, of playing with his dog during one of my many visits there.

About half a kilometre uphill from the aviary is a hermitage in which monks go into complete seclusion for meditation for periods upto 3 years.

A fifteen minutes walk downhill from the Main Monastery takes one to the old Rumtek Monastery, which was first built in 1730 by the ninth Karmapa but was destroyed due to a fire and had to be reconstructed to its present state.

The main puja or dances of Rumtek also called the Tse-Chu Chaams are held on the 10th day of the 5th month of the Tibetan calender around June. Dances called the Kagyat are also held on the 28th and 29th day of the tenth month of the Tibetan calender in the Old Rumtek Monastery.

After the XVIth Karmapa passed away in 1981, the search began for his reincarnation. But it was almost ten years later that a boy who met the requirements was traced in Tibet. Ugen Thinley was recognised as the XVII th Karmapa by the Dalai Lama. Ugen Thinley escaped from Tibet in 2000 and is presently staying in Dharamshall in Himachal Pradesh.

There is a regular bus service to Rumtek and taxis are also abundantly available. Whereas the bus fare to Rumtek from Gangtok is about Rs 20 one way, hiring a taxi to Rumtek and back would cost about Rs 350. Cheap accommodation is offered in the few hotels around the monastery. There are also a couple of shops and one or two tea shops. Half a kilometre before the Main Monastery is the Shambala Tourist Resort(☎03592-252240 or252243) which provides modern amenities in typical rural settings with tourist huts built in traditional Lepcha, Bhutia and Nepali style.The Martam Village resort (☎223314,236843) 10 kilometres ahead of Rumtek is located in the tranquil countryside and offers accommodation in nine thatched cottages built in traditional syle but providing all modern facilities: a good place to get away from the hustle and bustle of modern life.

Shanti View Point

On the way to Rumtek Monasterty you can halt for a few minutes to get a view of Gangtok from here.

The Nehru Botanical Garden

This garden is located just half a kilometre before the Rumtek Monastery on the highway. A mixture of well tended tropical and temperate plants and trees can be found here. A huge greenhouse containing many species of orchids has been constructed within the garden. A cemented footpath winds its way through the garden and is good for taking a relaxed stroll. The sprawling town of Gangtok can be seen on the hill opposite. The garden is an ideal picnic spot.

Science Centre, Marchak

If you have the time and inclination it is worth visiting. Located in a sprawling area, showcases many sciientific exhibits. It even has a portable planetarium. A popular picnic spot "Smileland" with a swimming pool exists nearby.

Ban Jhakri Falls

Situated about 7 Kilometers from Gangtok on the way to Ranka, these waterfall is a popular picnic spot. Ban Jhakri is a mythical magician whose wife was a witch who used to eat children. But Ban Jhakri himself was a protector of children. Different masks of Ban Jhakri have been put up at this spot. An Energy Park using Non-conventional energy like solar power also co-exists here. There are exibits especially educative for children like slides,swings that generate electricity when you use them and this is used to power a demonstration bulb or a speaker.

Kanchendzonga Tourist Complex

Situated midway between Ban Jhakri Falls and Lingdum Monastery Kanchendzonga Amusement Park(☎03592-210780, www.ktcranka.com) is a nice place to visit and enjoy games like dashing cars, 4 D Ride simulator, Musical Fountain, swimming pool, bowling alley, snooker. For overnight stay there are traditional huts available.

Pal Zurmang Kagyud Monastery, Lingdum

For those interested in Buddhism, a visit to this monastery at Lingdum which lies on a bifurcation on the Gangtok-Rumtek road towards Ranka can be fruitful.It is the seat of the incarnation of Zurmang Gharwang Rimpoche. Built in 1997, this monastery is palatial in size.

Changu (Tso-Mgo) Lake

A lake at 3753 m(12,310 ft)! Impossible you will say but it is a fact. Changu lake is situated 35 kilometres from Gangtok on the Gangtok - Nathula highway which forms a part of the old trade route from India to China. Before 1962, caravans of mules carrying goods used to ply on this route. The stretch of the route just below Karponang, 15 kilometres from Gangtok was particularly dangerous. Its steepness resulted in many mules slipping to their death into the ravine below. Karponang is at an altitude of 3000 metres: an ascend of 1500 metres from Gangtok in less than 15 kilometres. Slightly less than 10 kilometres away from Karponang is 15th Mile or Kyongnosla which lies on a saddle on the Chola Range and from where a panoramic view of part of Gangtok and other surrounding hills can be obtained. The road has less gradient and the vegetation adopts an alpine nature. About a kilometre ahead of Kyongnosla and about five minutes walk from the roadside is the Tseten Tashi cave which is about twenty feet high and so named after a naturalist of Sikkim who was also the Private Secretary to the Chogyal.

Changu Lake, which is hardly 20 kilometres away from the famous Nathula Pass and about 400 kilometres from Lhasa, falls in the restricted area and hence an Inner Line Permit, which can be obtained from the Police through the Tourism Department or travel agent, is required by visitors to visit this place. Foreign nationals are also permitted to visit this lake. Photography is now allowed and in fact parts of few Hindi films have been shot here.

Its cool, placid water harmonises with the scenic beauty around which is doubled by its reflection in the lake. A small temple of Lord Siva is constructed on the lakeside. Primula flowers and other alpine vegetation grow around the lake, which has an average depth of 15 metres, lend a pristine beauty to this place. A footpath along the lake takes one to a resting shed - a walk of about half a kilometre. During the winter months the lake becomes frozen. The lake itself derives its water from the melting snow on the mountains around. During the olden times, lamas used to study the colour of the water of the lake and forecast the future. If the waters of the lake had a dark tinge, it foreshadowed a year of trouble and unrest in the state. The lake has a few rainbow trout and if you are lucky you may catch a glimpse at them.

A small cab in which not more than 3 passengers are permitted can be hired for Rs900 to Changu and back. Hiring of a jeep which can accommodate upto 7 passengers will cost about Rs 1200/-. Rides on yaks and mules are also offered at the lake site. Tea and snacks are available at the shopping compex about 200 metres before the lake. It has a pay and use toilet. Some of the stalls even keep film rolls and offer jackets, snowboots and gumboots on hire.

Because of the high altitude, heavy woollens are required to be worn here throughout the year. There is no facility of accommodation for the tourist. It is advisable to visit the lake before noon as usually during the afternoons the weather becomes inclement. Those with breathing problems should avoid exerting themselves too much because of the scarcity of air at this altitude.

Sherethang Trade Mart

A small market has been set up at Sherathang 6 kilometers short of Nathula. Traders from China come here four times a week to sell their goods. A major attraction in the Mart is the Community Information Centre which is the highest Cyber cafe in the world.

Nathula Pass

Nathula at 4320 m (14400 ft) remained as the major pass connecting Sikkim to Tibet till 1962. It was through this pass that trade between the two countries used to be carried out with trains of mules carrying wool, gold, rock-salt and borax and taking back essential items of daily use from India. From Nathula, Yathung the erstwhile famous tradepost in the Chumbi Valley in Tibet is just 30 kilometres away. During clear weather, the road winding down the Chumbi valley can clearly be seen and on the eastern horizon looms the Chomolhari peak that is situated in Bhutan. The Chinese soldiers are also visible a few metres away from the barbed wire that marks the border between the two countries. The exchange of mail takes place every Thursday and Sunday with the Indian postman crossing over to the Chinese outpost and meeting his counterpart to carry out the transaction. An engraved stone also known as the Nehru Stone marks the visit of the Late Prime Minister of India Jawarlal Nehru to Nathula in 1958. The Nathula border was quiet during the Indo-China war in 1962. However because of a dispute over the demaraction of territory by barbed wire firing took place between the armies of the two sides in 1965. In 1967 there was a major confrontation in which many lives on both sides were lost. A memorial has been built in honour of the Indian soldiers who lost their lives in this battle.The trade route through Nathula was reopened on 6th July 2006 for a few items.

There are active talks taking place between China and India to resume full fledged trade between the two countries through this pass. When this happens, China would benefit immensely as it would have access to the Kolkata port reducing freight costs especially to places like Lhasa in Tibet.

The Nathula pass can be visited by Indian tourists only on selected four days a week. The Travel Agents in Gangtok can arrange to get a pass to visit Nathula and also arrange a shared taxi which would cost Rs 450/- per passenger both ways (including environment fees).

Baba Harbhajan Singh Temple (Baba Mandir)

This temple lies on the road between the Nathula and the Jelepla pass. There is a touching story behind the establishment of the temple. Harbhajan Singh was a sepoy in the Punjab Regiment. In October 1968, while escorting a column of mules carrying provisions, he fell into a stream and drowned. A few days later he appeared in the dream of a colleague of his and expressed a desire that a monument in his memory be built. His colleagues in the regiment considered the dream to be auspicious and felt that if they fulfilled his desire he would protect them from agression and mishap. The temple was thus built and has over the years acquired the status of a place of pilgrimage. Visitors leave a bottle of water which they then arrange to collect a few days later. It is said that drinking the water is wish-yielding.

Although long dead, it is understood that the sepoy has been promoted to the rank of Honorary captain and his salary is even sent to his home in Punjab. Once a year arrangements are made to send him on leave to his home town. A berth is booked in a train and his uniform placed on it. A soldier from the regiment accompanies.

There is a souvenir shop which also issues computerised certificates certifying your visit to this place. Just adjacent is a cafe.

Jelepla pass

Like Nathula, Jelepla also falls on the Eastern border of Sikkim. A half an hour drive from Nathula, this pass offers breathtaking scenery and overlooks the famous Younghusband Trail which was traversed by Younghusband in 1904 when he led an army on an expedition to Lhasa. During the old days, the traders in Kalimpong used to prefer this route for sending their goods to Tibet. At Jelepla, the Chinese positions are at quite a distance.

Menmecho Lake

This is another beautiful lake located twenty kilometres ahead of the Changu lake. The 2 kilometres length steep narrow road from the Baba Harbhajan Singh Temple reaches the lake. Quite big in size, it lies cradled between the mountains below the Jelepla pass and is also the source of the river Rangpo-chu which meets the Tista at Rangpo. Like the Changu Lake, it also derives its water from the melting snow around especially from the stream that originates just below the Jelepla pass. The lake is famous for its trout and a farm to cultivate these fish also exists nearby. Accommodation for the visitors coming here is available at the dak bunglow and tourist lodge near the lake.

Lampokhari, Aritar

Set amidst a thick forest this lake is situated in the South East corner of Sikkim a few kilometers away from Rhenock. Boating facility is available at the lake. There are a few hotels that provide good accommodation.

PLACES OF INTEREST IN NORTH SIKKIM

Kabi Longstok

Twenty kilometres on the way to North Sikkim, before Phodong, is Kabi Longstok where the treaty of brotherhood between the Lepcha chieftain, Tetong Tek and the Tibetan chief Khye Bumsa was signed. The spot where the treaty was signed is marked by a memorial stone and lies amidst the shadows of tall trees and cardamom fields. Slightly ahead is a small monastery.

Phodong Monastery, Labrang Monastery and Tumlong Palace ruins

All these three are located within an area of one square kilometre and about 40 kilometres from Gangtok on the North Sikkim Highway.

Phodong Monastery which belongs to the Kargyupa Sect (Karmapa), is situated about a kilometre uphill by a jeepable road that bifurcates from the North Sikkim Highway. Phodong monastery was built by the Chogyal Gyurmed Namgyal somewhere in the first quarter of the eighteenth century

The main annual puja is performed on the 28th and 29th day of the tenth month of the Tibetan calendar two days before Losoong when the religious Chaams or dances are also demonstrated.

Another kilometre uphill from Phodong Monastery on the same jeepable road is the Labrang Monastery which was built about one hundred years later

Phodong's French Connection *Contributed by Green Circle*

Madame Alexandra David Neel was a French explorer and writer who visited Sikkim in t he early twentieth century to study Buddhism. Besides visiting monasteries in Sikkim she also spent many months meditating in a cave near Lachen. When she finally left Sikkim in 1913-1914, Sidkeong Tulku, the Maharaja of Sikkim who was also the abbot of Phodong Monastery presented her with a bronze statue of Buddha as a souvenir. Her passion for Buddhism, took her to many other parts of Asia before returning to France in 1925. She published many papers about her travels and the mystiscism of Buddhism which brought her international recognition as an authority on the subject.

Before she died in 1969 at an age of 100, she wished that the statue should be returned to Sikkim.Her wish was fulfilled by her friend Mary Peyronnet who also was Secretary of the Alexandra David Neel Foundation. She visited Sikkim alongwith the statue in 1992. Amidst rituals and prayers, the statue was restored to its place of origin on 24th April 1992.

but belongs to the Nyingmapa sect. Just below the road between Phodong Monastery and Labrang Monastery are the ruins of the third capital of Sikkim Tumlong. In the beginning of the nineteenth century, the capital of Sikkim was shifted from Rabdanste to Tumlong which then remained the capital for almost ninety years.

The Raja's house is now in complete ruins covered with a thick canopy of bushes but we can conjure up an image of what it looked like from Dr. Hooker's account during his visit and imprisonment here in 1849. He wrote in the Himalayan Journal

> ***It was an irregular low stone building of Tibetan architecture, with slanting walls and small window high up under the broad thatched roof, above which, in the middle, was a Chinese looking square copper gilt canopy, with projecting eaves and bells at the corners, surmounted by a ball and a square spire. On either gable of the roof was a round topped cylinder of gilded copper, something like a closed umbrella.***

The chortens surrounding the Palace have however withstood the vagaries of nature and many of them can be seen.

There are many buses plying on the route on which Phodong lies. Taxis are also readily available for Phodong from Gangtok. Cheap accommodation is available at Phodong Bazar which also has a few shops.

Chungthang

Situated about 100 kms away from Gangtok on the way to Yumthang is the small town of Chungthang in North Sikkim surrounded by high mountains that seem to touch the sky. At an altitude of about 1585 m(5200 ft), Chungthang lies at the confluence of the Lachen Chu (Tista) and the Lachung Chu. From here also the road bifurcates for the Lachen and Lachung valleys.

The spot worth visiting at Chungthang is the rock on which legend has it, Guru Padmasambva rested and the imprint on it is said to be his footmark. There is a small opening in the rock which remains filled with spring water. Adjacent to the rock there is a small stretch of land where paddy grows, defying the conditions which are not conducive to the growth of this crop here. It is said that while here Guru Padmasambva had sprinkled a handful of grains on this spot and paddy has grown here ever since.

Chungthang is also a good place to halt for sometime for a cup of tea before proceeding onwards to Yumthang.

Lachung, Yumthang Hot Springs and Katau

Photographs of the natural scenes of Switzerland and Yumthang valley look so similar that it is difficult to distinguish between them. Yumthang which is at an altitude of 3658m (12000 ft) is situated about 135 kilometres from Gangtok in North Sikkim. But going there is like travelling 135 years back in time - it is so remote and almost untouched by the vagaries of civilisation. It is well known for its hot springs to reach which one has to walk a few hundred yards from the road and across a pedestrian bridge on the River Lachung. For the convenience of bathers a hut with two pools in which the hot spring water collects has been constructed. Hot water rich in sulphur, emanates from a spring just behind the hut and is diverted to the pools. It is difficult to imagine that water so hot in its natural form could be found in a place so cold.

Yumthang is now open to foreigners and has also caught the fancy of filmmakers and a part of some movies have been shot here.

Although Yumthang itself is located on a flat valley and is near the tree-line, the surrounding mountains seem to touch the heavens. The route to Yumthang from Lachung - adjoining the Singba Forest Reserve -has a very picturesque landscape and is lined with rhododendrons which bloom at their best in May. What is particularly interesting about the rhododendrons of the Yumthang valley is that they bloom in different colours unlike those in other parts of Sikkim which are usually red.

Tourists require an Inner Line permit which can be obtained with the help of the travel agent to visit this place. Visitors are not permitted to take their private vehicles to Yumthang. Yumthang has a Forest Department Rest House but tourists are normally accommodated at the Tourist Lodge named Yaksey 6 kms from Lachung towards Yumthang. Yumthang itself has no population and the few yakherders around are nomadic.

Another 23 kilometres ahead of Yumthang are the hot springs of Yumey-Samdong on the river Sebu-chu at the foot of the mountain on which lies the Donkiala pass that connects the Lachung valley to the Lachen valley.

From Lachung one can also do a half day trip to Katau 35 kilometers away. You cross the Lachung chu river and then skirt the Lachung monastery and then the Mini Hydel Project. Many waterfalls leap out of the hills. The army has ingeniously constructed a bridge over one of these waterfalls.

Rhododendrons are in bloom in the meadows as late as June whereas in Yumthang the rhodondrons wither away by mid May. You get glimpses of Lachung town once in a while. You then reach Katau at 13000ft. Even in the month of June you can see a lot of snow. Fifteen kilometers further is Patala on the Chinese border but is out of bound for tourists. So if you did not get to see snow and rhododenrons at Yumthang try Katau.

PLACES OF INTEREST IN WEST SIKKIM

Pelling

Over the last few years, Pelling somehow seems to have developed into a hub of tourism activities in West Sikkim. Till as recently as 1996, Pelling was a nondescript village with a few houses. But over the last few years, it has undergone a sudden metamorphosis. Upclass hotels and fast food centres offering continental, Sikkimese and South Indian dishes have mushroomed. What has prompted this rapid development is perhaps Pelling's vantage location as a take off point for Pemayanste monastery, Kechopari lake, Yoksum, Dzongri, Tashiding and the Chanshey, Kanchendzonga and Fambrong waterfalls and the Shinshor bridge. The area a few kilometres away from Pelling offers wilderness and solitude and is ideal for taking walks. The view of the Kanchendzonga range from Pelling is also breathtaking. The Pelling area has developed into a separate tourist destination with many tourists preferring not to include Gangtok in their itinerary perhaps because of the hustle, bustle and the noise of the capital.

The Government run Mount Pandim (☎ 03595-250855) at Pelling near Gyalshing is an upclass hotel.Hotel Fambrong(☎03595-250660) and Hotel Norbugang(☎03595-250566) also have well appointed accommodation. For hiring taxis from Gyalshing for Yoksum and other places, one may contact M/S Biju Chettri (☎03595-250673) at Gyalshing Bazar.

Pemayanste Monastery, Rabdanste Palace Ruins and Sanga Chelling Monastery

Pemayanste monastery at an altitude of about 2105 m (6840ft), is situated about 6 kms from Gyalshing town and less than a kilometre from Pelling. It is the most important monastery of the Nyingmapa order and was first built as a small temple in the late seventeenth century by Latsun Chembo. Later during the reign of the third Chogyal Chakdor Namgyal, Jigme Pawo who was the third reincarnate of Latsun Chembo extended and rebuilt the structure in the form of a big monastery. The main hall of the monastery has an area of about 180 square metres.

The monastery houses numerous religious idols and other objects of worship, most of which are priceless because of their antiquity. On the top floor of the monastery there is a wooden sculpture portraying the Mahaguru's Heavenly Palace Sangthokpalri. The main dance of the monastery is on the 28th and 29th day of the 12th month of the Tibetan calender, normally corresponding to the month of February three days before Losar. A particularly impressive

MAP OF PELLING

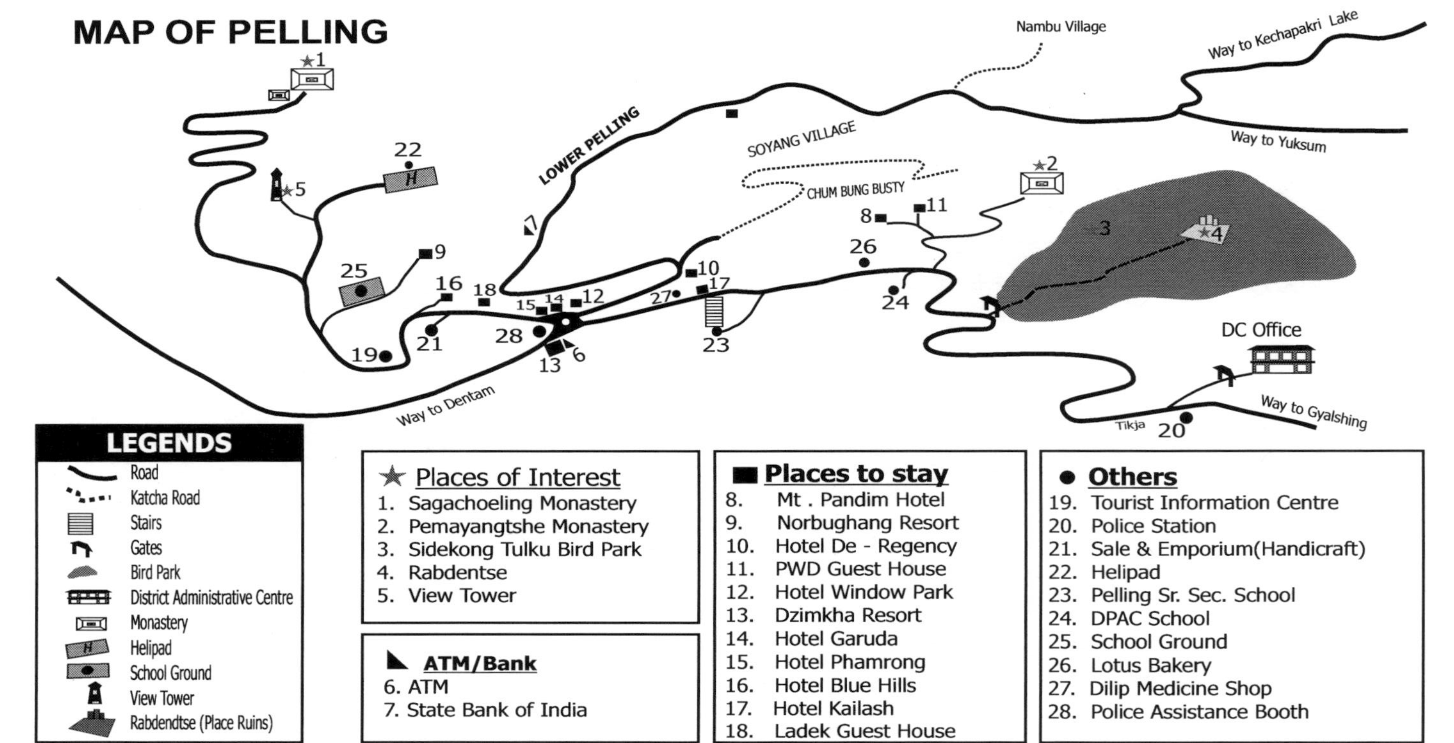

Chaam is on the second day that of the god Mahakal - a huge 8 feet high effigy. The highlight of the third day, is the unfurling of a huge thanka, the largest in Sikkim, depciting Sakya Muni the living Buddha, at the entrance of the monastery.

Rabdanste, which is a couple of kilometres from Gyalshing bazar and near the Pemayanste Monastery, was the second capital of Sikkim and was established in the late seventeenth century by the second Chogyal of Sikkim. It was abandoned towards the end of the eighteenth century because of the threat posed by the Nepalis and the capital was shifted to Tumlong. The Rabdanste Palace is in ruins and one has to trek about two kilometres from the main road near Pemayanste Monastery through a thick forest to reach it. The chortens around the palace have however withstood the elements of nature. The ruins are now being preserved by the Archaeological Survey of India and have been declared as a monument.

Sanga Chelling Monastery, considered the oldest in Sikkim, lies amidst a thick forested hill top opposite the Pemayanste Monastery towards the west. Less than a kilometre ahead of Pemayanste on the road to Yoksum is Pelling and it is from here that one starts walking to this monastery. The track is wide and moderately steep and it takes about half an hour to reach the monastery from Pelling.

Just adjacent to the Pemayanste Monastery is Mount Pandim Hotel suited for the upper class tourist. For tourists on a low budget, cheap but comfortable accommodation is available at the Gyalshing bazar. Daily bus services are available from Gangtok for Gyalshing.

Kechopari Lake

Kechopari Lake at an altitude of about 1951 m (6400 ft) is located on a bifurcation on the road between Gyalshing and Yoksum. Kechopari means the Wishing Lake. The water in this lake is placid and crystal clear. Not even a leaf can be seen floating on the water surface although there is a beautiful dense forest above the lake. It is said that if a leaf drops on the surface of the water it is picked by a bird. A trekkers' hut has been built near the lake for the convenience of the tourists. An hour's walk uphill from the lake takes one to a holy cave and a further one hour and a half walk uphill takes one to the highest point overlooking the lake and offers a bird's eye view. The lake looks like a footprint from here.

A ten minutes walk uphill walk from the lake is the Kechopari Monastery situated amidst a large stretch of flat land. A stupa which is a replica of the Swayambunath temple in Kathmandu flanks the monastery. This is perhaps the only monastery in Sikkim that has such type of a stupa.

Kanchendzonga waterfalls

The Kanchendzonga waterfalls are located about 15 kilometres away from Pelling on the way to Yoksum. The thunder of the icy cold water cascading down the granite rocks resounds in the surrounding. The sound is so loud that it is impossible to hear each other. A mist of water droplets from the waterfall lies suspended in the air and this can make your clothes cold and moist.

Yoksum, Norbugang, Kartok lake and Dubdi Monastery

Yoksum is situated 33 kilometres away from Pelling. The first king of Sikkim was coronated here on the throne made of stones close to the Norbugang monastery and the chorten. The footprint of one of the lamas, Latsun Chembo, who consecrated the king can also be seen close to the throne. The small but beautiful Kartok lake is also situated in Yoksum and is a nice place to spend a quiet moment. About a two kilometres walk uphill from Yoksum is the Dubdi monastery which is the oldest in Sikkim. Besides the trekkers' huts which can be booked through the Kanchendzonga Conservation Committee (☎03595-241211 or 241213). Hotel Tashigang (☎03595-258218) as well as many other hotels offer good accommodation. Yoksum is a takeoff point for Dzongri.

Fambrong waterfalls

Though not as majestic as the Kanchendzonga waterfalls, Fambrong does offer a spectacular sight. These waterfalls are located about 10 kilometres away from Tashiding towards Yoksum.

Tashiding Monastery

This is another important monastery belonging to the Nyingmapa order and is about 40 kilometres from Gyalshing by road via Legship. It lies nestled on the top of a hill that looms up between the Rathong river and the Rangit river and is surrounded by a profusion of prayer flags that flutter in the air. There are also many chortens dedicated to some Chogyals and other religious personalities of Sikkim. Carved skillfully on stone plates surrounding the monastery are holy Buddhist mantras like "Om Mane Padme Hum" by the master craftsman Yanchong Lodil.The monastery was built in 1717 by Ngadak Sempa Chembo during the reign of the third Chogyal Chakdor Namgyal. The sacred ceremony of Bumchu is held here at midnight of the 14th and 15th of the first Tibetan month. A description of this festival is given elsewhere in this book.

There is a bus service from Gyalshing to Tashiding. A trekkers hut is available for the tourist at Tashiding.

Changey Waterfalls

These waterfalls are located about 10 kilometres from Pelling on the road to Dentam.

Singshor Bridge

This suspension bridge is located about 25 kilometres from Pelling and about 5 kilometres ahead of Dentam towards Uttarey. The bridge has been built over a gorge that is about a thousand feet deep. The building of this bridge was an engineering feat indeed.

Hee Bermiok Area

If you want to get away from the hubub of Pelling, then Hee Bermoik 28 kms away is an ideal location to spend your time in peace. The Hee Bermoik area is coming up as a favourite tourist destination with homestays and mountain biking. It is an area dominated by the Limboo population and those interested in Sikkimese culture will not be disappointed. It has its share of places of interest. First there is a Limboo Temple called Makhim with a bust of Srijunga the patron saint of the community who is also saint to be the inventor of the Limboo script. Close by is the Alley Cave. Another cave which involves a 2 hours trek is the ShriJunga Cave located at the confluence of the Kalej and the Reshi rivers. Close to this cave is the Srijunga waterfalls. 7 kilometers away from Hee bermoik is Rinchenpong famous for its two monasteries: Resung Gompa and Rinchenchenpong Gompa. Rinchengpong used to be the visited by the Governor General of Bengal in the 1860s. Later in 1920 Rabrindranath stayed at Rabrinath Smriti Van in 1920. He is said to have written a few poems while staying here.

PLACES OF INTEREST IN SOUTH DISTRICT

A holiday in Sikkim to many normally means a visit to Gangtok, Nathula Pass and for those with a little more time, a stay at Pelling or a trip to the Yumthang valley – all terribly crowded with tourists during the season time.

But for those who want to beat the tourist rush and venture into the off-beaten path there are many other places to see. South District which is the smallest of the Districts, encompassing an area of only 700 sq km, is not yet on the popular tourist circuit. It has moderate altitude ranging from sea level to about 10,000 ft and has a pleasant climate. Sikkim as a whole gets very heavy rainfall but surprisingly South District has medium precipitation even during peak monsoon. It is a region of hotsprings, tea gardens and towering statues. And Sikkim's two mighty rivers the Tista and Rangit meet at one corner of this district. It is an ideal destination to spend a memorable holiday far from the maddening crowds.

Namchi which is the capital is of South District is 90 kilometers away from the nearest railway station(New Jalpaiguri) and the airport (Bagdogra) of Siliguri in West Bengal.

If coming from Siliguri the following itinerary is suggested:

Siliguri-Namchi- Char Dham- Samdruptse-Purcha-chu Hotspring- Kriteshwar Temple(Legship)-Rabongla-Damthang-Temi Tea Gardes-Gangtok. You enter Sikkim at Melli near the confluence of the two mighty rivers of Sikkim: Tista and Rangit that also marks one corner of South District.

If you want to do the trek to the mountains tops of Tendong and Maenam, then a few hours halt at Damthang and Rabongla respectively have to be factored in your itinerary it taking about 3 hours each one way.

The reverse route can be traversed if travelling between Gangtok and Siliguri..

Where else can we begin the tour of South District but on a holy note: the **Sri Siddhesvara Dham (Char Dham) Complex** (inaugurated on 8th Nov 2011) with a towering 108 ft high statue of Lord Shiva presiding over it.Why spend time and money travelling all over the country on pilgrimage visiting the Four Dhams and the 12 Jyoti Lingas when you can do it here in Namchi within an hour. Then onward to the the holy Statue of **Guru Padmasambva** midway between Damthang and Namchi on the top of the hill of Samdruptse. Guru Padmasambva is the founder saint of the Nyngmipa sect to which most of the monasteries in Sikkim belong. Measuring 135 feet in height (and 151 ft from the ground level), the statue can be seen even miles away glittering

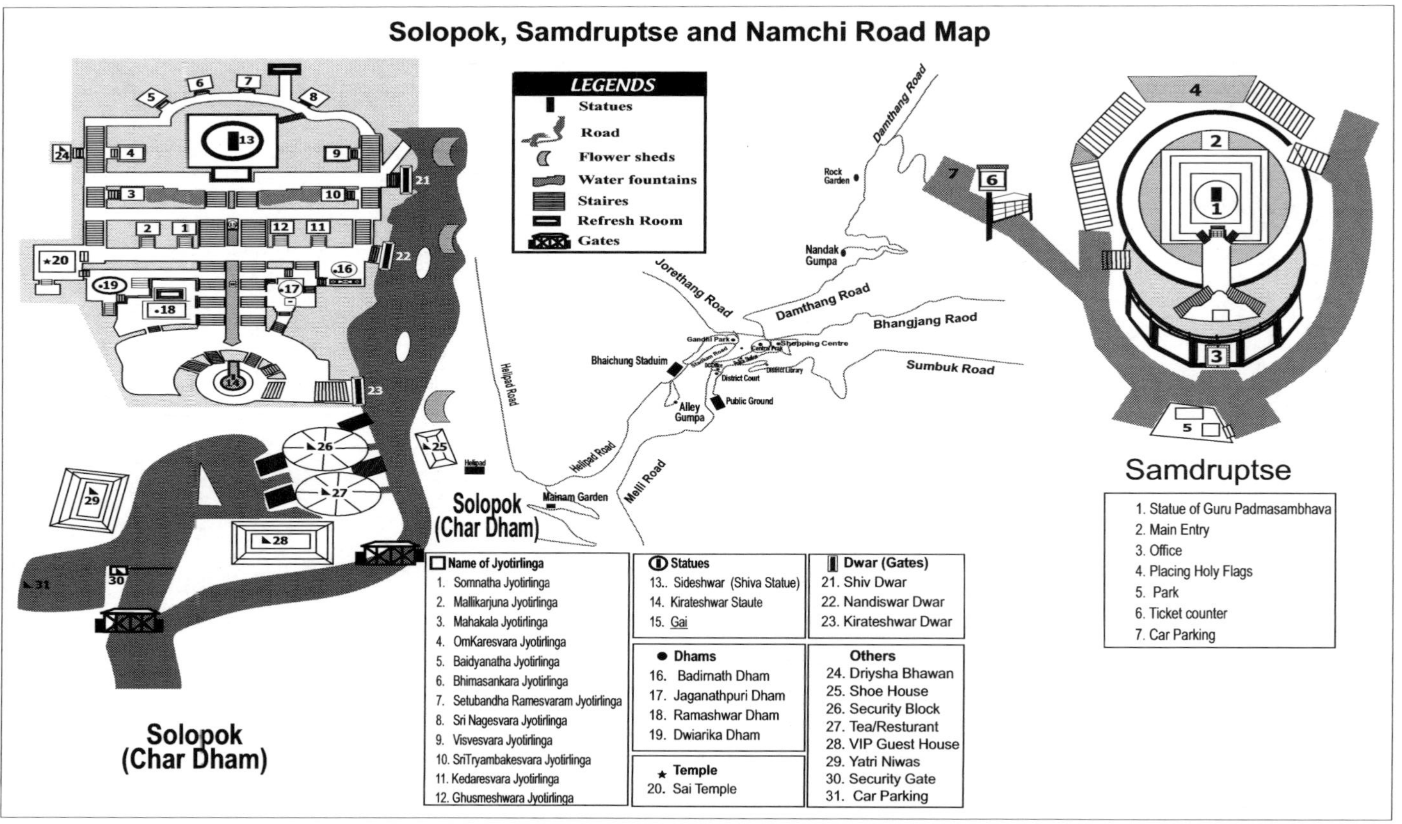
Solopok, Samdruptse and Namchi Road Map
LEGENDS
Statues
Road
Flower sheds
Water fountains
Staires
Refresh Room
Gates
Damthang Road
Rock Garden
Nandak Gumpa
Jorethang Road
Damthang Road
Bhangjang Raod
Sumbuk Road
Gandhi Park
Shopping Centre
Bhaichung Staduim
District Court
District Library
Public Ground
Alley Gumpa
Helipad Road
Melli Road
Mainam Garden
Helipad
Solopok (Char Dham)
Name of Jyotirlinga
1. Somnatha Jyotirlinga
2. Mallikarjuna Jyotirlinga
3. Mahakala Jyotirlinga
4. OmKaresvara Jyotirlinga
5. Baidyanatha Jyotirlinga
6. Bhimasankara Jyotirlinga
7. Setubandha Ramesvaram Jyotirlinga
8. Sri Nagesvara Jyotirlinga
9. Visvesvara Jyotirlinga
10. SriTryambakesvara Jyotirlinga
11. Kedaresvara Jyotirlinga
12. Ghusmeshwara Jyotirlinga
Statues
13.. Sideshwar (Shiva Statue)
14. Kirateshwar Staute
15. Gai
Dhams
16. Badimath Dham
17. Jaganathpuri Dham
18. Ramashwar Dham
19. Dwiarika Dham
Temple
20. Sai Temple
Dwar (Gates)
21. Shiv Dwar
22. Nandiswar Dwar
23. Kirateshwar Dwar
Others
24. Driysha Bhawan
25. Shoe House
26. Security Block
27. Tea/Resturant
28. VIP Guest House
29. Yatri Niwas
30. Security Gate
31. Car Parking
Solopok (Char Dham)
Samdruptse
1. Statue of Guru Padmasambhava
2. Main Entry
3. Office
4. Placing Holy Flags
5. Park
6. Ticket counter
7. Car Parking

in the forest. The colossal statue is made of copper, cement and concrete and was constructed at a cost of Rs 67.6 million.

Just a few kilometers before Namchi is the sprawling **Rock Garden** - a good place for a picnic. Namchi is also famous for its nurseries offering a wide range of orchids and other flowers and plants endemic to Sikkim. The town also hosts the colourful Namchi Mahaustav in November every year with traditional cultural programme and flower competitions. As of now Namchi does not have many hotels but of the few it has, Seven Hill Resort and Hotel Samdruptse can be considered for staying in if you are making an overnight halt.

Phurchachu Reshi Hot Springs are located about 25 kilometers from Gyalshing near Reshi on the River Rangit. One has to walk about ten minutes from the highway across the River Rangit by a pedestrian bridge to reach the hot springs. The water of these springs has medicinal value as it contains sulphur and can cure some skin diseases. People from all over the state and neighbouring Darjeeling come here during the winter months and spend days together lying submerged in the soothing water of the hot spring. There are a couple of trekkers' huts for the convenience of the tourists.

These springs are also considered very holy as one of the four holy caves is located here. This holy cave is called the Kadosang phu or cave of the occult fairies and lies on the south of the four cardinal points.

Shri Kiriteshwar Temple is situated at Legship (16kms from Gyalshing on the Gangtok-Gyalshing highway) on the banks of the River Rangit, is dedicated to God Shiva. It is said that many years ago a rock in the shape of a Shiv Linga miraculously appeared at the base of a tree. The temple has been constructed at this very spot. The temple complex also houses a Dharamshala (living accommodation for worshippers) and a community kitchen.

The temple is fast developing into a favourite stop over point for tourists going to Pelling and Yoksum.

The **Temi tea garden** carpets a sprawling area of the hill side overlooking the Tista river. Well manicured tea bushes interspersed with cherry trees present a visual delight. Temi tea has limited production but carries a premium value in the international market. Do not forget to sip Temi tea at the Café in the Tea Garden. If you have time a visit to the factory is also worthwhile.

Rabongla is situated almost midway between Gangtok and Pelling. It is worth spending sometime visiting the monastery and the park which has a 148 feet high statue of Buddha (Sakya Muni). Rabongla has many hotels providing reasonably good moderately priced accommodation. A nice place to stay is Mt. Narsing Resort. If you have time a side trip to Old Ralang and the New Ralang monasteries 10 kilometres and 15 kilometres away respectively is worth it. Further 5 kilometres onwards is the **Brong hotspring** but this involves a trek of about half an hour from the roadhead.

Of late Rabongla Monastery has been the venue for celebration of **Phang Lhabsol.** This a festival unique to Sikkim. It was popularised by the third Chogyal of Sikkim, Chakdor Namgyal. In this festival the snowy range of Kachendzonga is worshipped for its unifying powers.

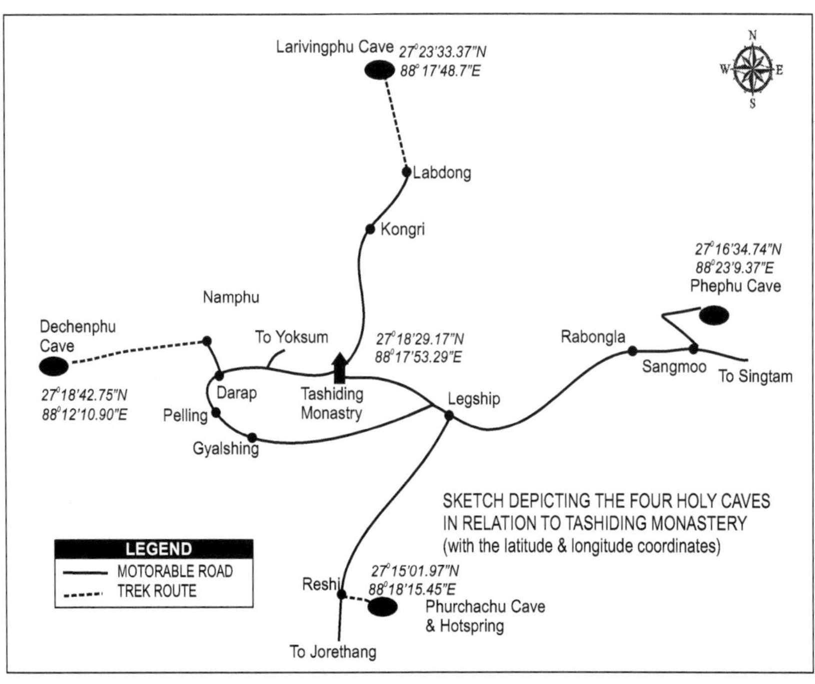
Larivingphu Cave 27°23'33.37"N 88°17'48.7"E
N
W
E
S
Labdong
Kongri
27°16'34.74"N
88°23'9.37"E
Phephu Cave
Namphu
Dechenphu Cave
To Yoksum
27°18'29.17"N
88°17'53.29"E
Rabongla
Sangmoo
To Singtam
27°18'42.75"N
88°12'10.90"E
Darap
Pelling
Tashiding Monastry
Legship
Gyalshing
SKETCH DEPICTING THE FOUR HOLY CAVES
IN RELATION TO TASHIDING MONASTERY
(with the latitude & longitude coordinates)
LEGEND
MOTORABLE ROAD
TREK ROUTE
Reshi
27°15'01.97"N
88°18'15.45"E
Phurchachu Cave & Hotspring
To Jorethang

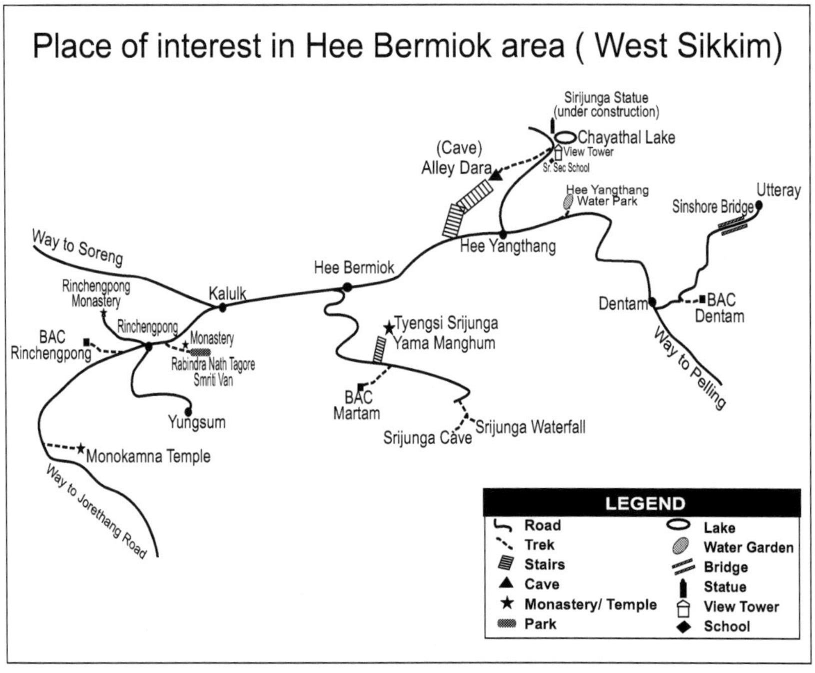
Place of interest in Hee Bermiok area (West Sikkim)
Sirijunga Statue (under construction)
Chayathal Lake
View Tower
Sr. Sec School
(Cave) Alley Dara
Hee Yangthang Water Park
Utteray
Sinshore Bridge
Hee Yangthang
Way to Soreng
Hee Bermiok
Rinchengpong Monastery
Kaluk
Dentam
BAC Dentam
Rinchengpong
Monastery
Rabindra Nath Tagore Smriti Van
BAC Rinchengpong
Tyengsi Srijunga Yama Manghum
Way to Pelling
BAC Martam
Yungsum
Srijunga Cave
Srijunga Waterfall
Monokamna Temple
Way to Jorethang Road
LEGEND
Road
Trek
Stairs
Cave
Monastery/ Temple
Park
Lake
Water Garden
Bridge
Statue
View Tower
School

SOME LESSER KNOWN PLACES

Four Great Caves

These caves are some of the lesser known places of interest and lie in the four different directions. These caves are Laringvigphu (old cave of God's hill) in the north, Kahdosangphu (cave of the fairies) in the south, Pephu (secret cave) in the east and Dechhenphu (the cave of happiness) in the west. Laringvigphu is considered as the most holy and it is a one day walk from Lapdang (Lapdang is 20 kms away from Tashiding by road). Dechenphu is also equally inaccessible and is a one day walk from Darap near Pelling. Kahdosangphu lies at Reshi hot springs on the Jorethang-Gyalshing highway. To reach the hot spring and the cave one has to walk about ten minutes from the highway across the river Rangit by a pedestrian suspension bridge. Pephu lies near Sangmoo which is situated five kilometres away from Rabongla on the highway between Singtam and Rabongla. One has to walk about half an hour downhill from Sangmoo to reach the cave which lies between the Tendong and Maenam mountains. Its cavern is said to extend to both the Tendong and Maenam hilltops. (For detailed information on Dechhenphu and Laringvigphu see the section on Trekking in Sikkim)

If you are visiting Bhumchu at Tashiding in March, then the following itinerary can be considered

Day 1: Attend Bhumchu and halt at Tashiding

Day 2: Leave Tashiding early morning and reach Labdang(Gurung Basti), 20 kms away and trek (approx 8 hours) up to Laringniphu Cave. Bivouac at the cave.

Day 3: Trek back to Labdang and then by road to Pelling. Halt at Pelling

Day 4: Pelling to Namphu by road (8 kms) and then trek about 7 hours to the Dechenphu Cave. Halt at the wooden hut close to the cave

Day 5: Trek back from Dechenphu cave to Namphu and by road to Pelling Gyalsing Legship and Reshi. Visit Phurcha chu. On to Rabongla and Sangmoo and visit the Holy cave Phephu. Return to Gangtok

War Memorial at Gnathang

During the last quarter of the nineteenth century some British soldiers were killed fighting the Tibetan Army at Lingtu close to Kupup. A memorial was constructed at that time in their memory at Gnathang a small village near Kupup.

Pendam Garhi

This fort which is now in ruins lies in Central Pendam (about 12 kilometres from Rangpo and 18 kilometres from Singam). The main wall of the fort now overgrown with bushes has withstood the vagaries of the elements and still exists. The wall extends 200 ft in length, 10 ft high and about 5 ft wide at the top. There are few enclosures in ruins and a temple of goddess Kali. The fort is about a 2 kilometres uphill walk by footpath from the road opposite Central Pendam Senior Secondary School.

The origin of this fort is not well documented but it is said that it was constructed during the reign of Chakdor Namgyal when his half sister

Pendeongmu in collusion with the Bhutanese was trying to snatch the throne of Sikkim.

Pendam Garhi has a good potential for developing as a tourist destination.

GOVERNMENT GUEST HOUSES, DAKBUNGLOWS

A map in this chapter depicts the Government Guest Houses where travellers can stay.

SHOPPING

Besides the places of interest, Sikkim also offers the added attraction of shopping.

Handicrafts

A wide variety of handicrafts are available for the tourist to take back as souvenirs, showpieces and even items of daily use in the Government Institute of Cottage Industry and the many curio shops in Gangtok. It is worth taking a few handicrafts back home to decorate your Drawing rooms as a remembrance of your visit to Sikkim.

Canvas wall-hangings depicting paintings on different aspects of Sikkim can cost from Rs 20 to Rs 200. Most of these paintings portray face profiles of tribals, eight lucky signs, dragons, religious processions etc. Thankas or religious scrolls can also be purchased but these are very expensive and cost above Rs 500.

Choksees are small wooden tables about one and half to two feet in height with intricate local Tibetan designs on the sides. They are collapsible and can easily be carried.

Carpet and rugs

Tibetan woollen carpets are very expensive and are adorned with intricate designs and patterns reflecting the art and culture of this state. Made of pure sheep wool, these carpets use brilliant vegetable dyes.

Jewellery

The exquisitely carved Dragon sets of silver and gold inlaid with precious stones are unique to Sikkim. These consist of finely designed dragons on ear-rings, pendants, finger-rings etc. and can be ordered either in silver or gold.

Tea

Sikkim tea, which is mainly grown in Temi Tea Estate, is famous the world over and carries a big premium in the world market. The tea is characterised by its exotic taste and flavour and costs about Rs 100 a kilogram. It sells by the brand name of "Solja" and "Kanchendzonga" and it is a good idea to carry a few packets back home.

Big Cardamom or Bari Elachi

Cardamom or Elachi grows in abundance in Sikkim and costs about Rs 150 a kilogram. A few hundred grams should be purchased.

Government Bunglows, Trekking & Log Huts in Sikkim

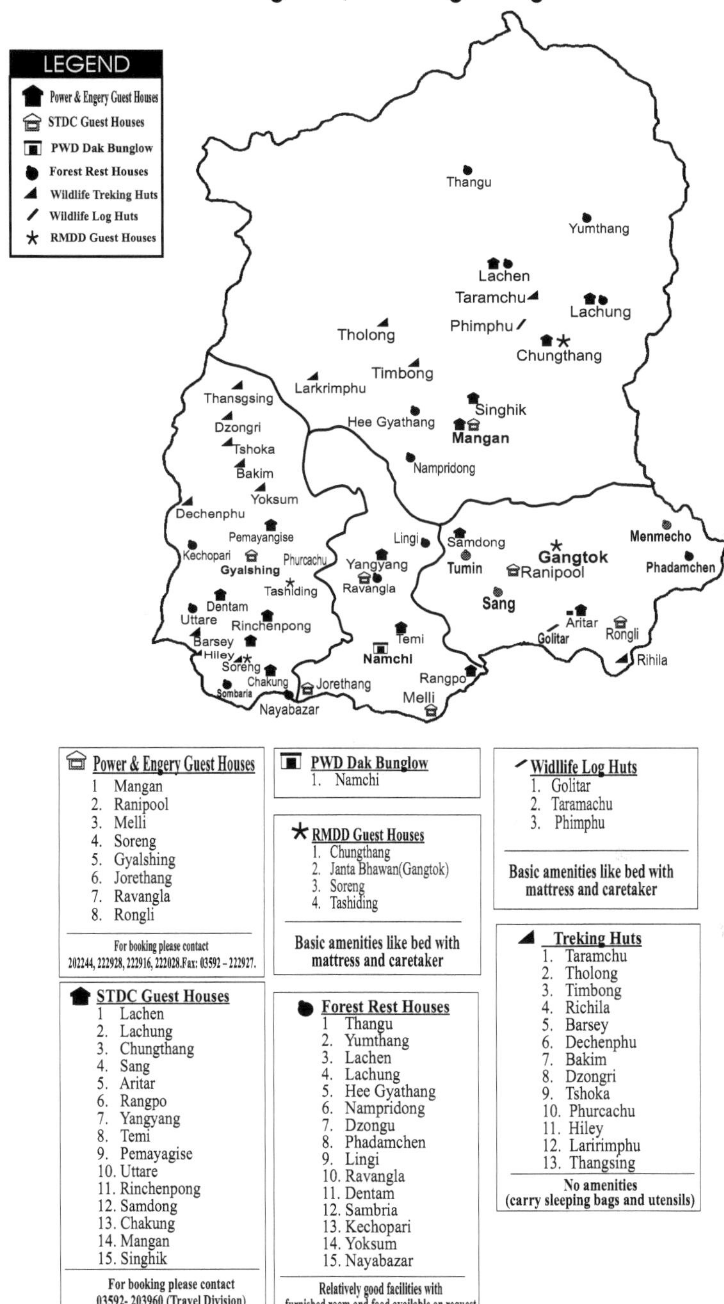

Power & Engery Guest Houses

1 Mangan
2. Ranipool
3. Melli
4. Soreng
5. Gyalshing
6. Jorethang
7. Ravangla
8. Rongli

For booking please contact
202244, 222928, 222916, 222028.Fax: 03592 - 222927.

STDC Guest Houses

1 Lachen
2. Lachung
3. Chungthang
4. Sang
5. Aritar
6. Rangpo
7. Yangyang
8. Temi
9. Pemayagise
10. Uttare
11. Rinchenpong
12. Samdong
13. Chakung
14. Mangan
15. Singhik

For booking please contact
03592- 203960 (Travel Division)

PWD Dak Bunglow

1. Namchi

RMDD Guest Houses

1. Chungthang
2. Janta Bhawan(Gangtok)
3. Soreng
4. Tashiding

Basic amenities like bed with mattress and caretaker

Forest Rest Houses

1 Thangu
2. Yumthang
3. Lachen
4. Lachung
5. Hee Gyathang
6. Nampridong
7. Dzongu
8. Phadamchen
9. Lingi
10. Ravangla
11. Dentam
12. Sambria
13. Kechopari
14. Yoksum
15. Nayabazar

Relatively good facilities with furnished room and food available on request

Widllife Log Huts

1. Golitar
2. Taramachu
3. Phimphu

Basic amenities like bed with mattress and caretaker

Treking Huts

1. Taramchu
2. Tholong
3. Timbong
4. Richila
5. Barsey
6. Dechenphu
7. Bakim
8. Dzongri
9. Tshoka
10. Phurcachu
11. Hiley
12. Laririmphu
13. Thangsing

No amenities
(carry sleeping bags and utensils)

Sikkim Liquor

A gift pack which consists of small 50 ml bottles of rum, brandy and other liqueurs is a good buy. Khukri and Fire Ball brandy are also good buys.

HANDICRAFT AND JEWELLERY SHOPS

Besides the Government Institute of Cottage Industry, Mandala Handicrafts Centre (☎ 206562) adjacent to the Tourism Information Centre, Kandoika(☎208115) in New market and Snow-white (☎205501) and Junction (☎221431) both on M.G. Marg all stock a variety of Sikkimese handicraft.

Traditional Sikkimese jewellery can be bought from Ramchandra Jewellers (☎ 222962) on the Lal-bazar Road. A wide variety of the famous "Dragon Sets" are available here.

COMMUNICATION AND INTERNET

Sikkim is extensive mobile coverage with all the major players like BSNL, Hutch, Airtel, Reliance etc.

While there are many privately owned cybercafes in Gangtok, the Department of Information Technology, Government of Sikkim has established many internet cafes called Common Service Centres all across the state in places as remote as Lachen, Lachung Yoksum and Nathula. Some of the Community Information Centres also have photocopying, lamination and Public Telephone facility. The Common Service Centres are listed below:

North

1. Mangan, District. Adm. Centre
2. Kabi, Panchayat Ghar
3. Phodong, Community centre
4. Hee-Gyathang, Sec School
5. Tingbong, Panchayat Ghar
6. Chungthang, SDM Office
7. Lachen, Sec School Hostel
8. Lachung, Sec School Hostel

South

1. Namchi,District Adm. Centre
2. Namthang, Panchayat Ghar
3. Jorethang, SIRD, Karfectar
4. Yangang, Panchayat Ghar
5. Sumbuk, Panchayat Ghar
6. Wak, Panchayat Ghar
7. Temi, Panchayat Ghar
8. Damthang, Panchayat Ghar
9. Ravangla, SDM Office
10. Melli Dara, Panchayat ghar
11. Lingi Payong, Panchayat Ghar

East

1. Gangtok, Near Power Secretariat
2. Pangthang, SAP Camp
3. Pakyong , SDM Office
4. Sichey Busty, DAC
5. Duga, VLO Office
6. Ray-Mindu, Panchayat Ghar
7. Rongli, SDM Office
8. Samdong,Panchayat Ghar
9. Rhenock, Panchayat Ghar
10. Sang, VLO Office
11. Pachey-Khani, Panchayat Ghar
12. Assam- Lingzey, VLO Office
13. Khamdong, BDO Office
14. Tintek, BDO Office
15. Sherathang, Nathula Trade Mart

West

1. Gyalshing, District Adm. Centre
2. Tashiding, Sr. Sec. School
3. Yoksam, Panchayat Ghar
4. Dentam, Panchayat Ghar
5. Mangalbarey, Panchayat Ghar
6. Soreng, SDM Office
7. Hee-yangthang, Panchayat Ghar
8. Okhrey, Panchayat Ghar
9. Daramdin, Panchayat Ghar
10. Kaluk, Panchayat Ghar
11. Chakung, Panchayat Ghar

The Common Service Centre at Nathula has been declared as the highest cyber cafe in the world by the Limca Book of Records 2007 Edition.

RAFTING IN SIKKIM

Rafting is a later entrant of adventure sport in Sikkim. Only the Tista and Rangit rivers offer long stretches which are ideal for safe rafting. On the river Tista, river rafting can be done from Chungthang to Melli. On the Rangit, the river is safe for rafting from Legship downwards. Both these stretches have now been opened for foreigners.

MOUNTAIN-BIKING IN SIKKIM

Mountain biking is another adventure that has been recently introduced in Sikkim. Most of the roads in Sikkim are negotiable by mountainbikes. This sport is definitely poised to become popular in Sikkim in the near future. Many mountain biking routes have been opened for foreigners. These have been spelt out elsewhere in the book. Many upclass hotels keep mountain bikes for hire.

PARAGLIDING

Paragliding is another adventure sport that is steadily becoming popular in Sikkim. Chumbong near Soreng in West Sikkim is presently one of the most visited spots for a paragliding experience. The Sikkim Paragliding Sports Cooperative Society (09733028538) located at Kazi Road and the Sikkim Paragliding Association(9735017094) located at Resithang Khelgaon near Bhan Jhakri Falls organize tandem paragliding from Thami Daragaon and Bulbuley to Resithang and from Chakung and Chumbong to Jorethang.

Besides places of interest tourists can visit Sikkim for its festivals and some other events These are listed below

Event	Period	Place
Maghe Sakranti	14-15 Jan	Jorethang
Lossar	Feb	Pemayantse Monastery
Bhumchu	March	Tashiding Monastery
Flower festival	March	Gangtok
Ramnami(chaite Dasain)	April	Aritar near Rhenock
Saga Dawa	May-June	Gamgtok
Phang Lhabsol	Aug-Sept	Gangtok/Rabongla
Losoong & Chaams	Dec	Enchey monastey
Governor Cup Football	Oct	Gangtok
Chief Minister Gold Cup	Oct	Namchi
Dasain/Tihar	Oct-Nov	All over Sikkim
Namchi Mahaustav	mid Dec	Namchi
Mangan Music Festival	last week Dec	Mangan

See the Government holidays on the website sikkim.gov.in for the exact dates. These vary considerably as they many of the festivals follow the lunar calendar

Travel Agents Associationof Sikkim 03592-201018 sikkimtaas@gmail.com can be contacted for further details.

TREKKING IN SIKKIM

Gangtok is a bustling, modern town teeming with package tourists and seems to be out of place with Sikkim. If you must see Sikkim you must go to the villages and country-side and one way of doing this is by trekking. Most of the trekking routes are few tens of kilometres from major towns but going there is like travelling many hundred years back into time. The best months to trek in Sikkim are March to May and September to November. However trekking at altitudes above 4500 metres should be avoided in March and April because the winter snow still persists on the ground and sometimes there is even heavy snowfall during these months making it difficult to locate the path. Most of the so called places on trekking routes in remote areas have just a herders' hut or a shed and some places have nothing at all but just wilderness and you wonder how they derived their names in the first place. The places have names that are whispers on the wind: Yoksum, Zongri, Varsey, Maenam, Tolung. Some routes are so remote that you can walk for days together without seeing a soul.

Trekking in Sikkim can be a wonderful experience- an antidote to city stress of daily life- and its memories are cherished lifelong. While trekking one relishes the pure air and the silence of the wilderness and feels the awakening of senses dulled by urban living. Although trekking can make you physically exhausted, it can heighten your spirits and stir your soul. And the gruelling trek can leave you famished when the most distasteful food tastes like gourmet fare. As one walks through the vales and dales and past quaint villages which time has forgotten, mountains take up strange and wonderful shapes and the beauty of the Himalayas unfolds itself before you. As you trek, identifying peaks, mountains, rivers and places around you becomes a good pastime. And whether you can climb the next hilltop becomes more important than anything else in life. From a distance these mountains may seem formidable and unapproachable but as you near them they seem to welcome you into the forests vibrant with life. They are so tantalizing near yet so frustratingly far. Although each and every nook and corner of Sikkim - from the sultry tropical forests in the south to the howling wilderness in the north and from the razor-edged Singelila range in the west to the undulating Chola range in the east - is a trekkers paradise, the following routes are worth a mention. These routes encompass all the treks that have been recently opened to foreigners.

(Yoksum is well organised for organising last minute treks to Zongri. For other trek routes you should contact a local travel agent atleast 15 days in advance so that he can make the necessary arrangements for permits, porters etc.

I had undertaken the following treks before the Government banned grazing in Alpine areas. The yakherder huts in which I stayed now do not exist:therefore carry tents)

Yoksum - Zongri Trek

Yoksum and Zongri are two places in West Sikkim between which there is a proper well beaten trekking track in the form of a bridle path. The best time

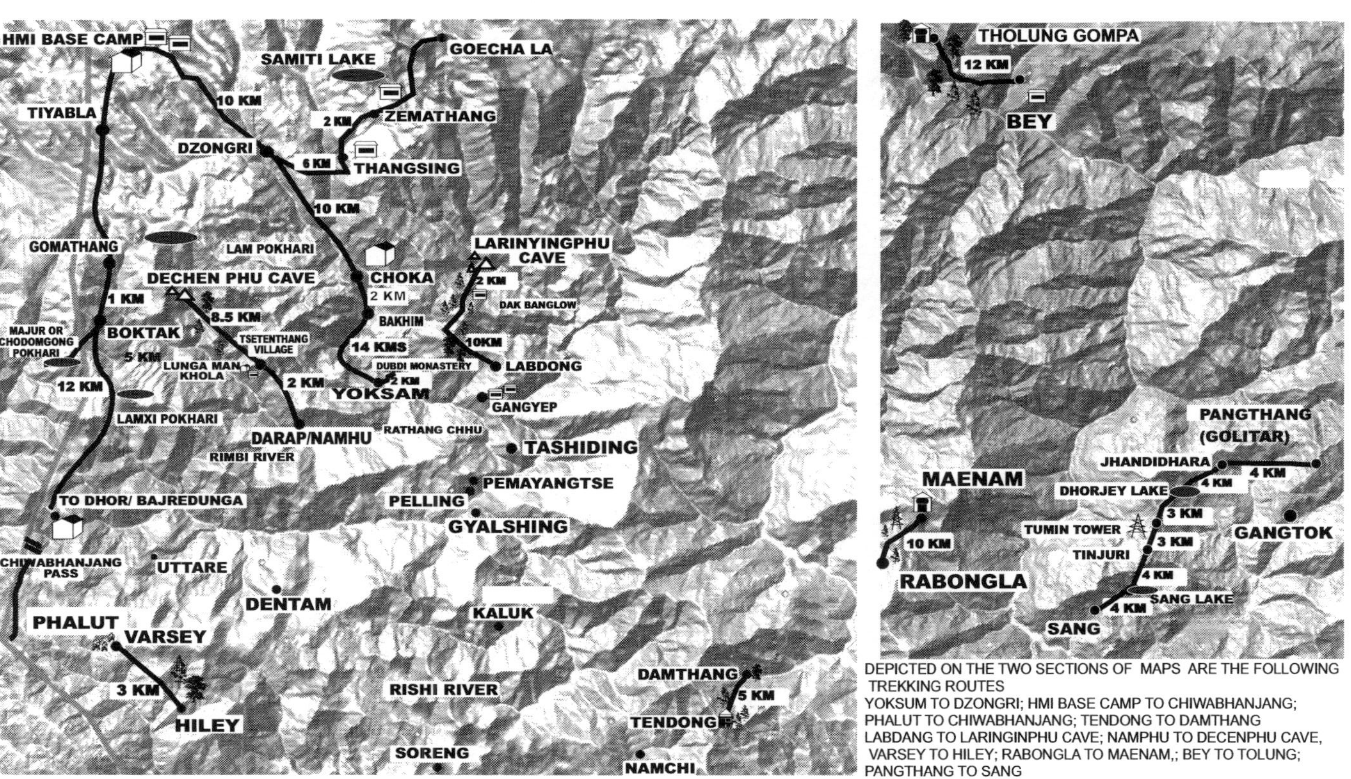

DEPICTED ON THE TWO SECTIONS OF MAPS ARE THE FOLLOWING TREKKING ROUTES
YOKSUM TO DZONGRI; HMI BASE CAMP TO CHIWABHANJANG; PHALUT TO CHIWABHANJANG; TENDONG TO DAMTHANG LABDANG TO LARINGINPHU CAVE; NAMPHU TO DECENPHU CAVE, VARSEY TO HILEY; RABONGLA TO MAENAM,; BEY TO TOLUNG; PANGTHANG TO SANG

to venture on a trek on this route is April to June and September to November. Tourism Department organises treks during autumn and spring. Till Yoksum there is a motorable road. To reach Yoksum, one must first come to Gyalshing from Gangtok or Jorethang from where regular bus services are available. From Gyalshing to Yoksum, one can either travel by bus or taxi. If travelling by own vehicle, one may opt to reach Yoksum via Tashiding taking the bifurcation road from Legship. Besides having many trekker's huts, Yoksum also has a private hotel which provides both boarding and lodging. Guides, porters and pack yaks are readily available at Yoksum. Tents, sleeping bags and other trekking equipment are also available for rent at Yoksum.

Yoksum was the first capital of Sikkim and it was here that the first Chogyal was consecrated by the three holy Lamas. The spot where this ceremony took place in 1642 can still be seen here. Overlooking Yoksum and about half an hours walk uphill is the Dubdi monastery one of the oldest in Sikkim.

The walk to Zongri begins with the track skirting meadows and meandering past huts. After an hour of a flat track which is crossed by small foot or two wide streams whose waters seem to be in a hurry to meet the river below, the climb begins. A walk of another four hours on a path lined with sky embracing trees and carpeted with leaves falling from the surrounding vegetation takes you to Bakim which has a trekker's hut. A further one hour climb and you are at Bakim. You may opt to halt at Chokha which also has a trekker's hut. Chokha itself is a small village consisting of about a dozen houses and a monastery. To cater to the tourists, most of these houses offer accommodation and food at a nominal cost.

The walk between Yoksum and Chokha takes about six hours but would vary considerably with the trekker's stamina. In a distance of about 16 kilometres one has climbed from Yoksum at 1780 m(5840 ft) to Choka at 3006 m (9860 ft)

Another steep climb of 10 kilometres which takes about 4 hours and you are at Zongri at 4030 m (13220 ft). Zongri has two trekker's huts and hardly any other habitation. From the Zongrila pass about an hour's walk from the trekker's huts, the view of the mountain ranges is heavenly. In front of you is the Kabur Dome and piercing the sky is the Mount Pandim. Mount Kanchendzonga with its accompanying peaks towers over you in the North.

At Zongri the bridle path ends and bifurcates into two footpaths: one leading to the Base Camp and the other to the Goechela pass. The base camp at 4573 m (15000 ft) is 9 kilometres away and takes about three hours for the average trekker to reach.The Base camp which consists of a number of trekker's huts is owned by the Himalayan Mountaineering Institute, Darjeeling which conducts a number of mountain climbing courses every year. The Frey Peak, Koktang, Kabru and Rathong look ominously close from here and tower above the HMI camp.

On the other route the Goechela pass at about 4942 m(16210 ft) is about 14 kilometres via Thangsing, Samiti Lake and Zemethang.

Base Camp -Boktak- Laxmipokhari-Garakhet Trek

If your feet are still itching to go ahead after reaching the Base Camp, you can take the route to the South on the Western border of Sikkim to an area that has a profusion of perhaps the most beautiful lakes in Sikkim and therefore it would not be inappropriate to call it "The Lake Trek". It is a domain of sky lacquered lakes, glacial valleys and chiselled peaks. The journey to and fro will take about four to five days. Long stretches of this route are trailess and therefore an expert guide who knows the area well will be required. Our guide who would also double as a porter was a skinny chap hardly weighing 40 kg but was capable of carrying goods weighing one and a half times more. The few shepherd sheds on the way are inhabited only during the grazing season from July to September and if you are trekking some other time make sure that all necessary provisions are carried. Although you can stay in the shepherd huts, it is a good idea also to carry tentage to meet any contingencies.

From the Base Camp, a steep climb takes one to a pass at about 4878 m (16000 ft) from where a almost vertical, knee wobbling drop reaches one deep down in a flat valley surrounded by huge granite cliffs. You ford across the river Runji chu whose water seems to gurgle and murmur as though annoyed at the feeble attempts by the boulders in it to stop its flow. Another vertical climb up and you are at Khangerden with its lone hut. This murderous trek of just about 6 kilometres takes about three hours. From Khangerden to Boktak through Tiyabla is relatively easy going and takes about six hours. If you start early in the morning from Base Camp, you can comfortably reach Boktak in the late afternoon. A night halt at the yakshed at Boktak and the next day you are ready to see the most beautiful lakes on earth in this untrampled remoteness. A halt in a yakshed can be an out-of-the- world experience. The yakherders seem to be completely oblivious of events taking place in the country or the world. Their life centres around yaks: they talk and think only about them. What matters to them most is yaks and nothing else. The other topic the yak herders discuss with obvious relish is the Yeti or "The Abominable snowman". Many of them swear that they have had encounters with the Yeti. Yetis, I was told, are bigger than the size of a man, with feet pointing backwards, long hair and are very dangerous.

During my visit, the preparation of our dinner at Boktak was presided by a yakherder a withered old man, whose wrinkled face and claw like hands illuminated by the glow of the fire gave him a witch-like appearance. The atmosphere was heavy and close, and a strong reek of smoke from burning rhododendron branches fought a losing battle against stronger reek of unwashed bodies. While having dinner we were regaled with stories concerning nothing else but Yaks and Yetis. I infact started believing that Yetis do exist and later that night, as a call of nature took me out into the freezing darkness, I did feel that a Yeti would come and pounce on me.

The yakshed is a crude structure whose walls are made of stone and the roof of planks that are weighted down by small rocks to prevent them from getting blown away during a storm. It is divided into two sections one for the lactating and gestating yaks and the other for the yakherders. The floor is covered with a thick layer of hay that serves as a mattress. As I lay resting looking at the stars through the chinks in the roof, I went off to sleep, inspite of the ding-dong of the bells from the ruminating yaks. This sound in fact acted as a lullaby. Somewhere in the night, I was rudely wakened by what seemed as a slap on my face. It was in fact a yak which had poked its head over the partition and was liking my face - perhaps the salt of my perspiration was too much for it to resist. I changed my position and lulled back into a restful sleep.

A moderate climb of about two and half hours Boktak through Chirpuk reaches you to the bank of lake Majur Pokhari. This lake at its centre has a green iridescent sheen feature shaped like the wings of a bird (Majur meanings wings of a bird) that glistens brightly. No one has been able to explain this illusion, but it is said that it is caused due to the reflection of light. Above the Majur Pokhari are two twin lakes called the Ram-Laxman lakes. It is worth mentioning here that during the trek one will come across a number of such twin lakes all called by the same name of Ram- Laxman. You return back to Boktak and halt at Gomathang one kilometre below on a riverside, which also has a yak shed. At night darkness closes like a lid on the mountains, shutting out the world, and the stars blaze to life in a sky suddenly too small to hold them.

The third day sees you taking the steep climb up from Gomathang to the lake Laxmipokhari. Laxmipokhari is a big lake cupped in a deep crater. The rim of the crater is so high above the lake level that it is easy to photograph the complete lake without using a wide angle lens. A steep switchback trail from the rim takes you to the lake-side where a small wooden temple has been constructed. As you invoke the blessings of the gods on the banks of this pristine lake, you cannot help thinking that it is here that god really resides and not amidst the din of crowded temples in the cities and towns. As though some gigantic chemical reaction was taking place, the lake spews out clouds of moisture in the form of mist and soon blocks out our view. A tint of sunlight suffuse in the mist gives everything an unearthly cast. From Laxmipokhari towards Garakhet is a relatively flat walk except before you cross the Dafley Pass which experiences howling winds almost throughout the year. Your path meanders past another Ram-Laxman lake and Bhut Pokhari before you reach the pass. While resting on this pass, I saw an eagle just above me in the sky which remained suspended in the air without moving or flapping its wings for a full five minutes. While I was wondering what were the laws of physics that enabled the bird to perform this gravity defying feat my porter reminded me that it was getting late and we were set to move on.

A moderate drop from the pass takes you to Lampokhari a lake whose length is considerably more than its width. Before you reach Garakhet you pass by a small lake called the Haspokhari which is in the shape of a swan.

You halt at Garakhet and on the fourth day walk up to Timbong pokhari just on the border of Nepal and Sikkim but not before you visit another set of Ram-Laxman and Bhutpokharis on the way. Timbong pokhari is about an hours walk from Garakhet and this lake is considered to be very holy and is oval in shape. Pilgrims from both Nepal and Sikkim visit it regularly. Devotees have strung small bells on the lakeside as it is believed it brings good luck. From

Timbong Pokhari you retrace your path backwards till Dafley pass from where a short cut takes you straight down to Gomathang bypassing the Laxmipokhari area.

The distant drone of an aeroplane far away over the rolling hills of Nepal is the only sign that reminds you that you are in the twentieth century.

After a night halt at Boktak, you reach Base Camp by late noon on the fifth day. On the way back I came across a herd of yaks that was being moved to the lower altitudes towards Uttrey in Sikkim as it was now autumn and snow had begun falling in the higher reaches. But while moving downhill the yaks have to traverse through a part of Nepal and making a couple of overnight halts in the other country. Although there is a sort of an unwritten agreement between yakherders to use each others grazing fields when the flock are in transit, overstaying sometimes has caused misunderstandings. Salt, which is an important ingredient in the diet of the yaks, seems to be a very scarce commodity on the Nepal side and there is a tendency by the yakherders from the other side of the border to procure it from the bordering towns of Sikkim and this sometimes causes a scarcity. I remember having bartered half a kilogram of salt that I was carrying in my provisions for a kilogram of yak butter: a good bargain indeed!

Instead of returning back from Garakhet to the Base Camp, one can trek further onwards along the Nepal border to Dhond, Labi and to Chiwabhanjang via Bajredunga which is hill feature that gets struck by lightning so often that it is littered with scorched tree and branches. No wonder it derives its name from Bajrewhich means Lightning.

Phalut-Singelila-Chiwabhanjang Trek

For this trek, it is more convenient to enter from Phalut that lies near the trijuction of Nepal, West Bengal and Sikkim. This route lies on the ridge of the razor-edged Singelila range that defines the boundary between Sikkim and Nepal. Phalut is approachable from Darjeeling by road. Just near Phalut is Toriphule which remains covered with beautiful yellow flowers most parts of the year and is in fact the real trijunction. The highest point on this route is a point called Singelila at an altitude of 3686 m (12089 ft) and after which the whole western range of Sikkim is named. The mighty Khanchendzonga range forms a part of the Singelila range and is named after this barrnen spot. I fail to comprehend how the mighty range has been named after this desolate spot. High intensity winds batter Singelila continously to such an extent that gravel tend to become flying missiles. One notices with surprise how the few flags on this hilltop manage to survive. From Singelila one can see Mt Kanchendzonga towering above and in the distant east the Chola range. On the west are the rolling hills of Nepal and far down below the Nepal village of Cheng Thapu can distinctly be seen. And far far away you can even see Mt Everest. In fact from many points of the Singilela range you are treated to sights of both Kanchendzonga and Everest. A fall on one side may land you a few hundred metres into Sikkim and a fall on the other side deep into Nepal. On the Singelila range the air is in a continuous state of turmoil. The clouds sometimes get shepherded from the Nepal side to Sikkim and sometimes it is the other way round.

One accosts yaks on almost every turn peeping curiously as you pass by. Yaks form the mainstay of the livelihood of the few people who stay here. In fact the people are here because the yaks are here. Yaks are used for their milk, meat, skin and hair. These are mostly sold at Darjeeling and its surrounding areas. Yak milk is very thick and the yield is barely a litre an animal per day. Yak milk is converted to cheese and butter.

During the winters when this area becomes snowbound and bereft of any vegetation, the yaks are moved to lower altitudes. During late spring, when the heat and the flies become intolerable the yaks begin their journey back to the upper heights.

During my visit, at the yakshed near Singelila a wizen faced old man wearing high Tibetan boots and a dirty black robe girdled at the waist came forth to greet us. Yaks were obviously his great enthusiasm in life. He smelt of them too. In one corner sat his wife vigorously shaking a goatskin bag. Milk is filled first in the goatskin bags and after it has curdled after a few days, the concoction is shaken to get the butter. From a transistor radio - which seemed so out of place here and almost an anachronism - the disembodied Hindi number "Choli ke pechey kya hai ...." was being played: our Bombay film industry was even trying to break the stillness of this wilderness.

Chiwabhanjang which forms a pass to Nepal is about a three hours walk from Phalut. At Chiwabhanjang are two small lakes known as Bhut-Pokaris. An inspection bunglow stands in ruins at Chiwabhanjang as a mute testimony of the British presence here in the old days to keep off the Nepalis from attacking Sikkim. It is also possible to reach Chiwabhanjang from Uttrey in Sikkim in about three hours but the trek from Uttrey to Chiwabhanjang is very steep.

Hilley-Varsey- Chiwabhanjang Trek

This route lies in the south-western corner of Sikkim. One has to first reach Hilley by road via Sombaria. From Hilley, one has to trek for four kilometres that takes approximately one hour to reach Varsey which is at an altitude of 3049 m (10000 ft). At Hilley, which is at an altitude of 2744 m(9000 ft), silver firs, hemlocks, magnolia and rhododendrons are found in equal abundance but as one approaches Varsey, the rhododendrons reign supreme and during the month of March they are a riot of red colour. The branches of trees all along the route entwine with each other to form a leafy canopy. Bright sunlight filters through a fretwork of rich green foliage lighting up flowers in splashes of colours. Butterflies of many hues flash like living jewels dancing from flower to flower. Above in the azure sky, big winds send clouds scampering here and there. A group of birds fly in jagged formation trumpeting. Nature itself seems to exult.

At Varsey there is Shambhala Rhododendron Resort with comfortable rooms and attached bathrooms for the tourists. One has to walk a few hundred yards ahead to catch a view of Chiwabhanjang on the Singelila range. Far below the village of Burikhop can distinctly be seen.

From Varsey, Chiwabhanjang can be reached in a trek of about three to four hours.

Damthang-Tendong Trek

Damthang is 14 kilometres from Namchi on the Gangtok-Namchi (via Temi) road. A number of buses ply on this route from Gangtok. To reach Tendong from Damthang one has to walk for about one and a half hour on a footpath through thick forest of the Tendong Forest Sanctuary. Different species of vegetation struggle with each other to obtain a foothold in this thick forest. The trunks and branches of trees are heavily festooned with clinging, beard like moss. Yearning for sunlight, vines clamber up the tree trunks. Gigantic ferns take the form of giant garden umbrellas. In the near darkness of the forest, shards of sunlight filter through the thick canopy of trees. Insects trill and rasp, leaves whisper, little creatures walk through the underbrush leaving ripple of rustlings and birds whistle their territorial claims.

Tendong at an altitude of 2640 m(8660 ft) is situated on a small plateau on top of the mountain. From here the view is just spectacular. Perhaps no other place in Sikkim offers a better panoramic view of the mountain ranges in the state than Tendong - it is like sitting in the centre of a huge amphitheatre. On the east one can see the full Chola Range, on the west the Singelila range and the towering Kanchendzonga. In the North East can be seen the Paunhri peak with the surrounding mountains. Darjeeling, Gyalshing, Nathula, a part of Gangtok and the rolling plains of Siliguri can all be discerned from here. Both the sunrise and sunset are breathtaking from Tendong. As one watches, rain slashes through the brilliant sunlight and a rainbow leaps across the landscape below. From other parts of Sikkim Tendong looks like a volcano - and legend has it that it was in fact once an active volcano which is now dormant.

There is another legend of the Lepcha tribe that saved itself on its summit during the great flood that once inundated the world - the story has a likeness to that of Noah and his Ark and Mount Arrarat which Tendong is said to be. It is said that during the great deluge, the Lepchas first sought refuge at the Maenam peak some kilometres away but when the waters started rising fast, they moved to Tendong. There seems to be an anamoly in this legend given that Tendong is much lower in altitude than Maenam. Tendong however is clear of any high rise features nearby and therefore gives an impression of being much higher than Maenam. Tendong is also worshipped by the Lepchas in a festival called the "Tendong Lho Rum Faat" which literally means Worship of Tendong.

Two small one-room monasteries exist here - one quite old and in the verge of ruins and the other a newly constructed one. An observation tower, three stories high, on a similar pattern of the one at Tiger Hill Darjeeling has been constructed here for the convenience of tourists. As dusk falls, the nocturnal animals come alive. A cricket clicks and is followed by hundreds of others until the whole forest around Tendong reverberates with a deafening din. Sudden silence for a few seconds and then again the cacophony.The lights of

Siliguri, Darjeeling, Gangtok and other towns twinkle in the night and it looks as though the galaxies themselves had descended on the earth.

Dawn brings its share of spectacular sights. The eastern sky slowly lights up and the snow-clad peaks become crimson and then glistening white. As the sun rises, the crowns of the smaller mountains are brightened up one by one and then slowly the probing rays enter the deepest of the valleys and the gorges revealing verdant forests soaked in hundreds of shades of green and sparkling white rivers. Suddenly these rivers far below start steaming like a Turkish Bath and soon a white sheet mist blanks out the scenery.

The twin peaks of Tendong and Maenam have been very beautifully personified by Dr. Pawan Chamling in his peoms Perennial Dreams. He has made them as witnesses to the travails of the downtrodden. An excerpt:

This holy ridge and Mount Maenam
Have witnessed boundless woes and pangs
And endless tears and sacrifice
Of toiling people dwelling in Himalayan ridges,
In green upland leas, in hamlets and villages,
Beside the Rongnyit and the Rongnyu rivers
And in the foothills of the Tendong and the Maenam monts
These holy monts have witnessed
Horrendous bloodshed of these working people

Rabongla - Maenam -Bhaledunga Trek

Towering above the town of Rabongla, is the Maenam hilltop. One has to trek three hours uphill from Rabongla through the Maenam Wildlife Sanctuary teeming with Magnolia, Rhododendron and small bamboo to reach the hilltop which is at an altitude of about 3235 m (10612 ft). These trees, like giant sentinels seem to guard the path. Flowers clamber over trees while mosses, ferns and creepers more reckless and more ambitious climb the soaring trunks. A small hermitage - almost in the middle of nowhere- containing the image of Guru Padmasambva nestles here.

The view from the Maenam summit is picturesque and breathtaking. The town of Rabongla lies sleeping far below and through the gaps in the mountains one can see the rolling plains of West Bengal lazily stretching out with the clouds resting on them. As the sun rises, these clouds become buoyant and form a heavenly curtain of mist. In the west an amazing vista of the sparkling peaks of the Kanchendzonga range spreads before you.

A walk of another half an hour on the same ridge takes one to Bhaledunga - a peculiar looking cliff that protrudes out and resembles the head of a cock. This distinctive looking feature can be seen from miles away and during the old days used to serve as a guiding landmark to travellers. From the tip of this cliff, there is a vertical fall of fifteen hundred metres and one does require a strong head to be able to look down from here. Far down the river Tista can be seen snaking its way like a giant python through the valley. During my visit, in the lingering fire of a July sunset, the Tista seemed to possess its own incandence glowing silver, then rose and finally mauve.

From Maenam one can take the steep track to Yangyang then further walk down to Singchuthang (Mangley) on the banks of the river Tista and then reach Sirwani and Singtam on the National Highway. This walk takes about six hours.

Trek to Laringnygphu

The Gazetteer of Sikkim compiled by H.H. Risley in 1894 makes a brief mention about the 4 holy caves of Sikkim- the traditional abodes of Guru Rimpoche and Lhatusun Chhembo situated in the four cardinal directions surrounding Tashiding. About Lharinyingphu – the old cave of the God's Hill – he writes " It is situated about three day's journey to the north of Tashiding along a most difficult path." In the south is Kahdosangphu adjacent to the hotspring of Phurchachu. Pephu lies between the Tendong and the Maenam mountains. De-chen phu lies in the west and can be approached from Nampu near Pelling. The four caves somehow can be likened to the four Dhams that we have in Hinduism

Having visited all the other three holy caves earlier, I had a longstanding desire to trek to fourth one too – the holiest of them all - Lharingingphu..

The 20 kilometers bumpy vehicular road from Tashiding via Chongrang, Gangyep and Kongri to Lapdang has made the Lharinyingphu cave considerably less inaccessible although it still involves a formidable and daunting seven hours arduous uphill trek.

After spending the night at the RDD Dak Bunglow at Tashiding, we have arrived at Labdang, also called Gurung Busty, early in the morning. Labdang is slowly gaining importance because of the Relli chu power project that is coming up just a few kilometers below. The Voluntary Health Association of Sikkim has also taken major initiatives in the heath and social sector in Labdang. A community centre cum dak Bunglow has been set up by them here. The village of Dhupidara can be seen across and further away Mangnam over which rises Maenam. Towards the north, the peaks of Narsingh partly draped in clouds loom over head. Labdang is the take off point also for treks to Kasturi Oral.

We will be bivouacking and making a night halt at the cave and therefore a quick check of whether we are carrying everything required – sleeping bags, provisions, candles, utensils and so on

The older route to the cave by walking down from Kongri to Relli chu and then taking a steep uphill climb up via the village of Rungdung used to take two days to traverse to the cave and one day back. The Tourism Department, Government of Sikkim has recently carved out a shorter route to the cave by constructing a cobble stone path making accessibility much easier for those seeking spiritual merit – a very noble task indeed!

We walk four kilometers in the northerly directly through cardamom fields to reach the Relli-chu. We are now within the Kanchendzonga National Park. We negotiate a log bridge precariously laid out across the river. In fact last monsoon, the original bridge had washed away by a wall of water that came gushing down wreaking destruction and subsequently changing the course of the river. Because of this there was immense damage downstream to the upcoming Relli Chu Project and the NHPC Hydel Station at Legship.

We jump across rocks on the river bank and reach the cobble stone foot path. About a kilometer walk and the footpath suddenly disappears. Almost one hundred meters of it has been washed away by a huge landslip that had perhaps caused the Relli chu river to be dammed resulting in pondage and subsequent flooding. Clinging to stones and digging our feet into the mud for a foothold we negotiate this extremely dangerous landslip. We come across labourers repairing the footpath. I ponder that it is only because of their efforts that this harsh terrain is being converted to a readily accessible area and thank them from the bottom of my heart. We have to negotiate three smaller landslips. From here onwards it is a steep climb for about four hours through a thick forest. We stop once in a while to drink water from the innumerable small streams that cross our path.

Birds twitter and butterflies flit; a monal pheasant crosses our path. The thunder of Relli-chu flowing far down below resounds in the vaslley

Something incongruous like a mirage appears in this wilderness: a Dak bunglow. The tin roofed Dak Bunglow consists of three big rooms: two dormitories with attached toilet one for ladies and the other for gents. Three or four bare beds lie scattered in each room. Between them is a dining hall and kitchen. It must have been quite a Herculean task lugging the building material from the road head thirteen kilometers below. The Dak Bunglow does not have any caretaker and pilgrims are expected to just open the doors and walk in.

A signage outside the Bunglow says that the Cave is 1.5 kilometers away. Although dog tired and tempted to spend the night here we decide to instead biouvac at the cave itself as we have come to know that there are no pilgrims ahead of us meaning that accommodation is available at the cave which cannot accommodate more that six to seven people. This one- and- a half kilometer trek is almost vertical and takes a full hour to cover. The cliff marking the cave becomes visible through the gaps in the trees: in fact one of the caves is clearly visible. The last two hundred meters involves a short downhill walk and then a clamber through rocks to reach the cave.

Lharinyingphu is in fact a combination of four caves. Three caves lie adjacent to each other on a ledge on the edge of which grow thick foliage of cane and small trees. The first cave is the main one, the second is shallow and has a spring water source which is used by the pilgrims for drinking and washing utensils. The third one is small essentially used for bivouacking and spending the night. The fourth cave is a further ten minute uphill walk from here and offers a good view of the surrounding area. All the caves have colourful Lungtas strung across their entrances and stone altars with the floor littered with coins and discarded brass butter lamps.

It is late afternoon and our feet are weighing tons. On the narrow ledge in front of the caves we light a bon fire and cook our food. Devotees have left utensils, crockery and cutlery and I realize that we could have come here

Trekkers negotiate the hills

The tower at Tendong

A temporary bridge over a stream

Mountaineers over a crevasse

A jeep negotiates a snow bound road

Tourists board a helicopter at Gangtok for mountain flights

Larignimphu-the holiest cave

A cairn marks the Chiwabhanjang pass

Tshoka near Dzongri

The temple at Gurudogmar lake dwarfed by the snowy peaks

Kanchendzonga towers over the author at Green Lake

A roadsign highlightingthe need to preserve the environment

A COLLAGE OF ALPINE FLOWERS THAT GROW AT ALTITUDES ABOVE 15,000 FT

without carrying our own. Sadly, there is also a lot of litter around: plastic bottles, food wrappers, tins and left over food. Perhaps a mechanism of disposing this garbage would have to be developed. Notices should be put up exhorting the pilgrims to carry back their garbage to the road head and disposing it properly.

It is soon dusk. On the southern horizon the lights of Darjeeling come on and it looks as though the galaxies have descended on the earth. After partaking to an early dinner, we crawl into the cave and lay out our sleeping bags on the hay that has been so thoughtfully been laid out by the earlier pilgrims. The altar at the corner of the cave is adorned with the picture of Guru Padmasambva. The sweet scent of burning incense and the soft glow of light from the butter lamps quickly lulls us off to sleep.

The twittering of birds wakes us up early next morning. We enter the first cave the entrance of which has a small bust of Lord Buddha. Further inside there is a small gap just wide enough for a person to squeeze through that leads to a cavern about 10 feet high. From this cavern there is a labyrinth of tunnels inside with altars at the end of each. We crawl our way through these tunnels and offer our obeisance and prayers by lighting lamps and incense. Besides coins, butter lamps and khadas, people have made an assortment of offerings here: torches, pens, books and I even spot a transistor radio!

We walk back to Labdang covering the distance in about six hours. The journey has been a spiritually uplifting experience and has taken us to one of most hallowed corners of Sikkim.

This route has a good scope for being promoted as a part of the Buddhist circuit in the state. Pilgrims visiting Tashiding monastery during Bumchu in March should consider including Lharinyingphu as a part of their itinerary.

Trek to Dechenphu- The cave of Great Happiness

Dechen phu continues to defy easy accessibility. It has the highest altitude amongst the four caves and involves a one day daunting and murderous trek – taking you from almost 5000 ft to 10000 ft above mean sea level.

Fourteen kilometers downhill from Pelling is the village of Namphu at about 5000 ft above mean sea level and it is here till where the vehicle goes. We have arrived at Namphu and dawn is just breaking. It is a rather melancholic day: a faint drizzle and an overcast sky. I ask my porter who is also doubling as a guide the general direction of the cave. He points almost vertically upwards and says, "There, behind those clouds". We will be making a night halt at the cave and therefore a quick check of whether we are carrying everything required – sleeping bags, provisions, candles, utensils and so on

A twenty minute steep downhill walk and we are at the banks of the River Rimbi. Fed by the monsoon rains and melting snow, the river is gushing and thundering. The water has been harnessed a few kilometers downstream to generate electricity. Without crossing the river, we walk along its banks for about forty minutes to reach the village of Rimbi.

In this remote village, salesmanship also thrives. The lady shopkeeper from whom I purchase candies and chocolates to munch on the way says that there are no shops further up and recommends that we purchase all our last minute requirements from her. She charges Rs 30/- for a bottle of coke that ordinarily costs Rs 20/- at Gangtok. "Carrying Costs" she justifies succinctly. I think she has a point there so without arguing proceed onwards.

The track here bifurcates with the one on the right going towards Chawri and Zongri. We take the track on the left leaving the Rimbi river and walk along its tributary the Lungaman Khola. We now get a taste of the steep climb that lies ahead. The track at a moderate gradient passes through maize fileds, meadows and grazing grounds. In slightly less than an hour we are at Tsetanthang a picturesque village with a predominant Limbu population – which seems to be untouched by the ravages of civilization. In a hut an old man, surrounded by sheep wool, is using a "Charka" to spin out thread that would be used to weave wool carpets. We come across a man whose face has been badly disfigured - he was mauled a few years back by a bear that he tried to chase out of his farm. We must be at 6000 ft for that uncouth white scar of Pelling on the opposite hill looks to be at the same level.

We pluck out the leeches that are sticking to our feet and legsa and take a quick breakfast in one of the houses. Refreshed, we are set to move again. For the next six hours we just climb, climb and climb. There is not a single habitation on the way. The foot path is kutcha and is lined with thick vegetation and trees of magnolia and rhododendrons. The foliage is so thick that even the sky is not visible. At places the track becomes bouncy and soft because of decaying vegetation that has compacted over ages.

Mid way, the vegetation begins to thin out and gradually gets replaced by pine, cane and shrubs. Through a gap in the clouds we can see the cliff on which the Dechenphu is situated. The cliff face glistening white is a sheer drop of about a thousand feet. It reminds me of Taksang Monastery in Bhutan which is also situated on a cliff.

We finally reach the cliff face. The path bifurcates with the one on the right going towards the Singelila range – a further four hours walk away and onwards to Nepal. Far in the east we can see the roof of the Tashiding Monastery against the backdrop of the Rabongla ridge and in the southerly direction, the Pemayanste Monastery. After negotiating a narrow path that has skillfully been sculpted on it we are at the hut just below the cave and on the base of the cliff. The cliff looms ominously above us. The hut has been constructed by the Rural Development Department for the convenience of the pilgrims. It has a single room measuring about 30 ft by 15 ft and has a tin roof and walls made of wood planks. The floor is just hard ground covered with hay and grass which act as cushion. We lay out our sleeping bags, rest a while and after a cup of tea prepared by our porter on firewood get ready to pay our obeisance at the cave just about 300 feet away.

The track leading to the cave is very narrow and lined with a profusion of prayer flags (Lungtas). The mouth of the cave is about 6ft high and about 5 ft wide it becomes a cavern inside about 8 ft high and then after 15 ft rapidly truncates to about a height of 2 ft. One can crawl in further and after 20 ft reach a small hole on the cliff side. The smallness of Dechenphu as compared to the other three holy caves in Sikkim is sufficiently compensated by its altitude and the fantastic view around. A small statue of Buddha adorns the mouth of the cave. The floor is littered with coins and discarded brass butter lamps. We offer khadas, light butter lamps and incense and ring the bell the sound of which echoes in the hills. It seems many students visit the cave as we find books kept at various places in the cave seeking blessings of the Buddha. The cliff is pocked with few smaller caves but these are not very significant. Lungaman Khola flows just below our hut and we use its pure mineral water for drinking, cooking and ablutions

As dusk falls, the nocturnal insects come alive. A cricket clicks and is followed by hundreds of others until the whole forest below the cave reverberates with a deafening din. Big water drops seeping out of the cliff continuously bombard the roof of the hut. All this noise does not disturb us at all. We are dog-tired and lull off to sleep. The lights of Darap, Pelling down below us and Darjeeling on the Southern horizon twinkle in the darkness.

The loud twittering of birds wakes us in the morning. Just half a kilometer ahead perched on a hillock a lama from Bhutan has put up a shack of twigs and hay. He has been here for the last one year and we are given to understand that he would continue to be here for another two years meditating in complete silence not talking to anyone. We are moved by his faith and perseverance. We visit his hut and reverently place a small bag of rice at the entrance of the shack.

We walk six hours down to Rimbi village and then undertake then uphill climb to Namphu thereafter. Did I hear a blare of the motor horn? We are back in the cacophony of civilization.

Tolung Monastery Trek

The Tolung Monastery was first built in the reign of Chogyal Chakdor Namgyal in the early part of the eighteenth century. It contains rare and valuable scriptures and artifacts of other monasteries that were brought here for safety during the invasion of Sikkim by the Nepalis during the late seventeenth century and the early nineteenth century. A brass chorten within the monastery contains the ashes of one of the incarnates of Lama Latsun Chembo, the patron saint of Sikkim. All the relics are kept sealed in thirteen boxes under the supervision of the Government of Sikkim. Once every three years in the month of April the relics are shown to the public in the monastery complex. The last display of the relics was held in May 97. The old monastery has been demolished because its structure had become weak and a new one has been built in its place.

Tolung at an altitude of 2488 m(8160 ft) ft lies in the sparsely Lepcha populated Dzongu area of North Sikkim and a permit is required from the District Collectorate at Mangan to visit it. To reach Tolung monastery, one has to travel by road upto Linzey. There is a daily bus service from Gangtok to a place slightly short of Linzey. From Linzey to Tolung is a 20 kilometres walk and takes approximately five hours along the thundering Tolung river, which is a boiling torrent at many places, through thick forests and cardamom fields. The track itself is easy but is surrounded by precipitous cliffs from which plummet down waterfalls in white plumes hundreds of feet into the narrow gorges to the valley floor. Birds tweet louder to make themselves heard over the sound of the waterfalls and the rivers. Perched precariously on these cliffs here and there are the huts of the hardy Lepchas. As one walks towards Tolung, the surrounding mountains on the top of which ice clings tenaciously even during the summer seem to close in. On reaching Tolung one can understand why the Sikkimese chose this place to keep the relics here out of the reach of the invading Nepalis. It is so secluded and perhaps because of its high altitude was easy to guard.

At Tolung there is a Pilgrims Hut. A further walk of about an hour along the Tolung river takes one to a religious spot called Devta Pani.

During my trek to Tolung Gompa, I found that I had forgotten to wear my watch and so I asked a Lepcha whom I met on the trail what the time was. He told me that he had never learnt to read a watch. I then realised that time was a meaningless concept here - there were no deadlines to be met and no tasks to be done that required hurrying. Time here itself moves at a different pace.

I passed an old cemetery and thought of the deceased who led a life that lacked in opportunities because of the circumstances that prevail in a rural environment. Because of this many were not able to bring out their dormant capabilities. Perhaps if given a different upbringing, many would have become celebrities in some field or the other.

A stanza, from Thomas Gray's Elegy written in a Country Churchyard, which seemed so apt here, echoed in my ears

Full many a gem of purest ray serene,
The dark unfathomed caves of the ocean bear,
Full many a flower is born to blush unseen,
And waste its sweetness on the desert air.

Tashi View Point - Tinjure -Sang trek through Fambongla (Trek on Gangtok's Western Horizon)

Right from my childhood I used to stare at the huge hill opposite Gangtok spanning from Rumtek Monastery to Pangthang. It seemed to rise in front like an impregnable green wall. A lot of questions used to run in my mind. How do you get there? Did it have a forest with wild animals. What was there on the other side - another mountain? It was only when I was fifty years old that I ventured there and got an answer to my questions.

This relatively easy trek can comfortably be covered within a period of one day. Tinjure lies on the highest point on the Rumtek hill opposite Gangtok. One has to reach Golitar four kilometers ahead of Tashi-View Point first by vehicle and then walk a few kilometres that takes less than an hour on the road to Pangthang and Dikchu till the Log-hut of the Forest Department. From here the bridle path begins skirting the Experimental farm of G.B. Pant Institute at a moderate gradient and takes one through the dense Fambonglho Forest Sanctuary to the top in about two hours. The last stretch of half an hour is rather steep and one has to dodge under trees that have fallen across the path. A profusion of cane plants appear and these form a leafy tunnel over the track letting in hardly any sunlight. At places where the bridle path breaks the ground is soft and bouncy because of decaying vegetation that has accumulated and compacted for ages.

During my trek , a heavy shower of rain the previous night had left the forest sparkling and a brilliant shade of green. The spring was trying to coax the buds on the trees to bloom. Every bird in the forest seemed to fill its lungs with the sweet, fresh air and sing its heart out. The insects were equally vociferous. Now and then you startle a deer, which scampers off with graceful, flying leaps over the long tufted grass. Scores of jubilant bullfrogs serenade you from every pool and pond. You smell the sweet scented fragrance a forest gives off after a storm, the perfume of flowering shrubs and the smell of damp moss on the tree trunks.

We are now at Jhandi Dhara also somethimes wrongly called Tinjure.It has a three storey wooden Observation Tower festooned with prayer flags on concrete stilts and the view from here is just breathtaking. It overlooks both Gangtok and the Tista valleys and on the northeastern horizon towers the Kanchendzonga range with specially Siniolchu in all its splendid grandeur glittering against the blue sky. Gangtok looks as though someone has strewn the hillside with matchboxes of different colours. In the south the omnipresent volcano shaped Tendong peak looms against the backdrop of the Singelila range. Peeping out from the forests of Tumlong the monastery of Phodong looks like a small ladybird. On a clear day even the plains of West Bengal can be seen.

From Jani dhara we walk on the ridge of the mountain.On the right side is the Tista valley with the river Tista snaking its say through. On the left you catch glimpses of the Gangtok town, the Lingdum Monastery and the Rey Mondu Monastery. The path is without any steep gradients but the foilage is very thick as a result of which walking speed is considerabley slow- two to three kilometers an hour. There are no springs or streams on this route and soon we run out of drinking water. But there are a lot of juicy wild strawberries growing all around and we varaciously eat them to quench our thirst. The forest guard accompanying us points to to the paw marks of bears on the trees. We come across a small lake- Dharey after two hours. After another one hour we cross by the the Tumin Watch tower. A walk of another two hours and we are at Tinjure - the highest point on the hill opposite Gangtok.A downhill trek of an hour and we skirt past the holy Sang pokhari and shortly thereafter we are at Sang Bazar where our vehcile is waiting to pick us up.

The trek covering a distance of about 20 kilometers. has been an exhilirating experience. The mountain was not just a 2 dimensional green wall but a world teeming with trees, birds butterflies and wild life

Pastanga to Khedi Trek

Undertaking the trek on Gangtok's Western horizon, prompted me to explore the other mountains surrounding Gangtok. Why not visit Khedi at 2800 metres perched on at a vantage point on the mountain towards the

TREKKING ROUTES TO KHEDI AND RICHILA

South East direction from Gangtok. This mountain lies straddled between the Rolep chu and Takchamchu. Khedi itself offers breathtaking views of the Chinese Border and Nathula and was enroute on a less trodden trade route to Tibet via Menal and the Changu Lake till 1960. The takeoff point for Khedi is Pastanga at 1400 metres which is a 30 kilometers drive from Gangtok via Ranipool and Assam Lingzey. From Pastanga a trail of moderate climb through thick forest of oak and magnolia trees takes you to ChauriKharka in about 3 hours. Chauri Kharka at about 2000 metres is nestled in a beautiful meadow. The only habitation here is a shpherder's hut where you can if you like rest and have a cup of hot milk.From here onwards the vegetation profile changes dramatically. Rhododendron trees and a Malingo a variety of Bamboo become in abundance. A steep climb of about an hour and a half and you are Dobatey - which means two ways in Nepali. Before reaching Dobatey you can get glimpses of the Palace and Deorali areas of Gangtok town. From Dobateythe track bifurcates- one going towards Khedi and the other towards Rametay Dara and onwards to Machong near Pakyong. From Dobatey to Khedi is a trek of a moderate climb lasting three hours which includes visits to two small lakes Pothi Pokhari and Bhaley Pokhari both located at two separate bifurcations about 200 metre distance each from the main trek route. Khedi is a huge undulating stretch of land on the mountain top. The Nathula Pass with the bright Red Conference Building of the Indian Army can clearly be discerned from here. And on the western direction waves of mountain form a front drop to the mighty Kanchendzonga range. It is worth halting overnight at Khedi for which you would have to carry tents.

The Khedi Ecotourism and Ecodevelopmengt Promotion Society (KEEP),(Mobile 9733026037) located at Pastanga can provide guides, tents and other logistics for you to undertake this trek.

Trek to Richila on the Bhutan border

Can you be in Sikkim, Bhutan and West Bengal at the same time? A visit to Richi la on the trijunction will enable you to do just that. The Pangolaka range defines the 33 km long boundary between Sikkim and Bhutan and meets West Bengal at Richila. A part of this range and the Richila can clearly be seen from most parts of Gangtok It is the last mountain on Gangtok's horizon in the South Easterly Direction.

The best way to reach Richila is from Aritar, close to Rhenock. Aritar is fast developing into a favourite tourist destination with Lam pokhari as its major attraction. But visitors coming here do not have much else to do. Therefore for those for a liking for some adventure the 15 kiRholometres trek having a moderate climb to Richila from Aritar is worth including in the itinerary.

After an overnight halt at Aritar we reach the border at Haticherey 2 kilometres away. It is 4.30 am when we alight from the vehicle and commence the trek. We will be ascending from Hathichere's 5000 ft to Richila at about 10000ft in 15 kilometres : a rather moderate climb. We have obtained permits from the Forest Department Counter at The Tourism Office at Gangtok on payment of a nominal fees to enter the Pangolakha Wildlife Sanctuary. We are now in

West Bengal. On the hill opposite we can see the lights of Pedong and on the left Lava. Slightly above the lights of Kalimpong gleam and in the background Darjeeling twinkles in the night sky. Soon dawn breaks and the beautiful vistas around us becomes visible. After two hours and a half we are at Mul Kharga at 7,500 ft which marks the entry into the Pangolakha wildlife Sanctuary. We have ascended about 2500 ft in altitude in 5 kilometres:a relatively stiff climb. The Forest Department of the Government of West Bengal has a Guard House here manned by couple of their Forest Guards and it is here that we halt for about an hour for breakfast that we are carrying alongwith us.

We will now be trudging on a track that demarcates the Pangolakha Wild Life Sanctuary in Sikkim and Neora Wild Life Sanctuary in West Bengal. The path is lined mostly with maple, magnolia and oak trees. green foliage lighting up flowers in splashes of colours. Butterflies of many hues flash like living jewels dancing from flower to flower. Birds sernade us with an orchestra Cuckoo is the sopranoand the woodpecker the drum. Such forests are tempting targets for poaching and illegal tree felling and we did not come across any signs of either. The officers and staff of the Forest Department in charge of this Sanctuary seem to be doing a good job in maintaining it in such pristine condition. Sikkim is being plagued with an increasing population of vehicles leading to pollution. Such untouched areas therefore require to be fully protected to offset the concomitant emissions and reduce the carbon footprint.

After an hour we reach Ramethy Dara. The view from here is breath taking. The area suddently becomes bereft of any trees and gets replaced by "Maling" species of bamboos. We are now in Red Panda country. Although we do not see any of these creatures, I have an eerie feeling that our every move is being watched by them from their leafy hideouts. From Rametey Dara the path runs for a further two kilometres on a stream bed that has been gouged into the terrain perhaps over the last few centuries.

A few kilometres ahead and the vegetation gets replaced by a thick forest of rhododendron trees. Having light red trunks, these trees soar almost 40 ft above the ground. The space between the trees is populated with the ubiquitous ferns and the maling bamboos. We are finally at the Richila hut of the forest Department. It is a 20ft by 40 ft concrete structure with a tin roof and wooden bunks inside. A kitchen made of wood adjoins it. However most of the planks of the kitchen have been stripped off and have apparently used by visitors as firewood.

Sadly, the place is also littered with a lot of garbage – bottles, plastic wrappers etc. We feel that it is our moral duty to clean up this place of litter before we do anything else. We collect the garbage and burn it. The Government must have a mechanism in place to ensure that garbage in these pristine area are disposed off without harming the environment. It is understood most of the visitors coming here are from Bhutan. Perhaps putting up signages advising trekkers not to litter might help.

Just about 100 ft away from the hut is nestles a small lake Jorepokhari on the West Bengal side. Did Bhutanese forces cross Richila three centuries ago to help Pedi Onmgu's machinations to overthow her half brother Chogyal Chakdor Namgyal? There are no records to suggest the route they took but perhaps they came this way.

We are dog tired and after an earely dinner roll out our sleeping bags. But not everyone is heading to sleep - the nocturnal animals start trilling and clicking - but this is not disturbance and acts like a lullaby and puts us off to sleep.

Next day early morning we go to the actual trijunction which is about 500 metres away from the hut. It is a barren and rather nondescript spot with bushes growing all around - no landmark or plaque or pillar to indicate that we are at such a significant point. A cairn – a pile of stones with a small wooden stick is all that marks this place. Our altimeter reads 10450 ft. Dawn brings its share of spectacular sights. The eastern sky slowly lights up and the snow-clad peaks become crimson and then glistening white. As the sun rises, the crowns of smaller mountains are brightened up one by one and then slowly the probing rays enter the deepest of the valleys and the gorges revealing verdant forests soaked in hundreds of shades of green and sparkling white rivers.

From here we get a panoramic view of Sikkim. Opposite us is Pakyong, scarred by the upcoming airport strip. Further up Gangtok can clearly be discerned. On the Western border is the omnipresent Kanchendzonga range. Nathula, Jelepla and 17th Mile on the Eastern border of Sikkim with the Chomolhari peak in the background are all clearly visible. And in the South are the undulating hills of Bhutan and the Dooars. And far away below are the rolling plains of West Bengal. A few kilometres in the Easterly direction is a barren hilltop Pangolakha after which the entire range has been named glistening yellow in the sunlight.

The early morning sunlight seems to also activate the wildlife especially the birds. Twittering and chirping loudly they dart from tree to tree foraging for food. An eagle rides a thermal air-current and remains almost motionless in the air for a full minute and then suddenly the equations of the forces that are allowing it to hang like that change and it dives to land on a tree top.

Downhill we retrace the same path but after crossing Mulkharka we take a small detour and visit Phursey Lake. We skirt around its banks and then take the steep footpath down to Hathichere.

We are soon back at Aritar and then it is the journey back to Gangtok. It has been an exhilarating three day getaway -visiting a different world, a different eco-system - so unlike the noisy and maddening one that we are used to.

NORTH SIKKIM HIGH ALTITUDE TREKS

(This contains very useful information for mountaineers on expeditions to peaks in North Sikkim. Special permission from the Government of India is required to visit some of these places. Your travel agent will be able to help)

Lachen-Green Lake Trek

Green Lake may in the minds of many conjure up an image of a beautiful, exotic water-body green in colour. The Souvenir published by the Statesman on occasion of the coronation of the Chogyal in 1965 shows a painting of the Green Lake depicting it as a huge lake –the artist perhaps had never visited this area and had let his imagination run wild. Sadly the reality is that instead of a lake there exists here just a small shallow pond.

In fact, even a century ago there was no lake according to Douglas W. Freshfield who wrote in 1899: "The hollow enclosed between the converging moraines of the Zemu and Green Lake Glaciers has been very lately a lake, and was now a lake basin."

The absence of a lake is however sufficiently compensated by the splendid view around. Just a few kilometers away, the huge mass of Kanchendzonga towers above. The peaks of Simvo are a short distance away on the left. At the base of the Kanchendzonga is the Zemu Glacier full of a sea moraines - rocks and boulder and debris created by moving ice scrapping the mountainside - a veritable natural pulveriser. Once in a while the distant thunder of avalanches can be heard resounding in the emptiness.

Winds roar, avalanches thunder and glaciers groan. Powerful primal forces here create and destroy natural features just in a manner a sculptor shapes a statue and destroys it if it does not catch his fancy to build it afresh. The terrain here itself is in a state of flux - mountains are moulded into different shapes, streams frequently change course and lakes appear and disappear.

The nearest vehicle point for Green Lake lies on the Lachen- Thangu road. From Lachen 6 kilometres by vehicle on the road to Thangu and across the river Zema takes us to point called Zema I. We get down from our vehicle at the third bend after crossing the Zema River just below the abandonded SIB bunglows. We had arrived at Lachen the afternoon before and had hired porters who would be doubling as our guides. We had purchased last minute requirements and spent the night in the SPWD Dak bunglow.

It is early morning – still dark but high up over the mountain tops there is a faint glimmer of light signifying that dawn is breaking. The thunder of the Zema river below glistening white even in the darkness reverberates eerily in the valley.

Sleeping bags, tents and provisions on our backs and we are ready to begin the arduous three day trek that will take us from 10,000 ft to almost 17,000 ft above mean sea level. During this 35 kilometer trek we will not come across a single habitation on the way –only wilderness. Mules and yaks cannot negotiate this track, because of treacherous landslips enroute so you have to completely rely on porters to carry the provisions. A faint trail marks the beginning of our trek route which would for most part of the journey run parallel to the Zema river and then the Zema Glacier. From Zema I to Talem which is a walk of about 4 hours, the route is almost trailess, rocky and strewn with boulders. Shattered tree trunks are piled in an inextricable confusion. We cross many landslips and ford across a stream. We have been forewarned to watch out for shooting boulders and never attempt to cross this stretch if it is raining as shooting stones from above are inevitable. The Zemu river thunders below us and at places we cross almost a vertical hillside with no track at all and one wrong step can take us tumbling down into the river. A huge landslide has scarred the mountain across the river. It sets me thinking; surely this landslide has not occurred because of environmental degradation due to deforestation as there is no human activity here. It has perhaps been triggered as a part of a natural upheaval process.

At Talem which is on a flat stretch of land there are a few abandoned army bunkers. After a refreshing cup of tea made by our porters over firewood, we are ready to move further.

From here onwards, the track becomes slushy at places - sometimes even a foot deep. Luckily we are wearing full length gum-boots. From Talem, Jakthang takes about 3 hours to reach after crossing the Lonak La river. At Jakthang there is a 2 roomed wooden shed on stilts constructed by the Forest Department and set amongst a profusion of pine trees. Our porters who have now metamorphosed as cooks collect firewood and prepare an early dinner for us. We are dog-tired and it takes us no time laying out our sleeping bags going off to sleep on the hard wooden floor.

Early next morning again sees us on the track again. The walk from Jakthang to Yabuk takes about 5 hours. We have to literally wade through bushes at many places. At other places the branches of trees on both sides of the track entwine to form a cage giving you an eerie feeling that you are inside the skeletal remains of a huge prehistoric animal. The track gets more muddy. The last stretch of the route to Yabuk is steep. Yabuk has a two storied 4 roomed wooden shed on a stone foundation. We rest here for sometime and partake to some refreshments and tea and are ready to move again. We are at the edge of the tree line. Ahead there are no trees and the vegetation gets smaller and smaller as we go higher – bushes, shrubs and then nothing at all.

From Yabuk to Sona Camp the next halt is a gruelling walk of about 3 hours on a boulder strewn trailess area. These boulders and stones have spilled over from the Zemu glacier. One can easily lose the way but some good souls have set up cairns, which are a few stones stacked over one another, prominently placed over boulders to indicate the way. These cairns have many times helped save lives of travellers who have lost their way when the area is snowbound. The small stone hut at Sona Camp is in a dilapidated condition so we have no option to pitch but our tent here and rest for the night here the sound of the Zema river flowing just a few feet away lulling us to sleep.

On the third day, we are awake early in the morning. It is still dark but the stars shine bright in the sky and cast a ghostly light on the landscape. Soon dawn starts breaking on the eastern sky. The peak of Siniolchu, a few kilometres away across the Zemu glacier, becomes crimson as the first rays of sun strike it. It seems that God took special care when making Siniolchu. It is perfectly symmetrical and conical in shape and a sharp contrast to the shapeless masses of mountains around - a triumph of mountain architecture. Its summit a mere needle seems to pierce the fabric of the blue sky. Thin clouds start gathering on the mountain top, linger for sometime as though uncertain on where to go and then suddenly soar upwards. After walking for about 2 hours from

Sona Camp we are a flat stretch of land called the Rest Camp or the Marco Polo Camp - I do not know how it got its name. Did Marco-Polo come here? There is a track to the right from where one can reach the Muguthang valley after crossing the They la pass and then onwards to Thangu over the 19000 ft high Lungnala pass. It is a route many take to reach the Green Lake specially those who use yaks to carry their provisions. After catching our breath here in the rarefied air and marvelling at the snowy peaks around, we start trudging again. The few small shrubs look almost luxurious given the harsh landscape around. The stillness is tangible- holy. The only sounds that we hear are those of our breathing and the pounding of our hearts. Instinctively, we tend to talk in whispers lest we disturb the silence of the wilderness. We sight a herd of Blue Sheep but before I can focus my camera they have disappeared over the ridge. Why are they fleeing? This wilderness is their domain and we are in fact the intruders. About three hours of walk in this untrammeled remoteness on a slight gradient track and we are at Green Lake slightly before noon. The Sheep are in fact greyish in colour and you think that their name is definitely a misnomer. It is said that when these sheep walk on the snow the reflection of the sky tends to give them a blue tinge. The terrain now is completely arid, prehistoric and lunar. We almost expect to see a dinosaur amble by. It hardly rains here as the clouds are obstructed from reaching the lake by the snowy peaks that surround it. Green Lake receives an annual rainfall of only 50 cms as against 325 cms received by Gangtok.

We pitch our tents here rest a while and cook our lunch using the primus kerosene stove as there is no firewood here. We then start exploring. Where is the lake? We are amidst a huge basin and there at its centre is a small pond –the Green Lake. There is a deep crevasse adjacent to it and centuries ago the lake perhaps drained out into the Zemu glacier below.

We reach the edge of the lake basin overlooking Zemu Glacier. Across the moraines, the rampart of Kanchendzonga rises almost vertically. From the Green Lake, the Kanchendzonga ceases to be an object of restful meditation. The apparently smooth ridges resemble the blade of a knife, and here and there harsh granite shows through the snow. The slopes are broken and jagged. On the left is the Simvo peak ice spewing out from its glacier. The view is breathtaking. To be here is to feel the very pulse of creation.

The next morning we start our trek back and in two days are in Lachen. We have been to a lake that does not exist and reached almost an arm's length away from the bastion of the Kanchendzonga. It has been like an odyssey to a different world – where man is humbled and nature reigns supreme.

Thangu-Muguthang-Chorten-Nyimala-Green Lake Trek

This is an arduous trek that begins from Thangu that is 28 kilometres away from Lachen on the highway. It involves altitudes ranging from 3963 m(13000 ft) to almost 5488 m (18000 ft). From Thangu, a vehicular side road of about 5 kms takes you to Kalapathar. From this point, the steep climb begins. If you feel that you cannot walk the high altitudes, you can take a yak from Thangu. These sure footed animals are well adapt on walking on this route. Yaks meant

NORTH SIKKIM TREKKING ROUTES

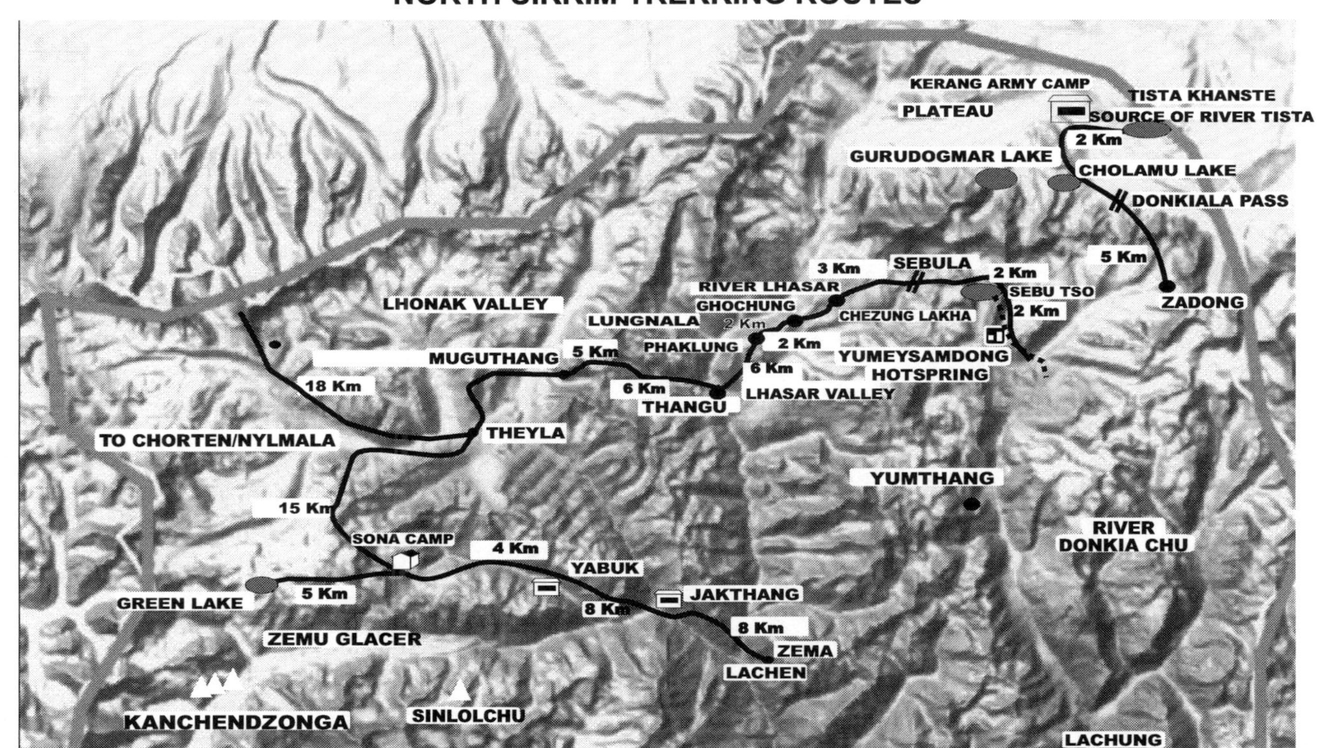

TREKKING ROUTES: IACHEN TO GREEN LAKE; THANGU TO CHORTEN NYIMALA; ZADONG, CHOLAMU TISTA KHANGSTE; THANGU TO YUMEYSAMDONG

for riding are of a cool temperament but even they can be unpredictable like the one I was given to ride made me feel like a rodeo cowboy and I decided that it was safer to walk. Within the next three hours, a murderous uphill walk reaches you to Lungna-la at slightly less than 6000 metres. Panting and drained of energy, you take a long well-deserved rest. Nothing moves except the few whisps of clouds overhead. The terrain is strewn with boulders and bereft of any vegetation except for a few enterprising Rhubarbs plants on the almost inaccessible cliffs and crags here and there. With the moving sun, surrealistic colours play on the rocks. It is a harsh landscape of forbidding grandeur. The Lungna-la pass itself is narrow and festooned with prayer flags. From here the view of the Lonak valley is marvellous and spellbinding. The valley is wide and flat and slightly undulating and green. The Nak-chu stream lazily meanders through it glistening white in the sun-light.

A knee wobbling downhill walk of about an hour and you are at the valley. Above you the mountains rise sharply. It are these mountains that do not permit moisture laden clouds to reach the Lonak valley which thus gets very low rainfall. However, anointed by the sparse summer rain, the valley exudes the green breath of life. You walk along the narrow Naku river stopping once in a while to drink its mineral rich water.

The Alpine plants around give a strong scent, which at this high altitude tends to give the traveller a headache. Aconites, which are said to be very poisonous ironically blossom in different colours.

Jatamasi plant which is renowned for its medicinal value and also used as an incense grows wildly here and the locals do good business selling it although it means sometimes climbing dangerous precipitous slopes. One also comes across a lot of Rhubarbs which adorn the mountainsides.

Muguthang at 4527 m (14850 ft) consists of a few huts built in typical Tibetan style. It is remote and undisturbed and preserves the murmurs of an ancient life. Surprisingly, there is a lot of greenery around although this consists mainly of small scrubs. The Government has even opened a school here although there are just two students in its roll and one teacher. Herds of yaks and sheep are seen all around. It is amazing to see how these beasts sit on the snow and doze off to sleep as though the snow was a mattress of cotton. The mainstay of the livelihood of this place are in fact these animals-the yaks for their milk, cheese, butter, meat and skin and the sheep for their wool- making life almost self-supporting here. These products are highly in demand and the profits are good. Even the droppings of the yaks finds good use as fuel. The yakdung is patted into cakes and stuck to the stone walls of the huts and let to dry - in the same manner as cowdung is dried in the villages in the plains.

During my visit to Mughthang, the village headman called me over for dinner. In his hut, chunks of raw yak-meat were let to dry over the fireplace and is eaten as such without cooking. The meat can last for months together and does not rot because of the cold and the low precipitation - less than 60 cm rainfall annually - thus inhibiting bacterial growth. A quaint smell of yak-meat, incense and burning yakdung permeated the air in the hut and it did take me quite sometime to get used to it. The lady wife was in one corner doing the cooking. She was heavily laden with gold ornaments - big ear-rings that seemed would almost tear her ear-lobe. A huge necklace with a pendant shaped in the form of a dragon adorned her chest. Each finger of her hands had a ring. I wondered how she was managing to do the cooking. In contrast to her ornaments, her baku - which is the local dress - was dirty. The room had a few faded thankas hanging on the stone walls. A statue of Guru-Padmasamva adorned the prayer altar in the other corner of the room. Packets of noodles and bottles of rum were stacked on the shelves near the fireplace. After a cup of butter tea and then a few rounds of Chang - the local beer made out of millet - dinner was served and consisted of Thukpa - noodles in meat soup, cheese, sheep-meat and rice.

A peculiar feature of the people, who are semi-nomadic, is that during winters when Muguthang becomes snowbound, they move their herds to higher altitudes instead coming down. There is a rationale behind this - at most of high altitude areas the winds blow stronger and this prevents the snow from settling down at one place thus leaving exposed the ground and vegetation which the yaks feed on.

An event which everybody looks forward to in Muguthang is the annual Yak race which takes place during the festival of Drukpa Teshi.

A further five hours walk on the Lonak valley from Muguthang takes you to wind-beaten Janak where the herders move their yaks during winter. From Janak a few hours walk ahead and you are at Chorten Nyimala- a pass that opens into Tibet.

From Muguthang, it is also possible to reach the Green Lake Base Camp. It involves a journey of five hours to reach Thechala and then a further five hours to Green Lake. As yaks can ply on this route, mountaineering expeditions using the Green Lake Base Camp, to attempt peaks in this area prefer to send their equipment this way.

On the map this land may belong to the Government but I have always felt that this rolling wilderness is in fact the property of the nomads who stay here. They can pitch their tents anywhere, graze their yaks anywhere - there are no restrictions at all.

Zadong-Donkiala-Cholamu-Tista Khangste trek

Most of the monsoon clouds reaching the Lachung valley precipitate before Yumthang but those venturing further north towards the Tibetan plateau have to encounter the last bastion in the valley- the Donkiala pass at 18400 ft. Overlooking the Cholamu plateau and the Roof of the World, and surrounded by snowy peaks most notably the Paunhri (Lonpo Kyangzong), the Donkia pass is like a nozzle that feebly sprays the plateau with what ever moisture that remains in the spent monsoon clouds.

Similarly mortals wanting to cross over from the Lachung valley to the Cholamu plateau have to encounter the Donkia pass and once they have done it they are depleted of energy and it takes them quite some time to get their breath back. Donkiala pass separates the upper reaches of Lachen valley from the Lachung valley and Hooker in his book "The Himalayan Journal" has rated it the most treacherous pass he ever traversed.

The motorable road ends thirty kilometres away from Yumthang via Yumey Samdong at a place called Zadong-at an altitude of about 16030 ft. We disembark from the vehicle and ask the driver to reach Cholamu via Lachen by the next day to receive us. From here to Cholamu Lake via the Donkiala pass is about a 8 kilometers trek and takes 5 to 6 hours for the average walker. We start walking along the narrow Donkiachu river. The climb is moderate but the progress is relatively slow because of rarefied air. The hillside is carpeted with alpine vegetation in a riot of colours – aconoonites, the rare blue poppies and a lot of other colourful flowers – I wish I could identity them. And dominating them like sentinels, are the yellow giant rhubarbs growing to about three feet in height.

After walking 2 hours, the Donkiala pass becomes visible. It looks quite near but takes a full hour to reach. We come across two small muddy lakes from which the river Donkiachu originates and flows into the Lachung valley. Glacial lakes look deceptively calm but are in a state of continuous flux and excessive melting of the glacier can cause them to burst their banks wreaking immense damage downstream- a phenomenon known as Glacial Lake Outburst Flooding (GLOF). A few years ago the glacial Tenbawa lake close by burst causing flash floods in the Yumthang and Lachung valley. A wall of water that gushed down, washed away bridges and caused a lot of damage to property. There is a need to monitor these lakes on a continuous basis through Satellite imagery and Synthetic Aperture Radar (SAR): any change in their size would be a signal for imminent disaster.

The last stretch of 100 metres to Donkiala pass is very steep and involves almost a vertical climb. Our bodies suddenly seem to weigh more than a ton and the legs almost crumble as the stress caused by rarefied air begins to take effect. Gasping and panting for air and feeling like a fish out of water, we finally reach the pass. But all our tiredness vanishes at the sight of the spectacular scenery around. Above the Donkiala pass spires of peaks rise their gloomy granite brightened by snow. The peak of Pauhunri (Lonpo Kyangzong) is silhouetted against the eastern sky. The relatively low altitude Chola range that delineates the eastern border of Sikkim suddenly soars up in the North to Pauhunri - the highest peak on the Eastern border of Sikkim – its ramparts scarred with many glaciers. From the Donkiala pass the view of the Tibetan plateau and its portion that juts into Sikkim as the Cholamu Plateau below us is marvellous. The plateau is flat as far as the eye can see but is broken here and there by small hillocks peppered with snow. Through powerful binoculars we can see the habitations at Tarksing and Geru in the Tibetan side. About 300 metres below is the lake of Cholamu and a smaller un-named lake above it. -both looking like emeralds . Slightly towards the west Tista meanders and breaks into many channels enclosing small oases of green vegetation sustaining wildlife and yaks on the plateau.

As we stand marvelling at the scenery below it begins raining heavily in the Lachung valley, whereas above and over the Tibetan plateau in sharp contrast it remains bright and sunny. I had read in books about how the high mountains of North Sikkim prevented moisture laden clouds from reaching the dry and arid plateau, but here I was seeing it actually happening before me.

A knee wobbling downhill walk of another one hour and a half takes us to the Cholamu lake. The reflection of the surrounding mountains doubles its beauty. Now, about the source of the Tista. Many consider Cholamu as the Source of the Tista. This is not true. The source of a river is defined as the furthest point from where a river starts flowing. Cholamu is one of the lakes in the river system that flows out as a stream to meet the Tista just a few hundred metres away. After walking the full length of the Cholamu lake we turn right and cross Tista and reach the Army Camp at Kerang. A cup of hot tea with the jawans and a rest of about an hour and we move onwards to explore the source of Tista. We walk for about slightly over an hour on the gently undulating land and are at the edge of a glacial lake. On the other side of the lake on the western base of the Paunhri is the Glacier – Tista Khanste which melts to form Khangchung Tso lake. Chunks of ice breakaway from the glacier - mini icebergs- float in the lake - tethering between solid and liquid state and then slowly melt away. It is from this lake the mighty Tista river takes birth as a trickle hardly a metre wide - the feeble beginning notes of which transform to a thunder few kilometres downstream- a river that tumbles and turns and trips overitself - its flow now being tempered downstream by the hydroelectric projects.

The plateau preserves an astonishing diversity of wildlife. A flock of birds that look like cranes swim on the placid ice-cold water. These birds are migratory probably coming from the northern latitudes. It strikes me that no natural or manmade borders are impregnable to these birds. Russia, China, India are to them one and the same - they believe in the true spirit of globalisation. It is a pity that man with a penchant for divisions cannot move freely from one place to another. A herd of Tibetan wildasses or kiangs as they are locally called, stand grazing on the other end of the lake. As there is a dearth of water on the Tibetan side, many animals cross over the border towards the lake. The plateau is teeming with marmots (big mice) , woolly hares and foxes. Once in a while a flock of snow flinches(birds) fly overhead.

Although deprived of any vegetation except sparsely growing scrubs, the plateau offers a stark beauty unparalleled perhaps anywhere in the world. The landscape here is similar to the fiery desert while the climate is that of the Tundras. Temperatures can rise to above 20 degrees celcius or drop below minus 20 degrees within a matter of hours: you can therefore get a sunburn because of the intense sunlight or a frostbite because of the intense cold.

The percitipation received by the plateau is less than 50 cms in a year as compared to Gangtok's 325 cms. Violent winds rage their force broken by neither trees nor scrubs. Howling with such a ferocity, these winds also sweep snow from the grass uncovering it for the yaks. The air is so rarefied and clear that the stars literally choke the sky and shine bright enough in the moonless sky to cast faint shadows and cause the snowclad mountains around to glisten eerily.

The intense sunlight and the high speed winds that the plateau experiences can be a good source of solar and wind energy. Use of solar panels and wind generators can easily meet the energy needs of the few hundred people who reside here.

Herds of yaks graze on the sparse vegetation and the few herders here make their livelihood by selling yak products. These herders follow lifestyles unchanged through the centuries. For us a visit to this area is an adventure but for the yakyerders it is just another day at office. For hardwork and acceptance of nature's sway, this moody and elemental place offers the herders in return the splendour of scenery. For a man from the city, staying in such a hostile environment would be unthinkable. But wouldn't a yakherder also find the city hostile, with its high decibel earsplitting noises and pollution that makes the air almost unbreathable? Such contemporary troubles like nuclear explosions and the depletion of the ozone layer seem deceptively far away. But these herdsmen are affected apparently in terms of increased Ultra-violet radiation and acid rain because of the avarice of their urban brothers.

In the most inshospitable places there is a wealth of hospitality. At a stone hut of the yakherder near Cholamu over a glass of hot Tibetan tea, which is a concoction of fermented tea leaves, yak butter and salt, I was told by one that the furthermost most of them had ventured was Thangu barely 30 kilometres away. Suddenly I start envying them for their lifestyles, which seem an anachronism in this modern age and has remained unchanged for centuries and untouched by the ravages of civilization.

Later I am told that the yak herder headman had been chosen for the post because he had the distinction of having visited Siliguri - for about a few months for medical treatment - and therefore considered as a person well exposed and wise with the ways of the world. Our vehicle has meanwhile arrived from the Lachen side and we are ready to leave.

In this anachronistic ambience, as I cast a longing lingering look behind of the Tibetan plateau, I am reminded of a stanza from Thomas Gray's Elegy written in a Country Churchyard that seemed so apt here

Far from the madding crowds' ignoble strife,
Their wishes never learned to stray,
Along the cool sequestered way of life,
They led their noiseless tenor of their way.

We begin our long drive back to Gangtok. I see an Uncle Chipps wrapper littered on the roadside. We are back into the 21st century.

From Lhasar valley to the Hotsprings of Yumeysamdong

One can never tire of the pristine beauty of North Sikkim. Most of it is untouched by the vagaries of civilization. But to experience it, arduous and daunting treks over high passes and fording rivers have to be undertaken. One such trek takes you from the verdant green Lhasar valley across the barren

Sebula pass and on to the hotsprings of Yumey samdong. The army had once upon a time thought of putting up a firing range in this area to test their big guns but mercifully this was shelved due to a public outcry.

Our trek commences at Thangu at a mind boggling altitude of 13500 ft. Situated on the banks of the Tista, Thangu, which is about 30 kilometers north of Lachen by road, has a sizeable military presence and also a thriving civilian population. It is an important takeoff point to the Cholamu plateau, Muguthang in the Lhonak valley and the Lhasar valley. Intense Ultra-violet rays and relatively good sunshine at Thangu coupled with good quality of soil result in the local vegetables especially radishes and turnips assuming huge proportions each sometimes weighing upto a kilogram.

It is a warm autumn morning and having had a nice night's sleep at the PWD Bunglow, we are all well poised to move. We walk in the north easterly direction and a moderately steep climb of three hours takes us to Phalung . From here the view of the Lhasar Valley about a thousand feet below is breathtaking. Through the Lhasar valley, the green river coils in a series of switchbacks, almost stagnant like a snake, until slightly further down it strikes straight and falling and changes colour to a white cresendo and bashes into the Lachen chu (Tista) at Thangu like a drunken pugilist. There is a plan to harness the Lhasar river by establishing a micro-hydel project to meet the energy needs of Thangu.

The Lhasar Valley abounds in alpine vegetation and medicinal plants. The valley is also home to semi-nomadic yark-herders during summer and autumn. These herdsmen move up to the plateau during the winter and spring when the valley becomes snowbound.

A further downhill walk of about an hour takes us to the abandonded clubhut of the Survey of India at Chechung Lakha. In the north, the Kanchengyao at 22600 ft is resplendent in a mantel of snow. On the right, is the Sebu-la pass, that leads to the Yumey Samdong Hotsprings at the upper end of the Yumthang valley. After partaking to lunch, we walk a few kilometers north to reach the base of the mountain that separates the Lhasar valley from the Lachung valley. We pitch our tents here for the night. Early next morning we.negotiate a three kilometer steep climb takes one to Sebu-la at 17000 ft. The pass is narrow and treacherous.

From the Sebu-la pass a knee-wobbling steep trek over glacial screes and we are at Sebu-Tso lake surrounded by mountains of Changma-Khang that seem to touch the skies. Medium sized, this lake is the source of the River Sebu-chu. We trek along the Sebu Chu on the banks of which are hundreds of Rhubarbs about five feet in height looking like sentinels. These are perhaps the largest biggest concentration of Rhubarbs one can get to see in Sikkim: in contrast the ones in the Lachen and Lhasar valley that hardly grow upto 3 ft and are far and in between. Half an hour later we are at a wide flat valley about half a kilometer wide in which the river Palo Chuuthang meets the Sebu Chu. We ford across the river Palo Chuuthang and leaving the river behind begin the gradual climb to reach a mountain top strewn with huge rocks and stones. This is the most difficult part of the journey. Jumping from rock to rock we takes about an hour to traverse just about a kilometer. A wrong step and you can land up with a fractured leg. The prayer flags that mark the Hot springs of Yumey Samdong can now be seen far below. We negotiate the steep downhill walk to the wide river valley below. The Sebu Chu reappears as a thundering waterfall almost 200 ft high on the left. We ford across an un-named tributary of the Sebu Chu and are at the hotsprings of Yumey samdong. Unlike other hotsprings in Sikkim which have one source, Yumey samdong has four or five hotsprings. People spend about a fortnight in the springs to get themselves rid of skin diseases, arthiritis etc. But we do not have that much time: being urbanites we are as usual in a terrible hurry. But we spend about an hour with our tired feet dipped in the soothing hot water sipping tea. I feel that this route can definitely be developed for trekkers visiting North Sikkim who want to try something more adventurous and venture into off-beaten territory.

A walk of another one kilometer and we are at the road side where our vehicle is waiting. The driver starts the vehicle and switches on the cassette player. The strident noise of a Hindi remix tells us that we are back in civilization.

MOUNTAINEERING IN SIKKIM

The first European to explore the Kanchendzonga area was Douglas W. Freshfield who reached its base in 1899 from the Green Lake Basin area. A German expedition led by Paul Bauer made the first attempt to reach the summit in 1929 followed by another attempt in 1931 and reached an altitude of 7927 m(26000 ft). In 1955 Charles Evans conquered Kanchendzonga a few feet below the summit from the Nepal side. In 1977 an expedition led by Major Prem Chand reached a few feet below the summit. In 1987 an Assam Rifles expedition attempted the peak. In 1991 an Indo Japanese expedition led by Hukam Singh and Yoshio Ogata conquered the peak.

The Kabru was first climbed in 1935 by a British C.R. Cooke. The Pyramid Peak was first conquered in 1949 by a Swiss R. Dittert. A British A.M. Kallas, climbed the Pauhunri in 1911. The summit of Siniolchu was first reached by a German in 1936. It was later again climbed by the famous Sikkimese Everester Sonam Gyatso. Pandim was climbed in 1993 by a team from the Sonam Gyatso Mountaineering Institute. Rathong was conquered by an Indian expedition in 1964.

TREKKING - SOME TIPS

Drinking unboiled water can lead to several intestinal diseases because of bacteria and parasites. As far as possible one should take only boiled water.

In snow bound areas, one becomes prone to frost-bite which manifests itself by causing numbness and loss of sensation of the limbs due to exposure to cold. Wearing warm clothing, thick woolen socks, gloves, snowboots can prevent frost-bite. If frostbitten, warming one self by sitting too close to the fire can cause burns. Just sitting at a warm corner near the fire can bring sensation back to the affected areas. Severe cases of frost-bite can cause gangrene and require immediate medical attention.

The glare and dazzle of snow can cause snow-blindness or photophobia. To prevent snow-blindness it is essential to use dark goggles in areas which are covered with snow.

Mountain sickness is caused by lack of oxygen at the high altitudes. The symptoms are headache, mild nausea, lethargy, vomitting. If no precautions are taken, mountain sickness can develop into Pulmonary Edema the symptoms of which are dry cough, difficulty in breathing, gurgling sound from the chest, watery sputum and tiredness. The remedy is immediate descent to low altitudes.

To avoid mountain sickness one should avoid excessive exertion and walk steadily. It is advisable to get a couple of days acclimatization at lower altitudes before moving to higher zones. For instance for people normally residing in the plains, acclimatization by halting for a few days at a place about 2000 metres high before moving to higher altitudes. This permits the red blood corpuscles in the body to multiply themselves and make the body attuned for more oxygen intake in the rarefied air. The mouth should be kept closed while walking as it prevents cold air from directly getting into the lungs.

Plenty of water, lemon-juice and glucose should be taken. Cloves, cardamom,ginger, maize or garlic should be chewed while walking. Alcoholic drinks and smoking at high altitudes should be avoided as these exert the organs of the body.

Food should be taken in smaller quantity but more frequently. If difficulty in breathing is experienced at night, a high pillow may be kept beneath the shoulders so that the weight of the body is lifted off the chest and the respiratory movement remains unhampered.

While trekking up or down steep climbs maintain a distance of about 10 feet between the persons before and after you. Rocks and stones coming loose from the person walking ahead of you can cause injury. Worse if the person in front of you trips he may fall on you if a safe distance is not maintained resulting in two people getting injured instead of one. An umbrella that can double as a walking stick is a useful thing to carry. When trekking in marshy and wet ground areas a trouser in which the last section of the trouser can be detached should be worn This will prevent the trouser from getting dirty and wet. If trekking in leech infested areas wash your socks with salt water and let to dry a day before and then smear with tobacoo powder. Alternataively wear knee high gum-boots.

It you have to walk across a terrain strewn with rocks and stones or ford across a river ensure that you step only on stones that are big in size. Stepping on stones that are small in size may result in it moving and causing you to lose your balance.

While negotiating rough terrains, keep your arms free: do not carry anything in your hands as you may require them to hold on to a rock or a plant if you fall. Use a small ruckback slung on your back and properly tied to your body to carry your bottle of water, camera, etc. Do not set up toilet near stream

A polythene wrapper carelessly thrown out of the occasional vehicle can suffocate the soil making it permanently sterile – this is the extent of the sensitivity of the alpine area. It is heartening that the Government as a part of its scheme for Green Taxis has now taken steps to prevent littering in the alpine areas. Vehicles plying here are now required to carry garbage bags or dustbins and the passengers have to use these to put the litter. When the vehicle returns back to its base the litter from these bags is to be emptied into the garbage bins. Diesel and petrol fumes are another bane to the alpine areas. Because of the rarefied air the noxious gases spread over wide areas within no time peppering the landscape with poisonous sulphur and nitrogen chemicals. The government could perhaps consider allowing only CNG vehicles to operate in these pristine alpine areas. Use food items that do not require cooking. We must prevent irreversible effects on the environment and it is our - including the tourists- duty to preserve the natural heritage that Mother Nature has provided us. Forests are not just a collection of trees harbouring animals; they are our life support system providing oxygen to other living things on planet earth. We cannot afford forests to disappear from earth as this would ring the death knell for all mankind.

As far as possible, firewood should be avoided, even by trekkers, with an aim to protect the forests and as an alternative kerosene should be used. Litter should be removed and paper products burnt or buried. Non biodegradable wastes like plastics, used cans and bottles etc. should be packed and carried back home. It may cost you little more in terms of poterage charges but you will have the satisfaction that you have left back a clean environment.

While trekking in this area it is a good idea to hire a local porter who can double also as a guide. This will enable the trekker to move faster and also prevent losing the way in the mountains.

Things to carry - a checklist

It can be quite a bad experience when in the midst of a long trek an essential item is found missing in your provision. I remember having forgotten to bring a match box on one of my treks and spent one full day without cooked food! The list given below spells out all the thinkable items required for a trek and would provide a good reference to check upon before embarking on the trail.

Food: Although tastes may vary from person to person, generally speaking the following is recommended.

• bread/buns • sugar • powdered or condensed milk • tea bags/coffee • butter • cheese spread • egg • baked beans • chocolates • jam • biscuits • water • lemons • glucose powder • brandy • dry fruits like cashew nuts/ raisins • fruit juice • Rice • dal (lentils) • refined oil/ clarified butter • mustard oil • onions • potatoes • seasonal vegetables (cabbages, peas) • tomatoes • salt & spices • turmeric • instant soup powder • fruits • precooked food like Paneer Butter massala • Sardines • Sausages

Utensils

For personal use

• steel plate • steel glass • plastic water bottle • flask

For cooking and cleaning
ladle • swiss-knife • two or three cooking containers • pressure cooker • portable gas cylinder • small kerosene stove and kerosene • soap and scrubber • matchbox

LPG gas ovens do not burn effectively above 10,000 ft and at altitudes above 12,000 ft they are useless because of rarefied air. At high altitudes use kerosene pump stoves (Primus) instead.

Camping gear: It is advisable to carry the following- tent, sleeping bag, carry mat.

For more photographs on the trekking routes see the following blog of the author: **www.sikkim-verma-travels.blogspot.com**

Thousands of tired nerveshaken, overcivilised people are beginning to find out that going to the mountains is like going home; that wilderness is a necessity..........

PLANNING YOUR TRAVEL

It is good to have an end of a journey but it is the journey that matters in the end...

SUGGESTED ITINERARIES

Visitors to Sikkim normally also include a visit to Darjeeling and Kalimpong in their itinerary. There are some who venture a step further and also include Bhutan in their programme. The Alternative I Itinerary has been tailormade for such tourists.

Alternative1 (Comprehensive 15 day Darjeeling, Sikkim Bhutan itinerary)

Day 1: Arrival at Darjeeling from Siliguri/Bagdogra after 3 hr road journey. If you opt to come via Mirik lake resort, it will take you 2 hrs more.

Day 2: Tiger Hill in the early morning (4am) by hired taxi, after breakfast visit places of interest in Darjeeling town which will take about 4 hrs, after lunch take the 3 pm toy train to Batasia and be back in town by 5 pm. Return to hotel after shopping souvenirs.

Day 3: Darjeeling to Kalimpong taking 2 hrs; Halt at Kalimpong for 3 hrs for sightseeing and lunch; Kalimpong to Gangtok taking 3 hrs. *Contact local travel agent on arrival at Gangtok for permit to vist Nathula on Day 5*

**Although Changu lake is open to tourists every day, visit to the Nathula pass is allowed for tourists only on Saturday, Sunday, Wednesday and Thursday. There is a quota on the number of tourists that can visit Nathula so during season time you may have a problem getting a permit at a very short notice. A Changu permit will also allow you to visit Baba Mandir and the Sherathang Trade Mart but not Nathula. A Nathula permit will allow you to visit all the places: Nathula, Changu, Sherathang, BabaMandir*

Day 4: Local Sightseeing - 3 point morning tour; and 5 point day tour (See Places of Interest chapter for detail itinerary of these points)

Day 5: Changu Lake, Nathula and back by hired taxi

Day 6& 7: Yumthang, Phodong and Back by hired taxi

Day 8: Gangtok to Rabongla (Buddha Park) Tashiding Monastery, Yoksum, Kechopalri lake to Pelling (breathtaking waterfalls on the way)

Day 9: Visit Pemayanste Monastery, Changey waterfalls, Singshor Bridge, Hee Bermiok area, Sanga Choelling Monastery and back to Pelling

Day 10: Pelling to Legship Shiva Mandir, Hot Spring at Reshi, Jorethang, Namchi for Statue of Guru Padmasambva and Char Dham and proceed via Manpur to Siliguri by hired taxi

Day 11: Siliguri to Phunsoling

Day 12: Phunsoling to Paro

Day 13: Sightseeing at Paro and arrival at Thimphu in evening (add one day if you intend to visit Taksang Monastery, near Paro)

Day 14: Sightseeing at Thimphu

Day 15: Thimphu to Phunsoling and Siliguri

Alternative II (for Trekkers)

Add days accordingly to your itinerary if you want to do the other treks indicated in the chapter on Trekking as follows

Panthang -Fambongla Sactuary-Sang -1 day
Yoksum Dzongri-Goechala and back -5 days
Lachen-Green Lake - Zemu Glacier and back -5days
Thangu-Lhasar Valley-Sebula-YumeySamdong -3 days
Rabongla-Maenam and back - 1 day
Damthang-Tendong and back- 1day
Namphu- Dechenphu Cave and back-2 days
Labdang-Laringnimphu Cave and back - 2 days
Uttrey-chiwabhanjang-HMI Base camp-Zongri-Yoksum -6 days

Does not include journey time to the trek start point

Alternative III(Buddhist Circuit)

Day 1: Enchey Monastery, Nor Gompa, Tsukllakhang Monastery, Guru Lhakang Monastery Chorten Tibetology

Day 2: Lingdum Monastery, Rumtek Monastery, Old Rumtek Monastery and back to Gangtok

Day 3: Gonjang Monastery (near Tashi View Point), Phodong Monastery, Labrang Monastery and back to Gangtok

Day 4: Gangtok to Phe Phu Holy Cave (Sajong),Rabongla (Buddha Park), Ralang Monastery and halt at Rabongla

Day 5: Rabongla to Bon Monastery (near Kwezing) Tashiding Monastery, Yoksum Norbugang and halt at Yoksum

Day 6: Dubdi Monastery (Yoksum), Kechopalri Lake, Pemayanste Monastery, Sanga Choling Monastery and halt at Pelling

Day 7: Pelling to Phurchachu Holy Cave at Reshi Hotspring, Statue of Guru Padmsambva and back to Siliguri or Gangtok

(You may also add treks to holy caves of Decehnphu and Lariningphu but this would entail an addition of 4 days to your itinerary)

Alternative IV (Sikkim Flora tour)

Recommended that this trek is done in the month of April when rhodendrons, Orchids and other flowers are in full bloom.

Day1: Flower Show in Gangtok

Day2&3: Gangtok to Pastanga to Khedi (Contact KEEP at Pastanga to organise your trek)

Day4: Damthang to Tendong

Day 5 to day 7: Gangtok to Singba Wildlife Sanctuary, Yumthang

(See chapter on Trekking for further details)

TRANSPORT AND OTHER TARIFFS

Helicopter

You can also fly from Bagdogra to Gangtok by the five seater helicopter. Only 10 kg of luggage is permitted per passenger. The fare one way per person is Rs 2200/- Avoid taking the helicopter, if you have to catch a flight or a train the same day. If the chopper flight is cancelled because of bad weather, you may miss your onward connection.

Taking your own Vehicles

Tere are no direct roads across the border between Sikkim and the bordering countries except at Nathula but no vehicles are permitted to cross over. In Sikkim, leaving aside restricted areas like Changu and Yumthang, you can take your own vehicles to all parts of Sikkim like Rumtek, Yoksum Pemayanste etc. The roads are generally good and even a dainty Maruti Car can negotiate most of the roads in Sikkim. But there are some stretches that are really bad and could give you a feeling of riding a horse that has gone berserk.

However good garages are available only at major towns and therefore it is wise to carry essential spare parts like fanbelt, ignition coil, CB point etc. It is also a good idea to keep a tow chain with you so that in case of a major breakdown you can ask a passing vehicle to tow you to where a repair facility is available. Fuel pumps are also far and in between and a jeriken to carrry extra fuel is essential. Be careful while driving on steep roads. Use the same gear to go downhill as you would to go uphill; this will ensure that the vehicle remains under control when negotiating steep downhill gradients: the engine acts as a brake. Lack of signages on road bifurcations can also confuse a traveller. Do not hestitate to ask directions from a passerby or a passing vehicle - that is if you come across one. Sikkim does not have a system of house numbers and to reach your acquaintance's home the direction will perhaps be "the house below the Pine tree"

There are no regular bus services to Changu and Yumthang. You have to avail of conducted tours or government approved taxis.

There are no restrictions in taking your own vehicles to all parts of Darjeeling. For Bhutan you can take your vehicle to the places your permit allows you to visit.

Transport, taxi, porter and other tariffs

If you are coming to Gangtok by bus or taxi with and West Bengal Number plate from Siliguri/Darjeeling you will be dropped at the Deorali Taxi Stand about a kilometer and half before M.G. Marg. You will then have to hire a local taxi to reach your hotel.

Till the late ninety eighties, the transportation scene in Sikkim was not good. The roads were bad and circuitous routes had to be taken. For instance reaching Yoksum from Gangtok used to take a good seven hours - an odyssey. Now you can do it in about four hours. Every morning shared taxis converge to Gangtok and other towns of Sikkim from remote villages and then leave back in the late afternoon.

The approximate charges of a small cab that can carry three /four passengers for various routes is as follows:

Gangtok local sightseeing:	Rs 400/- to 800(including haltage)
Gangtok to Rumtek and back:	Rs550/- (")
Gangtok to Nathula and back	Rs 1300 (")

Gangtok to Changu and back: Rs 900/-(")

(Package tours which include taxi fare, boarding and lodging to Yumthang cost approx Rs 2000/ per person.)

Gangtok to Yoksum:	Rs 1500/-
Yoksum to Siliguri:	Rs 1,500/-
Siliguri to Darjeeling:	Rs 900/-
Siliguri to Gangtok:	Rs 1300/-
Siliguri to Thimphu:	Rs 3,000/-

Taxi jeeps that can accommodate about seven to eight people are also available at about one and a half times the fare of the small cabs. Hiring such a vehicle to Yumthang and back would cost Rs 3200/- including one night halt.

At Gangtok, porters are abundantly available at the bus stands to carry your luggage to the hotel which are mostly all a walking distance away. Each porter charges between Rs 15/- to Rs 50/- depending on the distance. Taxis are also available at the bus stands and they charge approximately Rs 25/- per kilometre (taxis do not have meters).

The bus fare while travelling in the hills works out to approximately Rs 60/- for every 100 kilometres by ordinary bus. For Deluxe buses and taxis, the fare is one and a half times more than the ordinary bus.

For trekking, porters charge Rs 150/- per day to carry your luggage and provisions and can be hired at Yoksum. Yaks, for riding or carrying luggage can be hired at about Rs 150/- per day. Trekkers huts at Yoksum and other places on the Zongri route are without any beds and you have to sleep on the wooden floors, so bring along sleeping bags. Trekkers huts usually have two or three rooms with each room accommodating about 10 persons. Rs 50/- per person is charged per day for accommodation in the trekker hut for which the booking has to be done at the Travel Agents' Association at Yoksum. Sleeping bags, jackets, ruckpack and tents can be taken on loan at a nominal charge from Tourist Information Centre, Gangtok. Travel agents also have a provision for these items. Similar rates apply for trekking in the Darjeeling area.

The airfare (Economy Class) one way from New Delhi to Bagdogra is about Rs 7,500/- and from Calcutta to Bagdogra about Rs 3,600/-.The Helicopter fare between Gangtok to Bagdogra is Rs 3000/-. A 20 minute sightseeing mountain flight around Gangtok costs Rs 1,500/- . If you want to charter the 5 seater helicopter, it will cost Rs 1500/- per minute. If you intend to hire the chopper to fly near Kanchendzonga it will cost you over Rs 100000/- and only 4 passengers will be permitted.

The Three Tier AC railfare from Delhi to NJP and Calcutta to NJP is about Rs 1,300/- and Rs 600/- respectively. Add another 10% to calculate the Second Class AC charges. The Second Class railfare is about Rs 350/- and Rs 190/- respectively for the two routes. The Rajdhani train fare is 20 % more on what is charged in an express train.

A basic non-vegetarian meal (rice, chicken, vegetable) in an ordinary restaurant would cost approximately Rs 40/-. A vegetarian meal would be slightly cheaper. Vegetarian Bhojanalayas (restaurants) offer eat-as-much-as-you-can meals for Rs 30/-. Most of the hotels have bars and in Sikkim liquor is cheap.

For tourists on a shoe- string budget, low cost hotels which offer rooms for Rs 100/- or a dormitory bed for Rs 30/- are also available.

During the off-season (July to Mid-Sept and Dec to Feb), many hotels offer as much as a 50% discount on lodging.

TRAVELLING- USEFUL TIPS

Never have a tight schedule and always keep a few days extra on your itinerary. Roadblocks due to landslides, strikes and similar situations should always be kept in mind. Sikkim is accessible only through Siliguri and the Darjeeling area which are prone to strikes called by political parties and other organisations. During such times road communication is completely paralysed. A weather disturbance like a cyclone in the Bay of Bengal will invariably bring heavy rains in Sikkim: so check out the weather report before travelling.

It is a good idea to travel in groups of five or six as this will bring down the travelling and hotel charges per person considerably.

If visiting this region during the rush season (April to June and October to November) ensure that you have confirmed return reservation in the train or airline. It is also difficult to get reservations from here during December as schools close for winter vacations. Although incidents of mugging and snatching are almost non-existent in Sikkim, it is advisable to carry your money and passport close to your skin. A vest with two pockets is a good way to carry your money and important documents. Avoid carrying money and passport in a handbag as it can either be snatched or misplaced.

One should patronise the places like restaurants that look the busiest as you are sure to get fresh food there Places that do not have any activity are for some reason being avoided.

While travelling do not hesitate to talk to fellow passengers and ask them about places to stay and eat in. You can get valuable tips that can save you lots in terms of money and time

Do not be penny wise and pound foolish. For instance you may save Rs50/- by staying in a hotel in the suburb of the town you are visiting. However you may be spending Rs 200/- travelling to and fro to the town. You are there fore essentially spending more money.

Do haggle with porters to save a few rupees. You may end up missing an important train or bus connection in the time that you have wasted arguing with the porters. When you are spending thousands of rupees travelling spending a few more rupees will not make any difference.

Your residence/close relative telephone number and mobile number should be carried in your purse so that in an emergency your near and dear ones can be contacted.

If you have to withdraw money from an ATM, go to one which is besides its bank. In the rare event of your card being swallowed by the machine, you can seek help to retrieve your card.

Carry sufficient small change. You cannot expect change if you tender Rs 500/- for cup of tea in a stall in a remote village.

Unplanned and unexpected events should be taken in one's stride. One should learn to savour the time spent waiting for the road to open that has been closed because of a landslide. You can spend this time perhaps enjoying the flowers or the river that is flowing below. Or that one extra day spent at a place because of a strike should not make you jittery. These are all a part of the travel experience. You can fuss and fume or you can enjoy these moments.

While planning is good, too much of it can be detrimental and can take the fun out of travel.

There is this story of a knight who had to go out on a long journey: he planned for every contingency and carried with him every thing conceivable that he would require for the journey. But unfortunately the first bridge he came across collapsed under the weight of the goods that he was carrying and he drowned.

A Chinese philosoper has aptly said: *A good traveller has no fixed plan and is not intent on arriving*

Travel light so that you do not end up lugging huge bags of luggage. For instance three shirts and a couple of trousers and a sweater are sufficient for a ten day holiday. You are not going around exhibiting your wardrobe.

Keep your passport and hard cash in a Safe place on your body - a pocket perhaps in the vest. Your shirt should have at least one big pocket to keep your ticket and small currency notes which you have to access quite often. A small wallet that can be strung around your neck and kept below your your shirt is useful. A belt wallet is also useful specially to keep small change. A belt with a zip to discretely keep some rupees is also useful specially when you are travelling in places prone to mugging (not in this area of course!)

Luggage should have a label with your name, address and email id so that it can be restored to you easily if it is misplaced. Also mark your luggage with distinctive colour so that you can easily identify it especially at the airports.

Small children should have name plates with your contact address and telephone/mobile number so that in case they get lost in a crowd they can be restored to you easily.

THINGS TO CARRY

Keep a check list ready at a prominent place and use it to pack your things before travelling. It will help you pack within 5 minutes and get over the nagging "Have I forgotten something?" feeling before you travel.

Clothes: For the lower altitudes-light sweater, tee- shirts etc. For the higher altitudes - jacket with woollen lining, monkey cap, mufflers, wind-cheaters, long-johns, woollen socks and gloves. During the monsoons, a small umbrella, raincoat and gum-boots should be carried. Anti-glare snow-goggles & snowboots for snow prone areas.

Toiletries:

Soap	towel	toothpaste	toothbrush	shaving cream
face cream	shaving brush	razor with blades	hair-oil	comb
toilet paper	small mirror,	shoe polish & brush	washing powder	soap strips

Mosquito repellent will be required if travelling in low altitudes portable iron
For those with a nausea tendency, paper bags in which one can vomit and throw away may be carried

Miscellaneous:

Torch Match & candles small lock for the hotel room, Small alarm clock
lock and chain to secure luggage, Portable transistor/MP3 player
Medicine kit (see checklist below) Hot water bag if travelling to very cold places
Small Iron to press clothes spare spectacles if using spectacles
Guide book on the region Airline and Railway timetable ATM Card
Credit Card Cell/Cell phone charger Frequent flyer no card Visiting Cards
A photo copy of the important pages of your passport, ID Card, Driving Licence Address book containing all important phone numbers Universasl Adaptor(if from abroad)

It is particularly useful to have access to telephone numbers of the following so that you can enquire about train and flight timings and makelast minute changes, cancellations, report loss of credit, documents etc. :

Travel Agent where you booked your ticket
Airline Reservation Airline enquiry Railway Reservation
Railway enquiry Bank Credit Card Company
Debit card Company Hotel where you will be staying Taxi Service

Photography

Digital cameras have opened new avenues for the traveller.It would be worthwhile to carry the following and click away. Take as many shots as possible and delete the ones not required later on.

5Mega pixel 30 mm to 300mm optical zoom (Digital SLR Camera 8 Megapixel for professionals)
Macro lens for closeups 500 mm telephoto UV filter
Polariser Camera Carry bag Camera Stand
Spare memory card Battery charger Lens cleaner
Spare battery (in cold regions batteries can discharge very fast) Spare film
Spare film camera in case the digital camera goes defective

DISEASES & MEDICINES

This area is more of less free from any types of infectious diseases that the tourist may contract here. However you can contract diarrhoea if you partake to contaminated food or water. Drink only mineral or boiled water and do not eat stale food. Some people are found to be suffering from Tuberculosis: avoid contact with them. Places less than 2000 metres in altitude have mosquitos during the monsoons and therefore one should carry mosquito repellants. People prone to car sickness should carry adequate medicines: the roads have thousands of bends. To prevent diseases from amoebas, drink only boiled water. Bring along your customary medicines.

Medicine Kit

It may be worthwhile carrying the following while travelling or trekking:

Asprin like Disprin tablets & Vicks ointment for headaches;

Paracetamol like Crocin tablets for fever;
Antihistamine tablets like Avil for allergies;
Antiacidity tablets like Digene for acidity;
Laxative tablets for constipation;
Antidiarrhoeal tablets like Imodium or Lomotil and rehydration mixture for diarrrhoea;
Antibiotic tablets like Septran or Amoxcillin;
Prochlorperazine or Avomine for nausea for vomitting (useful for people who have a tendency to vomit when travelling by vehicle);
Diuretic tablets like Lasix for mountain sickness;

Iodex ointment & crepe bandage for sprains;
Antiseptic lotion like Dettol & cotton and bandage for cuts,
Water purification iodine tablets
Burnol ointment for burns & Vaseline to prevent chapping of the skin in windy places,
Multivitamins to supplement your diet if intake of good food is restricted;
Scissors and tweezers.
Other medicines that are normally taken for ailments should also be carried as per personal needs.

RESPECTING AND PROTECTING LOCAL CUSTOMS

Local cultures, local traditions and holy places should be respected and photographs of people should not be taken without asking for permission. Writing on the walls are a permanent example of environment pollution.

I do not like to feel at home when I am abroad...

ENTRY FORMALITIES AND PERMIT DETAILS

Sikkim

Foreigners can now visit many parts of Sikkim for a period of 15 days after obtaining a Inner Line Permit (ILP), without which a foreigner is not permitted to enter any part of Sikkim as the entire state is under the Foreigners (Restricted Areas)Order and Foreigners (Protected Area) Order. The State Government may extend the permit for a further period of 45 days in 3 spells of fifteen days. The following offices have been authorised to issue permits to foreigners:

1. All Indian Missions and Posts abroad
2. F.F.R.O s Delhi, Bombay, Calcutta and C.T.O. Madras
3. Immigrations Officers at the Airports at Bombay, Calcutta, Madras and New Delhi
4. Chief Secretary, Government of Sikkim, Gangtok(☎03592-202315)
5. Home Secretary, Government of Sikkim, Gangtok (03592-204290/203450)
6. Inspector General of Police, Government of Sikkim, Gangtok (☎ 03592-202747)
7. Assistant Director (Tourism), Government of Sikkim, Siliguri (☎0353-2432646)
8. Deputy Director (Tourism), Government of Sikkim, New Delhi(☎011-26115346)
9. Resident Commissioner, Government of Sikkim, New Sikkim House,14 Panchseel Marg, Chanakyapuri, New Delhi (☎ 011-26883026; 26113747)
10. Asst. Resident Commissioner, Government of Sikkim, 4C,Poonam, 5,Russel Street, Calcutta(☎033-2468983)
11. Deputy Commissioner,(☎0354-2254266) Darjeeling
12. Deputy Secretary, Home Department, Government of West Bengal, Calcutta
13. Tourist Officer, Rangpo (Border between Sikkim and West Bengal)

Individual foreign tourists may visit the following places for a period of 60 days:

East District

Gangtok, Rumtek, Pakyong, Barapathing, Rongli, Rhenock, Aritar and Rorothang

West District

Gyalshing, Soreng, Pemayanste, Khecopalri, Tashiding and Yoksum

South District

Namchi and Ravangla

North District

Phodong, Mangan and Singhik

For the purpose of extension of permits for individual foreign tourists in the Restricted Areas specified above, the powers have been degelated to the FRO, Gangtok and Superintendents of Police of North, West and South Districts for a further period of 30 days in 2 spells of 15 days each. This is being done for the convenience of foreign tourist who while visiting the outlying districts decide to stay on for sometime. Henceforth the foreigners will not be required to approach the Home Department for grant of such extensions. This delegation does not extend to permits for entry into Protected areas. Entry into the Protected areas like the Green Lake by individual foreign tourist is not allowed and they must form groups of 2 or more and travel through a Travel agent.

Group of two foreigners can also visit the Tsomgo (Changu) lake for one day. However they cannot visit Nathula.

Organised foreign tourist groups consisting of not less than two persons, sponsored by recognised Indian travel agencies will be issued permits upto a period totalling fifteen days for routes in the following areas:

East District

Gangtok - Penlong -Tinjure - Rumtek

North District

i) Gangtok - Chungthang - Lachen -Thangu
ii) Mangan - Lingzey - Sabrung - Talung Monastery - Kisong (except Yabuk)
iii) Mangan - Lingzia - Sakyong - Royot Patam (except Gochala) - Dzongri - Yoksum
iv) Yumthang - Phuni Punichoka - Tarum Cha chu - Chungthang
v) Dikchu - Phodong - Labrang - Namptham - Mangan - Maling - Singhik - Samartek - Chungthang
vi) Lachung - Yumthang - Yumey Samdong

South District

i) Sirwani - Temi - Damthang - Tendong - Namchi -
ii) Damthang - Tendong - Damthong - Rabongla - Maenam - Yangyang - Singchuthang - Sirwani
iii) Rabongla - Maenam - Borong/Polot - Tashiding
iv) Kewzing- Rayong- Tinkitam- Legship

West District

i) Yoksum -Dzongri (except Gechala)
ii) Yoksum - Dzongri - Thansing - Lampokhri
iii) Uttery - Chiwabhanjang- Dhond- Garakhet- Boktak- Dzongri
iv) Hilley - Varsey- Dentam- Singelila- Chiwabhanjang

v) Hilley - via Sombarey - Varsey - Soreng
vi) Hilley - Varsay-Dentam (except Pelling)
vii) Pelling - Sangacholing- Khechoperi - Yolsum - Dubdi- Sinon - Tashiding

Besides these, some mountain biking and white water sport routes have been authorised.

Areas other than those mentioned above can also be visited, for which a special permit, which is relatively difficult to get, has to be obtained from the Ministry of Home Affairs, New Delhi. The travel agents can help.

The routes which fall in protected areas for Indian Nationals for instance Yumthang - Phuni - Taramchu - Chungthang can be visited by them by obtaining a permit from the Sikkim Police on the same lines as visiting Changu or Yumthang. This permit is called a Protected/Restricted Area Permit(PAP or RAP). For routes falling in unrestricted areas for Indian Nationals like Hilley-Varsey-Dentam no permit would be required by them. If you as a foreigner and would like to visit any other protected place in Sikkim (which has not been specified above), like the Green Lake apply to the Home Secretary, Government of Sikkim, Tashiling, Gangtok, Sikkim or Joint Secretary (Foreigners), Ministry of Home Affairs, North Block, New Delhi at least one month in advance giving details about yourself, purpose and the dates of visit. After obtaining permission make it a point to be in Gangtok two to three days prior to your date of departure so that you can pay the environmental fees; the Government of Sikkim and the banks observes a lot of holidays so ensure that you are in Gangtok during working days.

Nationals of Pakistan, Bangladesh, China and Myanmar will not be issued permits without the prior approval of the Ministry of Home Affairs, Government of India, New Delhi.

Domestic tourists now require to be in possession of photo ID to enter restricted areas in Sikkim like Yumthang, Changu lake etc.

ENVIRONMENTAL AND SANCTUARY ENTRY FEES

Royalty has been imposed on mountaineering expeditions within Sikkim as per the rates and the conditions given below with the amendment that the local Sikkimese trekkers are to be exempted from payment of the fees on production of their valid identity card/certificate. The fee is to be imposed as an environmental fee with immediate effect under Wildlife (Protection) Act, 1972

(a) Climbing of Peaks-

Peaks above 8000 metres	US Dollar 8000
Peaks between 7501-8000 metres	US Dollar 7000
Peaks between 7001-7500 metres	US Dollar 6000
Peaks between6501-7000metres	US Dollar 5500
Peaks below 6500 metres	US Dollar 5000

(b) All mountaineering expeditions booked through registered travel agency located in Sikkim shall be eligible for a 20% rebate of the fees prescribed in (a) above. Expeditions sponsored by the Sonam Gyatso Mountaineering Institute at Gangtok and the Himalayan Mountainering Institute at Darjeeling shall also be given the same concession.

(c)For Indian expedition only 50%of the fee referred to (a) above shall be charged.

(i)For trekkers, the Environmental Fee is as follows:-

(a)For Foreign Groups -

For group of 5-10 members	US Dollar 300
For group of 11-15 members	US Dollar 400
For group of 16-20 members	US Dollar 500

(b)For domestic Groups-

For individual	Rs. 1000/-
For group of 5 to 10	Rs. 4,500/-
For group of 11 to 15 members	Rs. 6,000/-
For group of 16 to 20 members	Rs. 7,500/-

(The fee is for duration of the trek which is usually 10 days on the average).

In addition to the environmental fee, entry fees for Wildlife sanctuaries and national parks and other related fees like camera fees etc as prescribed by the Forest Department (☎ 281261,281724) situated in the Forest Secretariat, Gangtok will be charged.

I. ENTRY FEES IN THE KHANGCHENDZONGA (HIGH ALTITUDE) NATIONAL PARKS:

a) Rs. 180/- per head for first 7 days
b) Rs. 50/- per head per day for additional days

STUDENTS:

a. Rs 25/- per head for first 7 days
b. Rs. 10/- per head per day for additional days

II ENTRY FEES IN THE WILDLIFE SANCTUARIES (WLS):

a) Rs. 90/- per head for first 7 days
b) Rs. 15/- per head per day for additional days

II. A

a. Guide & Porter with team Rs. 5/- per head per day
b. Pack animal Rs. 5/- per animal per day
c. Tent pitching charge Rs. 25/- per tent per day

III. CAMERA OPERATION IN THE NATIONAL PARK AND WILDLIFE SANCTUARIES:

a. Still camera Rs. 10/- per camera per visit
b. Video camera Rs. 500/- - do -
c. Movie camera Rs. 2000/- - do -

IV FILM MAKING CHARGES FOREIGNER INDIAN

	FOREIGNER KNP	FOREIGNER WLS	INDIAN KNP	INDIAN WLS
a) Feature Film (one film at a time)	50,000/-	25,000/-	25,000/-	10,000/-
b) Documentary Film (one film at a time)	20,000/-	15,000/-	15,000/-	5,000/-

(Film making fee is in addition to camera operating fee).

V. ACCOMMODATION IN THE WILDLIFE LOG HUT (SUBJECT TO AVAILABILITY)

a. Rs 150/- per head per night.

STUDENTS

a) Rs. 50/- per head per night

VI. CONDITIONS:

1. The team shall enter the National Park and the Wildlife Sanctuary with an appropriate ENTRY PERMIT obtainable in the Wildlife Circle of the Department or in Wildlife Check Post in each entry point.
2. The team shall also ensure that necessary clearance for expedition in the restricted areas of Defence is obtained from the Ministers of Home Affairs and Defence of the Government of India and the State Home Department.
3. The team shall carry sufficient quantity of Kerosene oil and LPG for heating and cooking purposes and discourage use of firewood by members including porters.
4. The team members shall keep to the permitted route and places. The pack animals being used should be free from any cattle disease.
5 The team should ensure proper retrieval of garbages, poly bags, used tins etc. from the camping sites and route and abstain from polluting rivers and streams with human and kitchen wastes.
6. The team shall can enter with weapons which can decoy, injure or kill an animal, indulge in hunting and poaching of wild animals, kindle fire or leave any fire burning, destroy or remove any wildlife, trees, signposts etc. in the protected area.
7. The team shall have to apply in the form (supplied) and obtain permit for entry and other activity after paying necessary fees and shall also strictly adhere to the DOs and DONTs printed in the PERMIT.
8. The team shall also respect the mountains, lakes and the rocks which are sacred to the local people and shall abide by the law of the land.

Bhutan

Indian nationals intending to visit Bhutan which is a foreign country have to obtain a permit at Phunsoling: no passport is required. Foreign nationals in groups of six or more may visit Bhutan for which applications for visas should be made at least two months in advance to any of the following:

(i) The Department of Tourism, Tashichhodzong, Thimphu, Bhutan.

(ii) The Permanent Mission of Bhutan to the UN, 866 Second Avenue, New York.

(iii) The Royal Bhutanese Embassy, Chandra Gupta Marg, Chanakayapuri, New Delhi-110021. (☎ 011-26889230, 26889809)

(iv) The Royal Bhutanese Embassy, House No. 58, Road 3A, Dhanmondi Residential Area, Dacca, Bangladesh.

Foreigners other than Indian Nationals require certificates of inoculation against cholera and smallpox for entry into Bhutan.

MOBILE COVERAGE

You can keep in touch with your folks back home as the Sikkim and Darjeelings areas are well covered on mbile by BSNL, Airtel and Hutch. Some parts of Bhutan those bordering India have mobile coverage.

TRAIN, FLIGHT AND BUS INFORMATION

The railhead of Sikkim is New Jalpaiguri(NJP) in Siliguri from where trains are available to all major cities in India. Delhi can be reached between 21 to 32 hours depending on the train. Calcutta takes 10 to 12 hours and Bombay about 40 hours. The time table of the trains that pass through NJP can be seen at the end of this chapter.

Gangtok and Darjeeling have railway outagencies from where railway tickets can be booked for any section in India. Status of the trains running through NJP can be obtained from NJP Enquiry (☎0353- 2691555 or 2691808).

You can catch a flight for Delhi, Calcutta and Guwahati from Bagdogra airport in Siliguri. A helicopter service also operates between Gangtok and Bagdogra. Status of flights can be obtained from the Bagdogra Airport enquiry Jet Airways (☎ 0353-2538002;2538001) & Indian Airlines (☎ 0353-2551666). Status of the Helicopter service may be obtained from Helicopter Office(205492), Sikkim Tourism office or Gangtok Helipad (☎ 205277) or Bagdogra (0353-2531959;2551036). Details of the aircraft and helicopter timings are available at the end of this chapter.

Buses for Sikkim, Darjeeling, Kalimpong also originate the Tenzing Norgay Bus stand (☎ 2514920) at Siliguri.

Road condition reports between Sikkim and West Bengal can be obtained from the following :Sikkim Police Wireless 03592-202892, Tista Police Post03552-268270, Rimbi Police Post 03552-2262323. The road condition can also be seen on the website sikkim.gov.in

ROAD SIGNS AND SLOGANS

Driving in Sikkim is a pleasure with the beautiful scenery unfolding before you. However if it becomes monotonous the road signs and slogans of the Border Road Organisation(BRO) make interesting reading. It is as though the highway is personified and talks to you. These slogans force you to let out a chuckle.

All along the highway you will find signs that persuade you to be late, relax and take it easy that you actually start believing that being late is a good virtue. Some of these signs are

All will wait Better be late.
Better be Mr. late than late Mr.
Accident begins where alertness ends
Live and let live, Drive carefully
Eager to last then why drive fast
Reach home in peace not in pieces
Smile on drive takes you miles
This is not a rally enjoy, the valley
Drive with care make accidents rare
You have a licence to drive not to kill
Keep left it's the right way to drive
It is not rally enjoy the valley
Lower your gear a Slope is near
Life is short dont make it shorter
The Cat has nine lives You have only one.
Safe driving is more horse sense than horse power
Accidents breed when you overspeed
Mountains are a pleasure if you drive with leisure
While driving if you sleep your family will weep,
Safe driving is more horse sense than horse power.
Leave early Drive carefully and reach safely
Drive slowly Someone is waiting at home.
Caution and care make accidents rare
Fast drive last drive

Speed is a knife that cuts life
Better late than never
Safety first speed afterwards
Give away to earn a way
Be soft on my curves
This is highway not runway
Safety and speed dont meet
Take Heed Don't Speed.
Drive with card life has no spare
Don't gossip Let him drive
No hurry no worry be free
Alert today alive tomorrow
On the bend go slow friend
Overspeed is a misdeed
Hurry Burry spoils the curry
No need for overspeed
Blow horn don't get torn
Your hurry our worry
Beep Beep Don't Sleep
On the bend, go slow my friend
Drive like hell you'll be there.
Life is a journey complete it
Faster will see disaster
Overspeed is a Misdeed

Then there are road signs that speak against drinking and will make any person seriously think giving up drinking. Some of them are

Driving is risky after whisky
For safe arriving no liquor while driving
Drive on horse power not on rum power
Driving and drinking form a lethal cocktail
Drinking and Driving don't mix
Drink and Drive and You won't Survive
Drunken driving is injurious to health yours and others
Three enemies of road liquor speed and overload

There are even sensous road signs like

Feel my Curves, Do not test than.
Darling I love you but not so fast.

Or the stupid one

"If married, divorce speed" meaning that unmarried drivers have the liberty to drive receklessly.

Then there are the well deserved self praise road signs of the BRO.

BRO works today for your better tomorrow
BRO blood group" is zeal and enthusiasm
When the going gets tough the tough get going.
Snow clad mountains, schorching deserts, inaccessible pockets, BRO is seen everyone
Every wondered who defied death to build these roads- Border Road Organisation
BRO cuts moutains but joins the hearts

Some of the above roadsigns were picked up when I was in Ladhak travelling the Sriginar-Kargil-Leh-Manali highway but they are equally applicable to the terrain of Sikkim.

TOURISM INFORMATION OFFICES

M.G. Marg, Gangtok,
Phone: 03592 - 221634
Fax: 205647

New Sikkim House
14, Panchsheel Marg, Chanakyapuri,
New Delhi - 110021.
Phone: 011 - 26115346/26115171

SNT Colony, Hill Cart road, Siliguri,
Phone: 0353 - 2512646

NJP railway Station, New Jalpaiguri,
West Bengal
Phone: 0353-2690475

Bagdogra airport, Bagdogra,
West Bengal
Phone: 0353-2698030

Bellevue Hotel,
Chowrasta, Darjeeling,

New Sikkim House,
4/1 Middleton street, Kolkata
Phone: 033 -22817905

Sikkim House,
La-4, sector-III, Salt Lake City, Kolkata-
Phone : (033)23358757.

Upper Pelling, Near Girl's Hostel of
Pelling, West Sikkim

Jorethang Bazar, Opposite SNT

Ravangla Bazar
Below Dak Banglow
Alleyroad,Namchi,
Phone: 03595264557

Opposite police check post, Melli,
Phone: 03595-248536
14, Near Tourist Lodge, Rangpo,
Phone: 03592 - 240818

Lachen, North Sikkim
Mangan, North Sikkim

Travel Agents Associationof Sikkim
(TAAS) Opp Janata Bhawan, Paljor
Stadium Road,
Phone : 03592-201018
sikkimtaas@gmail.com

AIR TICKETS
Silk Route
Travels M.G. Marg, Gangtok
Phone: 03592-205492

Josse and Josse ,
M.G. Marg, Gangtok
Phone: 03592- 204682, 205534

Privilage Tours,
M.G. Marg, Gangtok, 9434407435

CAR HIRE
Plaza Tours and Travels, 9434075121

GOVERNMENT ACCOMMODATION OUTSIDE SIKKIM

Sikkim House -New Delhi
(a) 14, Panchsheel Marg, Chanakyapuri,
New Delhi - 110021.
Phone: 011 - 26115346/26115171
(b) Sewa Bhawan, L-12, New Delhi
South Extension
Phone : 011-26263255/56

Sikkim House - Kolkatta
(a) 4/1 Middleton street, Kolkata
Phone: 033 -22817905
(b) Sikkim House,
La-4, sector-III, Salt Lake City,Kolkata-
Phone (033)23358757

Sikkim House - Guwahati
Panjabari, Kalalchetri, Guwahati
Phone : 09706544588

MONEY CHANGER
Pankhuri Enterprises Pvt. Ltd, 6th
Storey, RCC Building MG Marg
Phone: 03592-201329

BANKS IN SIKKIM AND TELEPHONE NUMBERS

STD Codes: North : 03592 East: 03592 South: 03595 West : 03595

Reserce Bank of India, Gagntok Sub- Office: 201013/-201391/204362
NABARD, Regional Office, Gangtok : 20301/204173
SBI,Regional Office, Gangtok : 209931

SBI

BRANCH	PHONE No.
Gangtok	206091
Zero point	221274
Deorali	281938
Tadong	231869
Penengla	237168
Makha	244206
Rumtek	252248
Pakyong	257843
Singtam	233704
Majitar	246113
Makha	244206
Dikchu	245166
Gangtok	206304
Ranipool	251216
Rangpo	240026
Pelling	258503
Sombaria	254212
Lachung	214855
Chungthang	276903
Mangan	234247
Phodong	262932
Kabi	237253
Dikchu	245166
Namchi	263755
Jorethang	257368
Melli	248206
Namthang	241247
Temi	261818
Ravangla	260834
Hingdam	251094
Kewzing	260702

CBI

BRANCH	PHONE No.
Gangtok	202235
Rongli	255825
Rhenock	253914
Tadong	232262
Singtam	233295
Pakyong	257209
Rangpo	240852
Geyzing	250804
Nayabazar	257511
Mangalbaray	252211
Dentam	255292
Legship	250852
Soreng	253209
Namchi	264746
Rangpo	240852

BANK OF INDIA

BRANCH	PHONE No.
Gangtok	204388

ANDHRA BANK

BRANCH	PHONE No.
Gangtok	202905

AXIS

BRANCH	PHONE No.
Gangtok	221912
Rangpo	240241
Namchi	263393

HDFC

BRANCH	PHONE No.
Gangtok	201375
Rangpo	240315
NH-31A	203616

IDBI

BRANCH	PHONE No.
Gangtok	201184

SISCO BANK

BRANCH	PHONE No.
Gangtok	202605
Singtam	233287
Geyzing	251153
Mangan	234042
Namchi	264729
Jorethang	257009

INDIAN BANK

BRANCH	PHONE No.
Gangtok	203926

ICICI

BRANCH	PHONE No.
Gangtok	202454

PUNJAB BANK

BRANCH	PHONE No.
Gangtok	201396

BANK OF BORADA

BRANCH	PHONE No.
Gangtok	203216

UNION BANK

BRANCH	PHONE No.
Gangtok	202740
Ranipool	251830
Singtam	233777
SMIT	246022
Geyzing	250090
Mangan	210013
Jorethang	257334
Namchi	264985
Singtam	233777

ALLAHABAD BANK

BRANCH	PHONE No.
Gangtok	201289

DENA BANK

BRANCH	PHONE No.
Gangtok	205153

UCO BANK

BRANCH	PHONE No.
Gangtok	203164
Ranipool	251516

UNITED BANK

BRANCH	PHONE No.
Deorali	281656

INDUS IND. BANK

BRANCH	PHONE No.
Tadong	231585

IOB BANK

BRANCH	PHONE No.
Gangtok	204912

NADARD

BRANCH	PHONE No.
Namchi	264717

OBC BANK

BRANCH	PHONE No.
Gangtok	264189
Singtam	233280

CANARA BANK

BRANCH	PHONE No.
Gangtok	203589

CORPORATION BANK

BRANCH	PHONE No.
Gangtok	201336

BANK OF MAHARASHTRA

BRANCH	PHONE No.
Gangtok	206818

SYNDICATE BANK

BRANCH	PHONE No.
Gangtok	203420

SBS

BRANCH	PHONE No.
Secretariat	203325
Deorali	281381
M.G. Marg	203383
Ranipool	251297
Singtam	233858
Rangpo	240833
Gyalshing	250758
Namchi	263750
Jorethang	257370
Soreng	253207
Sombaria	254214
Rabdenste	250803
Rhhenock	253869
Rongli	255770
Mangan	234245
Pakyong	257837
Melli	248207
Ravangla	260885
Chungthang	276831
Temi-Tarku	261669
Dentam	255240
Sichey	284022
Rakdong	245088
Yuksom	241300
Yangang	243431
Rangpo	240593

TIME TABLE OF DELHI AND BOMBAY BOUND TRAINS THAT PASS THROUGH NEW JALPAIGURI (NJP){Railway station connecting Sikkim}

2436 Rajdhani Express(4,7) via Lucknow	2424 Rajdhani Express (1,2,3,5,6) for Dibrugarh on 3,6	4084 Sikkim Mahananda Exp 4084A Link Exp.	5645 Dadar Guwahati Exp. (Ex Bombay 3,6)	5652 Lohit Exp. (Ex Jammu 3,5)	5610 Avadh Assam Exp	4056 Brahmaputra Mail	5622 N.E. Exp	5647 Dadar Guwahati Exp. (Ex Bombay 5)	The timings mentioned indicate the time of departure; and the time of arr. in case of terminating station. Some trains run on certain nominated days of the week: these have the days of service mentioned in brackets after the train name in numbers from 1 to 7 (Monday as 1 and Sunday as 7)	5648 Guwahati Dadar Exp (Ex Guwahati 2)	5621 N.E. Exp	4055 Brahamaputra Mail	5609 Avadh Assam Exp	5651 Lohit Exp (Ex Guwahati 1,3)	5646 Guwahati Dadar Exp (Ex Guwahati 3,7)	4083 Sikkim Mahananada Exp. 4083A Link Exp	2423 Rajdhani Exp. (1,3,4,5,7) (Ex. Dibrugarh 6,7)	2435 Rajdhani Exp. (3,7) (via Lucknow)
		0640	↓ From Bombay	via Am-bala	0840	2105		↓From Bombay	↓ DELHI ↑	To Bombay ↑		0530	1525	via Am-bala	To Bombay ↑	1825		
0930	1400						0700		NEW DELHI		2020						1000	1420
	1850	1500				0310	1305		KANPUR		1340	2235				0915	0457	
1755				1445	1750				LUCKNOW				0520	1920				0620
		1750				0600	1550		ALLAHABAD		1050	1955				0630		
	2307	2100	1015			0845	1815	1015	MUGALSARAI	1850	0815	1726			1850	0345	0040	
	0223	0105	1405			1237	2205	1410	PATNA	1500	0440	1310			1500	2340	2055	
						1655		1945	BHAGALPUR	0855		0812						
				2120	2350				GORAKPUR	2325				1345				
						2145		0055	MALDA	0415		0355						
0425	0425	0425	1710	0605	0905		0105		BARAUNI		0120		1355	0400	1135	2045	1835	1835
0730	0730	0905	2150	1005	1325		0455		KATHIAR		2140		1015	0130	0715	1615	1550	1550
1030	1030	1450	0235	1430	1855	0305	0940	0615	NJP	2300	1710	2235	0505	2100	0215	1215	1230	1230
1730	1730		1300	2315	0500	1345	1845	1630	GUWAHATI	1330	0830	1145	2000	1130	1630		0600	0600

Other trains: Amritsar to Dibrugarh Express leaves Amritsar on 5, 1550 hrs; Dibrugarh to Amritsar Express leaves NJP at 500 hrs on 2. Jodpur Guwahati exp leaves Jodhpur on 2 at 23.30 hrs; Guwahati -Jodhpur exp leaves NJP on 5 at 1930 hrs. Capital Express (daily) leaves NJP at 1530 hrs arrival Patna 0400 hrs; leaves Patna 2250 hrs arrival NJP 1115 hrs.

TIME TABLE OF KOLKATA AND SOUTH BOUND TRAINS THAT PASS THROUGH NEW JALPAIGURI (NJP)

3045Howrah Guwahati Sarai ghat Exp (Ex Howrah 2,3,6)	3141 Teesta Torsha Exp (Terminates at Alipur Duar/Haldibari)	3143 Darjeeling Mail	5659 Kamrup Exp	5657 Kanchenjunga Exp.	5625 Banglore Guwahati Exp. (Ex Banglore 4,5)	5623 Cochin Exp(Ex Cochin 7) 5627 Trivandum Exp(Ex Triv. 5)	3147 Uttar Banga Exp(1,3,5) (Terminates at New Coochbehar)	3149 Kanchan Kanya (2,4,6)	STATIONS ↓ ↑	3150 Kanchan Kanya (3,5,7)	3148 Uttar Banga Exp (2,4,6) (Ex New Coochbehar)	5624 Guwahati Cochin Exp (6) 5628 Guwahati Trivandrum Exp(3)	5626 Guwahati Banglore Exp(Ex Guwahati 2,7)	5658 Kanchenjunga Exp	5960 Kamrup Exp	3144 Darjeeling Mail	3142 Teesta Torsha Exp(Ex Alipur Duar/Haldibari	3046 Guwahati Howrah Saraighat Exp(1,4,5)
	1340	1915		0625	↓	↓	2115	2115	SEALDAH	0645	0645	↑	↑	2035		0845	0635	
2200			1525		1405	1405			HOWRAH			0355	0355		0630			0600
2336		2120		0825					BARDAMAN					1735		0602		0349
0452	2243	0315	0010	1345	2110	2110	0525	0525	MALDA	2330	2330	2000	2000	1230	2200	2335	2055	2230
0925	0415	0815	0530	1810	0205	0205	1010	1010	NJP	1835	1835	1445	1445	0745	1630	1900	1530	1805
1700	↓		1600	0400	1215	1215	↓		GUWAHATI		↑	0500	0500	2200	0615		↑	1000

Two Toy Trains (Narrow Gauge) leave NJP for the 8 hour journey via Kurseong to Darjeeling at 0730 & 0900 hrs. Similarly two toy trains leave Darjeeling for NJP at 0825 and 0910 hrs daily.

5629 Chennai -Guwahati Express leaves Chennai on 1,4 at 2245

Similarly, 5630 Guwahati-Chennai Express leaves NJP on 5,7 at 2315 for Chennai

2509 Sealdah-NJP Superfast leaves Sealdah 2,7 at 0905;2510 NJP-Sealdah leaves NJP 1,6 at 0930 (Journey time NJP to Sealdah:10hrs)

AIRLINE AND HELICOPTER FLIGHT TIMINGS AT BAGDOGRA AIRPORT (Airport connecting Sikkim)

Indian Airlines

From (Dep. Time)	To (Arr. Time)
Delhi 1015	Bagdogra 1210 (Mon Wed Fri)
Bagdogra 1250	Guwahati 1340
Guwahati 1420	Delhi 1655
Calcutta	Bagdogra 1445 (Sun Wed Thu Fri)
Bagdogra 1525	Calcutta 1620

Jet Airways

From (Dep. Time)	To (Arr. Time)
Delhi 1030	Guwahati 1235 (Daily)
Guwahati 1310	Bagdogra 1355
Bagdogra 1430	Delhi 1630
Calcutta 1110	Bagdogra 1210 (Mon Tue Sat)
Bagdogra 1240	Calcutta 1340

A Helicopter leaves Gangtok daily on a half hour flight to Bagdogra at 1045 hrs; it takes off from Bagdogra for Gangtok at 1500 hrs. Sightseeing flights from Gangtok also arranged as per passenger requirements.

COMMONLY USED LOCAL WORDS

Many places in this area derive their from the physical, natural or manmade features they are associated with. Some places even get their names from the day on which the Hat (Market) is held. For example at Mangalbarey the hat is held on Tuesday (Tuesday is Mangal in Nepali).

Sikkim	New House
Denzong	Valley of rice
La	Pass
Chu	River
Tso (Tho)	Lake
Thang	Flat Land
Ri	A mountain
Kang	Perpetual snow
Rang	River
Ai	Sister
Yabla	Sir
Aku	Brother
Daju	Elder brother
Bhai	Younger brother
Bhowju	Wife of elder brother
Bhowari	Wife of younger brother
Kaka	Elder uncle
Mama	Maternal uncle
Maiju	Maternal uncle's wife
Phu Phu	Father's sister
Khancha	Youngest brother
Kanchi	Youngest sister
Cheta	Eldest son
Maila	Second son
Saila	Third son
Nati	Grandson
Natini	Grand daughter
Bhatij	Nephew
Keta	Boy
Keti	Girl
Chora	Son
Chori	Daughter
Nathula	The pass of the listening ear
Samdong	The place facing the bridge
Cholamu	The lake of the goddess
Khukri	Knife
Doko	Basket made of bamboo
Chembo	Saint
Tashi Delek	All purpose greeting, welcome, good luck

COMMONLY USED LOCAL PHRASES

In bigger towns of this region, people understand and speak English and Hindi. But in other places you may have problems communicating and learning the following Nepali survival phrases would be useful

Good Morning/Afternoon/night/	Namaste
Thank you	Dhanyanwad
Why?	Kina?
What?	Ke?
How?	Kasari?
Where?	Kaha?
When?	Khaile?
How much?	Kati?
Where is ....?	.... kaha cha?
What is this?	Yo ke ho?
Does this bus go to ....?	Yo bus .... jancha?
When does this bus leave?	Yo bus kati baje jahan cha?
How far is ....?	.... kati tado cha?
May I take a photograph?	Ma photo linu chakchu?
Please take me to	Mlayi .... lage do
Where can I stay here?	Mo kaha basno shakcho
Where does this road go?	Yo bato kaha chancha?
Do you have a room vacant?	Room cha?
Where will I get good food?	Ramro khana kaha payoncho
From where can I get ....?	....Kaha deke payoncha?
What is available?	Ke paincha?
Get me a cup of hot tea	Ek cup tato chay lano
The bill please	Bill laono
Please hurry	Chito
Please halt	Roko
Please move	Hino
How long will it take?	Kati time lagcha?
What is your name?	Nam ke ho?
Please come here	Yah auno hos
Who was it?	Kho thio?
Hot water	Tato pani
How much do I pay?	Kati paisa bhayo?
What time does it open?	Kati baje kholcha?
I don't understand	Ma Bujena
Can you repeat that ?	Feri Bhanno Hous
Can you reduce the price?	Daam Ghatayono Hous

BIBLIOGRAPHY AND RECOMMENDED READING

Sikkim and Bhutan, 1909	J. Claude White
Sikkim and Bhutan, 1970	V.H. Coelho
Himalayan Journal,1855	John Hooker
Gazetteer of Sikkim, 1894	H.H. Risley
Enchanted Frontiers,1971	Nari Rustomji
India and Tibet,1910	Col. Younghusband
Tours in Sikkim, 1922	Brown Percy
Sikkim the Mountain Kingdom, 1972	C.Y. Salisbury
Sikkim, 1873	J.C. Gawler
An Expedition to Lhasa 1906	Col. Younghusband
Report of a Mission to Sikkim 1885	Colman Macaulay
Among the Himalayas 1899	L.A. Waddell
Lands of the Thunderbolt 1923	Ronald Shay
Report on the State of Bhutan 1865	Ashley Eden
The Jewel in the Lotus 1957	B.J. Gould
Journey to Lhasa and Central Tibet 1902	S.C. Das
Sikkim Saga 1983	B.S. Das
Sikkim: A short Political History 1974	L.B. Basnet
Report of a visit to Sikkim and the Tibetan Frontier 1874	J.W. Edgar
Sikkim Coronation 1965	Coronation Souvenir Book Committee
Politics of Sikkim 1975	A. C. Sinha
Sikkim - A Statistical Profile	Bureau of Economics & Statistics
State Government and Politics: Sikkim	N. Sengupta
An Introduction to the History and Religion of Tibet 1991	N.C. Sinha
Sikkim 1989	R. Bedi
Sikkim - Himalayan Rhododendrons	Udai Pradhan, S.T. Lachungpa
Birds of Sikkim	Salim Ali
The Butterflies of the Sikkim Himalayas	Meena Haribal
Medicinal plants of Sikkim	L. Rai, E. Sharma
Introduction to Bhutan	Francoise Pommaret
History Culture and Customs of Sikkim	J.R. Subba
Perennial Dreams	Pawan Chamling

INDEX

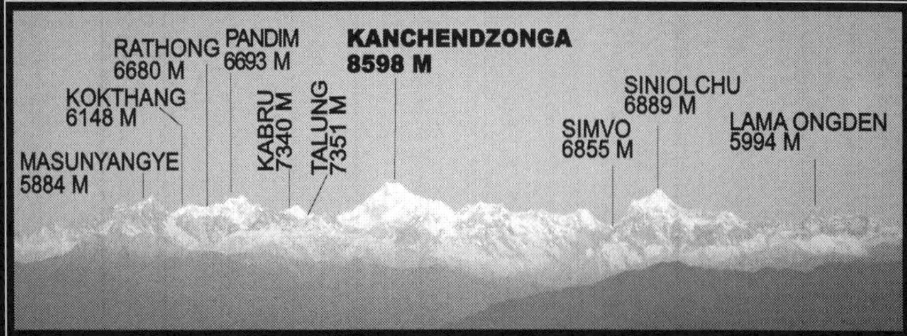

The best available and the most authoritative guidebook on Sikkim even referred to by the tourist guides and locals.

This book is useful for the following:

- Tourists, trekkers and mountaineers
- Scholars doing research on Sikkim
- Candidates appearing for exams
- Non Government Organisations(NGOs)
- Investors, Donor Agencies and Social workers

Highlights of this publication are:

- Detailed road, town and trekking route maps
- Information on places of interest
- Information on people, local customs, religion, history and culture
- Separate chapter on Buddhist festivals and dances
- Recommended itineraries with approximate tariffs to help plan the travel budget
- Information on permits and Survival tips for the tourists
- Updated telephone numbers of hotels, tourism, airline and railway offices
- Quiz on Sikkim

The author Rajesh Verma has extensively travelled and trekked in this area, photographing, researching and documenting all along. He has been mostly residing in Sikkim since birth and is presently Principal Director, Information Technology with the Government of Sikkim. A keen photographer, he has authored books on Ham Radio and Computers. His articles and photographs on travel have appeared in many publications and inflight airline magazines. Besides being associated with developing an internet website on Sikkim, he has also produced two interactive **CD-ROMs** titled **"Sikkim - A Land Beyond the Far Horizon"** and **"Rhododendrons of the Sikkim Himalayas".**

Made in the USA
San Bernardino, CA
08 June 2017